The Boy Who Loved Windows

The Boy Who Loved Windows

Opening the Heart and Mind of a
Child Threatened with Autism

P A T R I C I A   S T A C E Y

A Merloyd Lawrence Book

DA CAPO PRESS
A Member of the Perseus Books Group

Parts of this book originally appeared in *The Atlantic Monthly*.

Many of the designations used by manufacturers and sellers to distinguish their products
are claimed as trademarks. Where those designations appear in this book, and where
Da Capo Press was aware of a trademark claim, the designations have been printed in
initial capital letters.

First Da Capo Press edition 2003

Library of Congress Cataloging-in-Publication Data

Stacey, Patricia.
  The boy who loved windows : opening the heart and mind of a child
threatened with autism / Patricia Stacey.-- 1st Da Capo Press ed.
    p. cm.
"A Merloyd Lawrence book."
  ISBN 0-7382-0666-0
  1. Autistic children—United States—Biography. I. Title.
RJ506.A9S72 2003
362.1'98928982'0092—dc21   2003007605

Published by Da Capo Press, A Member of the Perseus Books Group
http://www.dacapopress.com
Da Capo Press books are available at special discounts for bulk purchases in the U.S. by
corporations, institutions, and other organizations. For more information, please contact the
Special Markets Department at the Perseus Books Group, 11 Cambridge Center,
Cambridge, MA 02142, or call (800) 255-1514 or (617) 252-5298, or e-mail
j.mccrary@perseusbooks.com.

Set in 12-point Bembo by the Perseus Books Group

1 2 3 4 5 6 7 8 9 10—06 05 04 03

To Cliff, Elizabeth, and Walker

Acknowledgments

First and foremost, I wish to acknowledge my sister, Paula Stacey, a gifted writer and editor, whose help here, as it has throughout my life, pushed me to stretch and grow, and of course, revise. I am grateful to my dear friend Julie Fisher who gave generously of her prodigious talents and companionship in delicious long discussions about this project. Cliff, my husband, tirelessly devoted his energy and support to me, and lent his architect's eye for detail. I wish also to thank my editor, Merloyd Lawrence, for her patience, her sensitivity, and her keen instincts and judgment, and C. Michael Curtis for his steady wisdom and for teaching me the importance of story. Thank you to Charles Everitt for his sense of humor and for knowing where this belonged. I am very grateful to my insightful first readers: Carol Edelstein, Robin Barber, and the Wednesday night writer's group, as well as Peter J. Smith, Andrea Dresdner, Tammy Barbasch, Elizabeth McKenzie, and Janet Sadler, and my superb fact checker, Elizabeth Shelburne. I am especially grateful to my amazing daughter, Elizabeth, for her willingness to share me with this project and for sometimes writing with me side by side. Thanks to my wonderful retreat companion Therese Sillars for her art of turning cheap paint into gold. I am extremely grateful to those who cared for my children so I could work on this project: daycare provider extraordinaire Donna Cavanagh as well as Carol and Robert Resnick, Polly Stacey, and Luke Dyson. Thanks to Peter Stacey, Jacqueline Stuart, Carolyn Thomas, and Roberta Montgomery for their support. Finally I wish to acknowledge the people at REACH for their courage and creativity.

A note about names: In the interest of truthfulness—and because I believe it's important to show that real people change real people's lives—I use actual names in this book. I have, however, changed the names of a few very minor characters to protect privacy. They appear as Victoria, Catherine, Lauri, and Lois.

Contents

As human beings, our greatness lies not so much
in being able to remake the world . . .
as in being able to remake ourselves.

—Mahatma Gandhi

I cannot say with true certainty when Walker's story began. It may have begun at conception—when two cells found each other, their parts separating, entwining, beginning their work of tinkering together a boy. Or perhaps this story began generations ago, building inexorably, like a landscape with all its faults and strange beauty. It might, too, be a modern story—something in the air, something in the water. Or it may have been precipitated by an injection (the hand of science with its innocent, and perhaps arrogant, need to improve on how we are born, or die). For my part, I can only say that it began with a suspicion that seemed to obliterate all future possibility and ended with everything being possible.

PART I

Sirens

To the Sirens first shalt thou come, who bewitch all men,
whosoever shall come to them.
—HOMER

THE DAY BEFORE my son was born, my four-year-old daughter, Elizabeth, and I were sitting in her room looking out at the treetops. That afternoon, mid-October in New England, the leaves seemed almost burning with color—yellow, orange, and purple—and I was trying to explain to her how something, before death, could be so glorious. At that moment I wanted to tell her everything, about the science of trees, about the odd and mysterious cycles that make up this life, the paradoxes. I had the perverse idea that she might want to know that the trees themselves were choking their own leaves of chlorophyll, but Elizabeth exclaimed, "Oh, I just have to be *there*—out there!" She ran down the stairs. I followed slowly, hefting my stomach, breathing like a geriatric. (By then I couldn't even see my feet.) Outside, the wind was up, a hundred leaves seemed to be raining toward us and she held her hands in the air, the way kids do on rainy days, as if she wanted to catch every living and dying thing in the sky. Afterward, I pushed her on the tree-swing and she jumped high into a pile of leaves, laughing and falling so deeply she almost disappeared.

What she didn't know those moments of that day in 1996, what I couldn't have known either, was that our lives were about to change forever. She didn't know that by six the next morning someone would put a needle into my spine, that I would flinch, that a doctor would urgently grab me by the arm and insist, "Now listen. Don't move. I've got to do this again. We've only got ten minutes to get that baby out." She wouldn't know that a baby boy, wrapped backward against my spine, would be pulled out and handed to his father who would be standing next to me. How could she ever imagine that when I saw her brother for the first moment, I wouldn't feel what I knew I should?

When does one begin to know a child? It seemed to me we had known Elizabeth from the moment of her emergence. I had been stunned by her gaze the second she came into the world: all head, pupils, awareness—pure consciousness. "The eyes!" "The eyes!" the nurses, doctor, and even a technician had all called out at once. She grabbed my husband's finger and hasn't let go since.

Yet Walker's birth was different somehow. Nothing seemed right. He didn't cry when he was born. The nurses tried to make him but succeeded in producing only a whimper, and then, when they'd handed him to Cliff and he lay in his father's arms, he looked like a small, skinned ferret—bloody, arms awry.

Did other mothers of newborns feel the way I did?

I remembered that my former boss had once said of his daughter: "She looked like hamburger when she was born!" What struck me was the absolute affection, humor, joy with which he delivered the information, as if to say: "My wet little wad of gristle was really a swan."

Even though the doctor told us that Walker was normal—that his Apgar scores were high—I was troubled less by how this baby appeared and more by some quality in his awareness. He had looked past me the first moment I saw him. In fact, his gaze became an obsession of mine in the hospital. He wouldn't look at me as he lay in the small plastic bassinet. He wouldn't look at me when he nursed, either. It was as if he didn't notice either Cliff or me, or Elizabeth, who, beaming, sat on the extra hospital bed, holding him in her lap. I felt an emptiness. The word that came to mind, a word I never told anyone, was "scarecrow." My baby, our baby, had a scarecrow quality—thin, loose, vacant.

I quietly decided that the way I might be able to find reassurance or cause for concern was through other people, through their reactions. I watched his visitors intently, studied them.

My day-care provider, Donna, came by with a good friend named Doris, a woman in her seventies. They both knew children, knew them exactly the way farmers know to read the wind, the signs of frost. Doris and Donna knew illness, too. Forty years earlier, Doris had lost a newborn in the hospital. They took it away from her and never let her see it again. She had raised two healthy sons and now worked at the school as a crossing guard. Donna had a son who was mentally retarded. Now in his twenties, he called her nightly at eight o'clock from his group home. First one and then the other of these two women held our baby in their arms and cried. I was reassured. If Doris and Donna could cry from happiness because of this baby, maybe this baby was going to be all right.

Still, concern, worry, came in hot little flashes. Toward the end of my five days in the hospital, I confided to my friend Monica that I didn't feel that the baby was "born yet," even though, of course, he was out. A woman with strong spiritual convictions, Monica suggested I pray he come into his body.

"Have a name yet?" asked the nurses. The truth was, Cliff and I hadn't been able to decide on a name before we had arrived at the hospital. We were both acutely aware that a name is synonymous with public identity. We wanted our son to be able to be whatever he wanted: musician or organic farmer or auto mechanic or mime, or, of course, president. But the process of naming seemed fraught with ill auspices. Choosing a name seemed arrogant, a dangerous alchemy; it was choosing a future. Finally, we decided on Walker after Walker Percy, philosopher and author of *The Moviegoer*. It seemed strong, philosophical, unique, which is what we hoped he would be.

Yet what he was, or was going to be, seemed to elude us, even as we committed the name to paper. Even before we sent the "name" form back to the hospital, Cliff and I had one of those talks that mark history for couples. Not a week after Walker was born.

I waited until the baby had fallen asleep, and whispering into the darkness, I spoke words I knew were treason for a mother to speak. I told Cliff I was worried something was wrong. It wasn't just that the baby looked pinched, ill at ease. He wouldn't look at me.

"People keep telling us that babies don't focus at first," said Cliff.

"It's not his focus, it's something different," I insisted.

I grappled for words to describe what was missing but ended up sounding melodramatic, like a disappointed lover. There was something missing in the "connection," none of those "oceanic feelings." The world hadn't "turned on its head."

Cliff's voice was serious. He spoke in a whisper and said, "I agree. He doesn't seem especially interested in us. I don't understand why he doesn't cry very much." He talked about his fear the moment the nurses fought to make the baby cry. "I don't understand why we have to wake Walker up to feed him," he added. We were quiet for a few moments, and he began to speak again. His tone was different this time, tender, his framing of the idea oddly artful. Cliff is not one for dramatics, yet he began, "But let me tell you a story." He described a boy who sometimes felt he was the black sheep of his family. Quiet, the brother of an outgoing sister, the shy boy spent a lot of time playing by himself in his room, reading and musing. He'd felt awkward about his quietness, his need for solitude, unfavorably comparing himself to his pretty, effervescent sister. Of course I knew Cliff was talking about himself.

"So, he'll be an architect," I said, feeling some relief, chuckling in the dark. "Just like you."

We had an explanation—one that seemed to make a lot of sense. Yet even if it wasn't the right explanation, I knew that Cliff was profoundly wise to be protective of our son's identity. We wouldn't want to judge our baby—wouldn't want to judge any of our children. And so I promised myself to be patient with this child, promised never to push him to be anything more than he was.

Yet within a week, we were back at our HMO to talk about Walker's lethargy, his lack of crying, his sleepiness. The doctor listened to the baby's heart and sent us home, saying, "Let sleeping dogs lie."

Remember, I told myself. *This is a boy. Boys develop more slowly. This is not Elizabeth.*

For the next week or two I determined to give Walker the peace he seemed to need. I put his baby carrier in the corner while I cleaned, held him as much as I could. He was quiet, rarely cried, and seemed to sleep constantly.

And so we fell into a pattern, the baby and I. Sometimes, if I was standing, I picked him up and gingerly moved him back and forth. While I made phone calls, or tried to work or clean with one hand, he lay in my arms heavily. He no longer seemed airy but seemed to be falling into me, somehow weighted.

Still, streaks of worry, the odd sharp or stinging sensation that disappeared as quickly as it came, seeped and intruded into our moments together. He seemed immeasurably ill at ease. I had the sense that he didn't fit in his own body, or that he was fighting back pain. But what kind of pain did this baby have? His face was pinched and crinkled, his posture awkward. He lay down as if he were on top of a ball, his back curled oddly sideways. Looking at him made me feel uncomfortable, and then guilty and even ashamed of the discomfort.

I began to judge myself as a mother. What was the root of these queer feelings? I knew that a mother's affection, if it was pushy, cloying, could be destructive. (I had friends who seemed permanently damaged because their mothers were too insistent that they become what they simply couldn't bring themselves to become.) I was trying to be honest with myself about who I wanted this boy to be. I remembered an essay my friend Roberta had written when we were in college, satirizing parents who try to produce geniuses of their children before they are even out of diapers. In her piece, someone injects a small violin bow into a mother's womb so a fetus can begin practicing Suzuki violin. Was I going to be one of those parents who were pushing, ever pushing, their children forward? Was I becoming one? Had I been too smugly proud of Elizabeth's precocity? I remembered feeling foolish to have intentionally listened to more classical music than I was accustomed to during Walker's gestation just because I thought it might help his brain develop.

Yet still I felt myself wishing time would push ahead so that Walker's scrunched-up face might be ironed out, filled by maturity.

Daily I waited for the eyes to come into focus. There was no way to talk about it. I wasn't even sure I wanted to.

One day I looked at Walker, and guessing he was sad or depressed, I thought he might be ready for some excitement. We had a tape of mostly Motown hits we'd made before Elizabeth was born. We played it often in the early weeks and months of her life: Otis Redding, The Supremes, and Aretha Franklin, who never failed to elicit joy in Elizabeth as a baby. I slid the tape into the stereo, turned it to play softly, . . . and started humming along . . .

. . . *And what you need, baby you got it*

All I'm asking, is for a little respect

I picked him up and tried to dance, *just a little bit.* His body shook. I checked his face; it seemed to be almost vibrating with discomfort. His eyes stared intensely into the distance. He was concentrating. Was he going to throw up? His head quivered and fell against my shoulder. I put him down quickly on a blanket (had I hurt his neck? I had heard babies could even die from too much motion). His hands flailed in space the way babies' limbs do when they think they are beginning to fall. He looked so frightened that it was as if he were going off a cliff. I quickly placed him back in the baby seat. He remained stunned.

I stepped backward and tried to understand what was happening. Why had he acted as if he were falling when he was on perfectly solid ground? I was concerned I might have injured him without knowing it but wasn't sure if I should feel guilty for the injury or feel hurt myself, for having been rejected. I had tried to go where I wasn't wanted. I tried to reason that Walker's birth had been three weeks early. Doctors didn't make much of it, but perhaps he was premature in ways I didn't understand.

When Walker awakened, later that day, I stood above him, watching. He gently looked up and I had the sense for the first time he might be trying to smile at me. From such moments, I was able to keep worry at bay for days, or at least hours.

Remember. Be patient. Boys are slower. He will show himself, in time. Anyway, if time wasn't for growing up, what was it for, then?

Yet by the time Walker was four weeks old, concern about his moods—was it possible for a baby to be in a depression?—or even concern about his feelings for me, seemed a luxury, a preoccupation too precious to be concerned with. His breathing, which in the first days had rattled a bit, grew so labored that he could barely sleep at night. He startled himself awake just to gather breath, seemed often only able to sleep between gasps. We called our HMO constantly and visited often. The doctors insisted there was nothing seriously wrong.

During this period, I became concerned about sudden infant death syndrome, which, in recent years, had been associated with respiratory failure. Convinced that Walker was a candidate, Cliff and I kept Walker in bed between us. (Books had argued that if there was no "crib," there would be no "crib death.") I elevated his head on my arm, taught myself to wake up if the spells of holding his breath lasted too long.

Walker didn't relate to us much the winter he was two and three months old, yet he was so uncomfortable, who would expect him to? Still, I wondered why he was so weak-seeming. His head was like a pumpkin weighing down a thin vine. The doctor said he was "perfect."

The way I describe our worries suggests that we were wringing our hands constantly, making doctors' appointments at every turn, feeling hopeless. I did call the HMO many nights because Walker couldn't breathe, and I knew something was wrong, yet most of our days were routine, everyday. Walker nursed, Elizabeth came home from preschool. We attended holiday parties. The larger issues were often overshadowed, obscured by day-to-day responsibilities—the phone ringing, cleaning and laundry. Those bigger questions: When does the soul enter the baby? Does it evolve with growing awareness? Is the soul born at conception or when the body is born? What is the key to the mystery of relationships? How do you know a baby? How do a mother and child come together without language? Answers, or even the reason I might be pondering such heavy concerns, were difficult to pin down—smoke blowing away in the wind.

Moreover, during this time I was beginning to wonder about my own life: I'd had a second child. What would I do in two or three years, when the baby was more independent? Would I continue to teach, or write more?

Still, in spite of our worries, Walker was a sweet baby—especially charming in sleep, when his face softened and his tiny red hands, usually clenched, opened a bit to show a lifeline. In spite of his strange poses, Walker was growing handsome; our neighbor insisted he looked like James Dean, especially in the handmade brown or red cotton berets a friend had sewn to keep his head warm.

By the time he was four months old, Walker was looking at us occasionally. We sometimes wondered if he was farsighted, since usually we were only able to win his attention from across the room or if we stood above him, never up close. Once or twice, his gaze was so intense as to be disarming, as though he was looking right into us; yet most of the time he seemed only vaguely interested.

Our thoughts about who this boy was were veering wildly. For a period of time, when Walker was three months old, we believed he might be remarkably gifted. He was showing his sister's affinity for language. "Say 'I love you,'" we'd say.

"Ah ew uh," he imitated, "Ah ew uh." Of course, he didn't know what it meant. Still, in those second and third months, we had moments of shared joy, a growing sense that Walker was emerging.

Yet as the months moved on, he somehow didn't. As he became four months old, five months old, it seemed as if a heavy veil, or shadow, lay between us and our son. He was growing increasingly unresponsive, deeply uncomfortable, morose. His pattern, if he had one, eluded us. He was a puzzle.

The doctors were not worried; we were.

One day when Walker was four months old, I was in the bathroom brushing my hair. I had propped him against the wall so he could see more. *Thud!* I looked down to see him lying sideways with his head on the hardwood floor. He must have taken a hard blow, yet he lay there as if nothing had happened. *Why wouldn't a baby cry when he felt pain?*

Walker's habits, and even his instincts, were not what we were used to, or what anyone had given us to expect. He continued to strike peculiar postures. Most babies fall over their parents' shoulders like flour sacks when they're being burped; Walker struck an S shape, arching as if he were doing pull-ups, balanced on someone's shoulder. When I held him this way I had the sense he might climb right out of himself up to the ceiling.

Now why would a baby fall into hysterics, after not crying for days, then suddenly sleep?

Why would a baby recoil when someone put a rattle in his hand?

Why would a baby sleep the very second you let go of him, but not while you're holding him?

And then, as mysteriously as it had appeared, Walker's talent for language was gone. When he was four and a half months old, he could no longer repeat our sounds: "Say 'I love you.'"

When I asked him to perform this little trick, he now turned away.

I remember the sense of guilt I felt when I realized he would no longer speak the way he had before. I had pushed him too far again.

I would let him do it on his own schedule; I resolved to give him more time.

Yet by the time Walker was five months old, it was clear something was wrong. We knew we were losing him; he was slipping away into the shadows. "Perhaps he's just uncomfortable because of his perpetual cold," suggested our family practitioner casually. Yet by now Walker still couldn't look at me at close range. Worse, he gazed away more often than he looked at us. He seemed more interested in the light that flooded into the house through the slatted blinds than in our daughter or us. He searched the windows, obsessively, compulsively. *What was it about those windows?* They seemed somehow significant to him. When he looked out, which he did now almost constantly, it seemed he wasn't just staring blankly but that he was reading something into the light, or the frame, or the blinds, as if there were an entire scene being played out for him there between the dust motes and the windowpanes.

One night when he was four and a half months old, Walker was in the bathroom with Elizabeth and me. He was lying in his baby basket; she was in the tub.

Elizabeth plunged her hands into bubbles and produced a plastic frog. It squeaked. Walker began laughing—uproariously, hysterically: the first time we had ever heard our baby laugh.

Elizabeth jumped out of the tub and squeezed the frog in his face: *Squeeeekkkkkk!* We saw a baby we had never seen before—a child of boundless joy and energy, laughing, responding, asking for more with quivering, excited hands. It was one of the first times brother and sister had any connection at all. Their laughter harmonized, filled those great bathroom acoustics with high-pitched mirth. Elizabeth squeezed and squeezed as Walker laughed and laughed. This was the moment I had been waiting for. We were a family, finally.

One more squeeze. *Squeeeeek*. And nothing.

Squeak again. But no reaction. The veil had fallen.

For days, perhaps even weeks after that, Walker seemed profoundly sad, disinterested. No matter how we positioned his body, he always, much like a needle on a compass, found his way to the light, staring out the windows, obsessively, incessantly.

Light was his true north. And the rest of us remained somewhere just to the east or west or south of his gaze, never in view.

You'll Have to Wait

BY THE TIME WALKER was six months old, we had little doubt that he was seriously ill. He was riddled with eczema and continued to struggle to breathe at night. He moved jerkily and could barely grab a toy. More difficult to describe, but just as compelling, was the deepening sense he was suffering some disturbance of the soul—he flailed in space, could still not look at us at close range, and there was the maddening, inexplicable affinity for windows.

Finally, Cliff and I managed to talk our way into the office of a senior pediatrician at our HMO in the nearby town of Amherst, Massachusetts.

The doctor came in quickly, with an oversized duffel bag. He wrapped a tape measure around Walker's head and measured him in all the ways it's possible for a doctor to measure a baby, checking his length, his reflexes, his muscle tone. Then he tried to talk to Walker. "Walker," he said firmly.

Walker didn't respond.

The doctor dug into his duffel and pulled out a red, fuzzy ball and began waving it in Walker's face. "*Walker!* WAL-KER! . . ." he said first firmly, then animatedly, and finally yelling.

Walker lay staring out the window, impassive, ineluctably drawn to the light.

The doctor took a seat, removed his glasses, and began. He explained that we needed to prepare ourselves for the limitations of our son's abilities. He was delayed in all areas of development. He might never walk or talk—and cognitively? The doctor hinted broadly that our son might be mentally retarded, perhaps even severely. He pointed out Walker's low body tone, his inability to turn over properly (Walker had been using his legs when he should have used his arms to swing his weight, so he flopped onto his stomach; such compensation was highly problematic for reasons I didn't understand). The pediatrician wondered if Walker was perhaps blind or deaf.

Although we knew something was wrong with our son, we had a feeling that the assessment wasn't accurate. We tried to express our perplexity—the uncanny sense that something was missing from this examination. It's true that Walker *was* a distant baby, yet we'd had many moments of connection at far range. Could this strange behavior have something to do with his allergies? We felt certain he was suffering from them: the eczema, the congestion, the discomfort.

The doctor shook his head. Allergies didn't often exist in babies.

We wanted to know if there was a name for his problem. Wasn't there an X-ray or test to find out what was going on?

"No," he said. "There's not a pediatrician in the country who's going to give you a diagnosis at six months old. You'll have to wait."

I queried him about cerebral palsy.

"Cerebral palsy affects the muscles, but not the intelligence," he said, shaking his head. I knew what he was implying. He was saying we couldn't count ourselves among those lucky to have a child with healthy intelligence.

Walker at that time had a small bump on his forehead. I often wondered if his behavior hadn't in some way been linked to it. Now, sitting in the doctor's office, I found myself hoping, in a rather desperate way, that the protrusion was malignant. (Cancer, the old scourge seemed a welcome comrade, operable, removable, compared to what the doctor was intimating.)

"When was the last time you met a baby with cancer?" the doctor asked dryly.

"But he could imitate our speech when he was three months old," I insisted.

The pediatrician assumed a sympathetic expression and looked at the floor.

This not looking was becoming familiar—our son couldn't do it, and now, neither could his doctors. We left our HMO and spent hours the following weeks in pursuit of a specialist with an explanation, but the doctors could offer none. Instead, they could only recommend that we call our local early intervention program, REACH. But we had already done so, at the recommendation of our day-care provider, Donna, whose son as I have said was mentally retarded.

Twenty years ago, Massachusetts was among the first states to introduce a statewide early intervention program, providing therapeutic "home-based" support to developmentally delayed children up to the age of three, and their families. Now, under the federal Individuals with Disabilities Education Act, all fifty states provide such services, often free of charge to families.

The director of REACH, Darleen Corbett, suspected that she knew what was wrong with Walker, before she met him. Yet she was reluctant to tell me over the phone.

"It could be a lot of things. He's only six and a half months old," she said.

I insisted. Finally she was bold enough to reveal her suspicions.

"Your son may have sensory integration disorder," she said. "I can't be sure until I see him, but this certainly sounds like S.I. to me."

"S.I.?"

"An extreme form of sensitivity." She explained that it tended to pervade a variety of systems simultaneously. "A child with S.I. dysfunction is likely to have allergies as well as being sensitive to a variety of stimuli."

"Stimuli?"

"Well, touching. These babies often don't like to be touched. Or to be exposed to light. He may be very sensitive to light."

"I doubt it," I said. "He loves to stare out of windows."

There was a pause.

"Is that what someone does with sensory integration problems?"

"Yes," she said. "Often."

The mystery that was Walker was falling into place—the allergies, the aversion to touching. Windows.

"We'll see you in two weeks, then," she said, bringing the conversation to a close. Still, I couldn't hang up. For the first time in months, someone had answers.

"Please," I insisted. "How serious is this problem? Can you tell me if it's possible to cure it?"

"I'm not saying I know for sure what your son has."

"But a cure?"

"Cure . . .?" she said, and her voice trailed off. "I don't know. But it may be possible to desensitize someone. We'll talk about that more when I see you."

I couldn't let her hang up. "Please," I said, stalling. "Give me something I can do."

"You can help by not smiling too broadly when you're close, and by playing with him."

"But he doesn't like to play."

"Find the brightest, flashiest toy you can find. Take him by the elbow and bring his hand toward it. If he's not going to come to the world, the world will have to come to him."

—

Nights under the single gray kitchen light. Walker, six and a half months old, strapped into his car seat, nowhere near able to sit up. Always looking aside toward the white blinds, even at midnight. The light was brightest off their white surface, or his head was cranked upward facing the bulb on the ceiling.

If light were air, I'd say he was trying to inhale it.

But there was a new problem. Shortly before the appointment with the pediatrician who had waved the ball in Walker's face, our family practitioner had called to say Walker had fallen off the charts for weight gain. He had descended below the lowest chartable weight for his age— below the fifth percentile. *So his body was slipping away too now.* The pediatrician gave me a quota of several ounces a day of rice cereal I needed to somehow force into him. He ate, but awkwardly. I often spent forty-five minutes trying to feed him the cereal, but food fell off his lips in clumps like snow slipping off a roof in spring. He seemed uninterested in eating. I sometimes found myself shaking with the effort.

For two weeks, before the director arrived from REACH, I worked with Walker every chance I had. I laid him on the bed or the floor, but usually in a baby seat, so he could face me, though he didn't seem to want to look. Over and over I held his elbow, bringing it forward, wrapping his tiny, desireless fingers around various objects.

One day I went by myself to our Unitarian Society for a Sunday service while Cliff stayed at home with Walker and Elizabeth. I sat in the balcony alone, not listening to the sermon. Instead, I focused obsessively on a baby, about six months old, sitting in her mother's lap in the pews below. The baby was drinking up the world with her eyes, with her fingers, with her tongue, I could see that. She was filling her senses, loading the huge cup of her wanting. She was pushing up from her feet, moving her hands out toward the world, flirting with the woman in the box next to her, grabbing everything around her, as if she hadn't eaten for days and she were all mouth and stomach. She fingered the pews, pulled her mother's hair, played with her collar, grabbed at the hymnal, wantonly touched a stranger's face. The mother looked frustrated; she probably wished she could relax, listen to the sermon like everyone else. *She doesn't realize she has a healthy daughter. A brilliant daughter,* I said to myself.

That night, after Walker had eaten what he could, I put him up on the table in his car seat as usual. Cliff was upstairs, already asleep. So was Elizabeth.

"I have a present for you," I said softly. "I bought it today when I was out. Back in a second."

I returned to the kitchen and stood in front of Walker with a bag from the toy store. I began to tell him I bought just what Darleen Corbett at REACH told me to buy and was in the midst of pulling at the bag when, in the moment, Walker's hands flew up, shook wildly, and fell. The bag had made a loud popping noise as I'd opened it.

"Did I scare you?" I whispered. "I didn't mean to."

Whew! I thought to myself, *Is this what Darleen Corbett meant by sensitivity? The mere sound of a bag opening tears through my son's nerves?*

I took the bag into the bathroom, opened it slowly so Walker would not hear the crackling, which suddenly struck me as very loud, and brought out my secret weapon. I produced a brightly colored object that looked like a little solar system, slightly larger than two hands clasped. The toy was a sphere, composed of heavy wires covered in bright, soft plastic—yellow, blue, red—perfect for grabbing and chewing and sucking, all those activities that other six-month-olds delight in.

When I came close, Walker's face was turned hard to the left, his head seemed to meld with the car seat, his back arched forward. I knew then that he had been shocked by the abrupt assault of the bag, yet I couldn't help somehow taking his retreat personally. *It is as though he can't get far enough away from me,* I thought.

I tried to move into his line of vision, smiled and cooed. Darleen had told me not to smile too broadly around Walker. He needed a calm, even face. Now, I barely lifted the corners of my lips, trying to win his gaze. He turned harder to the left.

Perhaps I could interest him in something else. I nudged the toy against the back of his limp hand. Nothing. I placed the solar system into his palm.

He didn't respond.

I took his arm by the elbow and moved it forward, the way Darleen had described. Over and over I held his elbow, bringing it forward, wrapping his lifeless fingers around the thin plastic tubes.

"Look!" I said, waiving the bright object in his face.

I put it in Walker's lap. His fingers twitched a little, though the movement might not have meant anything.

His fingers moved again.

I brought the toy closer, wrapped his fingers myself around one of its blue tubes. He clung to it for a moment. *Was he trying to hold on?*

I pulled the toy into the air. His hand stayed grasping for a moment, as if it had been glued to the blue tube, stuck there. Still he wouldn't look my way or at the toy.

My head fell into his lap. I was exhausted—and fought my emotion. And then we went to bed.

Grasping

IT WAS HIGH NOON; the sun was forcing through the window. Walker still obsessed with the light. What was this tendency to move toward the sun— was it like a plant's tropism, or was he attracted to something else: patterns? The blinds with their horizontal slats: dark, light, dark, light. Whatever it was, it was hypnotizing, charming his nascent mind. I tried to attract his attention, but my smile, as muted as I could make it, was no match for the sun.

My next opportunity was at lunch. This time, some improvement. I noticed that his grasp on the wires was firmer.

Yet was he holding harder on purpose?

I pulled his fingers away and put the toy just beyond his reach. He twitched, his hands flailed around, his knuckles knocked against the toy. My hand was shaking now too—that had to have been desire. I felt sure of it—at least I thought I felt sure. I held the toy up higher. The hand flew to it and grasped. *Damn,* I thought, *it was desire.*

Within two weeks Walker was grabbing the toy every chance he had, lifting it to his mouth, sucking it. Doing what babies do.

Nuances are difficult to record. Some of our happiest times can contain dissatisfactions, moments of worry, distress, boredom. Some of the most dismal and distressing moments can contain some element of whimsy, lightness, salvation. Philosophers from several traditions know about this. They refer to the double-edged sword of experience—that we are always carrying heaven and hell with us in each moment. And then there's the way that moments have of coloring and informing each other; as we compare one to the next, we adjust our expectations and aspirations. So when we were given the name, the term "sensory integration disorder," I had felt for a time a sense of relief. We had a name. We had a goal. We had a problem that might even be less threatening than cancer.

I was feeling extremely positive about the progress we had made, was nearly buoyant the afternoon after I thought I saw some improvement. Soon after, Cliff and Elizabeth and Walker and I visited Cliff's parents. I sat happily in the family room explaining that Walker was just extremely sensitive. I tried to explain the progress we had made—that we had moved his elbow, winning in the effort his interest in toys. They frowned, looked away, said "Hmm," skeptically. Cliff wouldn't come to my defense.

"What's wrong?" I asked in the car on the way home. "Why didn't you help me explain to them Walker's difficulties are not necessarily that bad?"

"I'm not sure I believe it," he said.

"What do you mean? The director of REACH did say it was possible to desensitize someone."

"I don't think we're out of the woods yet, Pat."

"What do you mean?"

"I looked up sensory integration on the Internet. Thousands of cross-references. Most of them to autism."

The light changed and the car made a hard left, a ninety-degree turn.

One day I took Walker in his stroller and walked into town with my friend Julie, she with her child and I with mine, strollers moving in tandem down the street. On the way home, Julie's baby, Kezia, played with a small pig on wheels and looked up at Julie from time to time. Walker kept his face at an angle, forced away from me. The motion seemed to deepen his concentration, his obsession with the peripheral. He was cranking his back around, uncomfortable. It had been wrong of me to take the walk. I felt sure that as we did Walker was evaporating, casting off more ounces. Julie began talking about a problem, the kind of conflicts that women often share; she had a friend whom she didn't feel close to any more. What should she do?

Friends? Closeness? Didn't Julie know that I was wading through chest-high water? I'm not even sure I was able to answer her. But what I knew was that everything was changing, the sky was changing, and the air between us was changing. I had the strange sensation that the street was shrinking. Friendship? Lost friendship? My fingers ached.

I hadn't seen Julie for three weeks when I was able to get away to see her at a local restaurant called Paul and Elizabeth's for dinner. We ordered our usual vegetable fried rice with tofu and a large roll to share. Julie was grappling with the question of having another baby. An acupuncturist had advised against it, since Julie's immune system had been compromised since her pregnancy. Still, she was wondering what to do with her life. She wanted to have a child, but she also wanted to study something called the Alexander technique (a method for improving coordination).

"I'd like to study the Alexander method in the fall, but if I do, I won't be able to have a baby until the summer," she began, pondering. "If I have the baby right away, I won't be able to begin studying until two years from now. I guess I could try to get pregnant in the winter. . . . " Her thinking went on like this. Julie was doing what we all do, trying to plan a life inevitably complicated, hoping to rein in what is wild and unmanageable about life with a child when you're a woman who hopes for more than just children. Yet all the while, as she was talking, my back was getting hot. I felt myself leaving my body, somehow floating over the tinkling glasses and the sparkling tables, the ferns. "Damn, Julie," I suddenly blurted out. "Don't you get it? Nature resists planning, Nature *resents* planning. You may never have a child! Your child may have Down syndrome and you won't work for years."

Julie looked down at her lap. Her hands began shaking, her chin. Tears fell.

I tried to explain myself, tried to back out.

Friendship was changing.

The director of REACH, Darleen Corbett, came for her assessment. Walker lay across one of Cliff's arms. She opened a large canvas bag and pulled out a red plastic apple with a bright painted-on face. Walker looked at it. He seemed interested. She tipped it to the side, and as it rocked it chimed an achingly sweet, high-pitched music. Walker looked down at the floor and soon fell asleep.

Later, during our interview, Darleen said evidence was growing that Walker indeed was suffering from S.I. disorder.

"How can you tell?" I said. "He's been sleeping the whole time you've been here."

She held up the apple. "Who else but a hypersensitive baby would sleep the minute you showed him this? Babies sleep to protect themselves. This toy is remarkably stimulating—the color, the bright face, the chime."

"You mean even that child's toy was too much for him?"

She nodded yes.

Walker slept for nearly an hour as we discussed his and my medical history and alternative therapies. When he finally stirred, Darleen brought Walker to a blanket and produced another toy, red with concentric circles. She held it in front of him, as if she were doing a snake charmer's dance. A stunning woman with blond hair and full lips, she seemed to be luring Walker into her field of attention. He followed the toy with his eyes—something I had never seen him do before. It was as if you could change a person just by acting a certain way. How could this woman who had never met our son lure him, entice him, draw him into her spell? And why was this toy attracting Walker when the apple made him fall asleep? What was she doing differently? It seemed that I had spent hours playing gently with Walker and had rarely if ever seen such high levels of attention.

For a week I was happy, explaining to my friends that Walker was capable of more than we realized.

Yet within days, the wheel was turning again.

Within a week, Darleen brought Arlene onto Walker's case. Arlene was a physical therapist with training in motor (movement) problems and sensory integration, and she came to give Walker a full evaluation.

Oddly, when Arlene met Walker, he wasn't at all the baby he had been in the specialist's office, or for her director. In fact, he seemed to have swung dramatically in the opposite direction. No longer dumbstruck, he seemed electric, a caricature of excitement. Walker's head swung from side to side, he was laughing, almost maniacally, and his arms and legs were moving up and down, down and up—rapidly, repetitively—as if he were sprinting through the air upside down.

Folding her long athletic legs under her, Arlene positioned herself gingerly in front of Walker and studied him in obvious alarm. We pressed her for an explanation but she chose her words carefully. While she spoke her gentle words, I translated them into my own. She didn't want to damn Walker before she gave him a chance.

She said that he had severe low upper-body tone. She stressed the word "severe" as she watched him lying on the floor. His thin arms seemed sunken toward the ground as if he were supporting something heavy.

"Is that something we can change?" Cliff asked. "Can't he exercise, build up some muscle?"

"This kind of weakness comes from the brain," she explained.

"You mean muscles have something to do with the brain?" I said, perplexed.

"Yes," she said.

"But what could be wrong with it?"

Both Arlene and her supervisor shrugged.

I wanted to know if we could give him some tests, but to my astonishment, Darleen Corbett said, "You can give him an MRI, but I don't recommend it."

"But why?"

"I think it will just confuse you—give you an idea about your son before you know who he is."

"An MRI?"

"I've seen kids with brains that looked shot full of holes like the surface of the moon who were fine—other kids with perfect MRIs who were very ill. You don't want to be thinking of your son that way, as damaged or full of holes while you're playing with him."

"So what can we do to help him?" Cliff asked.

She put her hands around Walker's thin arms, one around the upper, one around the lower, and pushed his forearm toward his elbow as if she were trying to snap it in place. "You can do this."

Great, I thought. *They're telling me my son might not walk or talk, is weak in the upper body, and we will start by pushing on his arms. How can any of what you're doing amount to anything?* Yet another voice said,

They're giving you something to do at last. I wrapped my fingers around the arms and pushed.

On her first official therapeutic visit a few days later Arlene and I talked, and we watched Walker. I noticed that he changed dramatically the minute she entered the room. His body began moving more and more, his hands swinging. Now he was making that odd sprinting motion through the air, something he had rarely done when he was alone with the family. Yet he wasn't oriented to Arlene or relating to her. It was almost as if he was too excited to even look at her.

I asked her about autism, but on this first visit she could only repeat: "You have a very sensitive son."

"Do you think he has autism?" I repeated.

She shook her head. No one could know.

PART 2

What's in a Face

AND SO, WE BEGAN OUR WORK with Walker, Arlene and I. We began
in a darkened room. No matter how we altered his position, his head continued to move like that needle of the compass to the light. Light was still his
true north. But in dim light, with drawn shades, Walker slowly moved his head
away from the window. What he looked at then was not us, but objects. Toys.

"Why objects?" I said to Arlene. "Why won't he look at me? It's
hard not to believe he just doesn't like us."

"Because faces have an amazing amount of information in them,"
she said. "Especially the eyes. Right now that's too much information
for him. Right now he prefers objects."

"Here," she said, "hold Walker closely." She described with Walker's
body, from head to toe, a crescent moon shape. "Keep him this way,"
she said, "curled in a ball." I held him gingerly in the mock fetal pose.
Arlene pulled my arms in tighter to make a firm fit.

"Why?" I said.

"It helps brain development," she said.

"You're kidding. You mean how the body is positioned can actually change how the brain grows?"

She might as well have been telling me to make sure Walker's crib
faced east. Yet I believed her. You didn't *not* believe Arlene.

"Does he know who you are?" she said to me one day. "Does he miss
you when you leave the room?"

Now I didn't answer.

Arlene was supposed to stay for an hour each week. Sometimes, she stayed for three. The goal with Walker was to attune his senses to each other and to an overwhelming world—not just so that he would be a happier baby but so that he might be able to resist the sirens that beckoned him inward. From the time she began working with Walker, Arlene made clear what was at stake: If Walker couldn't maintain his focus on the external world, he would not be able to learn. Her therapy might not be able to reach him, but she was eager to try. During these visits she worked intently to try to gain Walker's attention. I knew she wanted eventually to take him the next step, beyond toys to the human frontier, to where he would be giving *us* his attention, but she made it clear she wasn't sure it was possible. She stared down at the baby on the floor often, her brow knit just like his, and used the word "worrisome."

One day Arlene brought a thick wool fleece. She pulled her long legs apart, put the fleece on the floor within that V, placed Walker on it, and positioned her hand firmly on his chest. "I'm trying to turn off some of his senses," she said, "particularly the proprioceptive, the sense he has of knowing where he is in space. If we can quiet his proprioceptive, we might be able to reach his attention." I was beginning to understand: If she could keep him from that searching, lost hand-flailing on the floor, moving his arms as if he were falling through outer space, he might be comfortable enough to look at us—just as when the lights were dim, she could keep him from being seduced by those siren windows. Only then might he be able to "learn," as she called it.

She drew a toy from her bag, a tube that moved in and out like an accordion, and let him touch it. She pulled it away, challenging him to grab from a farther and farther distance.

The next visit, she brought a set of colorful stacking rings, the kind babies place around a plastic post. She enticed Walker to grab a yellow ring, which he did readily. Over and over they played this game. They worked with these plastic donuts, for hours it seemed. Him grabbing. Her grabbing. She talked all the while, in soothing, alluring tones, her mouth turned up at just the right angles.

"Why the light?" I asked Arlene. "Why would light be attractive to a child who's sensitive?"

"I don't know," she said. "Perhaps because it is stimulating some-how. Or perhaps because it's like a great void, a great nothingness."

"You mean it blinds him . . . like snow blindness."

"Yes, possibly," she said.

One day, when in our darkened room, I held him tightly in a ball as Arlene instructed me to do. Now that one of his senses was somehow "turned off," Arlene thought he might be able to use his energy to look at me.

"Hold him close," said Arlene. "Now, try to get his attention, but don't smile too much. That would be too much for him." I held Walker firmly and waited. He looked up at me, and his large round green eyes penetrated mine. Suddenly his hand rose to touch my face. I shivered—seven months old and he'd never come this close before. Yet within the instant, his hand flew in the other direction; his eyes looked away as if looking at me had been painful.

"It's not that he doesn't want to," said Arlene, "It's that he can't."

Exhausted by the effort, Walker fell into a deep sleep without warn-ing. While he slept, I tried to find ways to make it all right for Arlene to tell me her deepest worries. (I needed to know those worries. If I had an adversary, I felt compelled to know what it might look like at its worst.) But Arlene played her cards closely.

"Have you ever seen a baby with these exact problems of Walker's? The low upper-body tone? The sensory integration prob-lems?"

She considered Walker for a long time. Walker lay struggling to breathe in his sleep.

"No."

"How long have you been doing this?"

"Fifteen years."

"Have you seen babies who were sort of like this?"

"I guess," she said.

"What has become of them?"

"Some do all right. Others . . ." Her voice trailed off.

Talking about what was at risk was clearly difficult for Arlene, and I'm not sure I wanted to know. She knew this, and she felt she needed to protect me.

Still, the gray areas, the not knowing, the waiting was maddening. I called REACH's director, Darleen Corbett, and told her I needed to know what she and Arlene were thinking about Walker.

"I've got to believe he's going to pass those physical milestones," she said. "What we're not sure about are the psychological ones. We don't know if he's capable of interaction, or reciprocity."

I knew what that meant. It meant my son might never learn to love.

"You must strive for reciprocity with him."

But how?

———

That summer, my mother came from California for four weeks to take care of our daughter, Elizabeth, who had turned five that spring. One day I brought Elizabeth to swim at my mother's hotel. In the solarium, I passed a thin, tall man sitting on a lounge chair next to the swimming pool. Cross-legged, stiff-backed, arms outstretched in either direction, the man moved his hands through the air, swami-style, wrists rotating as if he were drawing a pattern of circles. As he drew in the air, he watched his hands. An hour later, he was unchanged. I knew what to call his problem. No one but Cliff had used the term when talking about Walker, but it was clear they were worried about autism. Both Arlene and her director had expressed their alarm at the level of Walker's unrelatedness, his tendency to pull inward, the peculiar motions of his limbs.

Yet why wouldn't they address the problem of autism outright? Why not encourage me to do research? Why not encourage me to know as much as I could about the problem? I confess, I was reluctant to read about it myself. I was afraid of seeing my son in the portraits I might run across—kids banging their heads against walls, staring at the ground, rocking senselessly, incessantly. Every time I brought up the subject, Arlene skirted it, still as if to say (though she would never say so), "You don't want to damn your son."

When I was in high school, my mother was working toward a master's degree in psychology. As part of her research she often visited a boy named Adam who was living in an institution thirty miles north of our town in the suburbs of Los Angeles. Every week my mother went to see Adam, and each week she tried to make Adam love her. The boy seemed indifferent to her charms. Instead, he talked only of math, of numbers.

Her idea was to woo him to be close to her. She thought a gift might bring about the transformation, so she decided to buy him a calculator.

She clapped her hands, then rubbed them together, scheming how she might be able to bring some pleasure to a boy who seemed somehow unaware, unused to, or even bored by pleasure.

"How did it go with Adam?" I asked when she came home after delivering the calculator.

She slumped on the couch. "He just threw it on the ground."

"Why?"

"I just don't think they know how to care, or relate." She stared off toward the window of our front door. "When autistic people are born, they won't conform to their mother's body. They just lie there stiffly. They don't want to be hugged. They don't want love. It's something they're born with."

My mother's teachers had insisted that people with autism recoiled out of some primal revulsion to love, affection, and human interaction. This was the reason they didn't want to touch. Yet what was the meaning of not wanting to be touched?

I had a psychology professor in college who had worked with autistic patients. His entire purpose seemed to be to try to make them seek out human touch, as if touching were synonymous with interacting and caring. He'd even made a movie about the effort called *The Psychologist Who Wore Tennis Shoes.* He had arranged for a camera to film him standing next to an autistic boy in a small boxlike room the size of an elevator. The floor of the room was metallic, wired with electricity. With cameras rolling, someone flipped the switch. The barefoot boy with autism flew into the arms of the psychologist in tennis shoes.

Such was the psychologist's proof that one could force contact with an autistic patient. Not a very optimistic vision. And what was his point? That under coercion or mortal danger we can force someone to interact? And anyway, love wasn't jumping into someone's arms to avoid pain. That was survival.

———

It was a night in mid-May. Walker and I were in the bathroom. I was brushing my teeth. I looked at Walker's face as he sat propped in a large basket near me. He seemed disturbed, yet I could tell he knew I was there with him; I felt his presence with me.

He was still covered with patches of eczema, still struggling to breathe.

"Walker," I whispered, staying as calm and even-toned as I could.

He didn't answer. I looked up into the mirror at myself. *Thud!*—a banging as if an anvil had fallen. I knew Walker had fallen again, this time from a propped position out of the basket onto his head. As I moved toward him, I braced myself for the scream that was inevitable. Of course, Walker had been unresponsive in the past, yet I kept expecting reactions from him. No scream came. I looked down at him. He lay on the floor, his head staring straight ahead, the ball and claw foot of the bathtub threateningly close to his eyes. I stood up, to take a broad view. Oddly, he was posed in the same position he had held when he was propped up in the basket, as if the floor had moved ninety degrees instead of him.

"Walker," I whispered, but he was emotionless, frozen. I picked him up and held him, felt his heart. It wasn't exactly racing, but it was quick, birdlike.

I brought him downstairs near my desk, and holding him in my arms I logged onto the Internet. It was 1997 and I had just learned how to use a search engine. I punched in all the words. Infant, brain, disease "head." Hydrocephalus appeared, a disease in which the brain expands because of a buildup of fluid. I considered for a split second, remembering that the pediatrician at our HMO had found Walker's head a bit large for his body. "The brain of children with this disease once exploded from pressure." I scrolled down to find photos of the skeletal remains of babies' skulls that had burst in slow motion, bones bending backward like crown roast, like overbloomed flowers bending back in decline.

Into the hard silvery light of the computer screen, I stared for a long time, not sure I wanted to go forward. I knew that autism was about emotional withdrawal. Cliff and I had discussed it over the phone while he was at work, just the day before. It seemed clear that Walker was headed for an autistic retreat. Now I looked at my computer screen. All I needed to do was type in the word. But I didn't.

I remembered once reading a theory of how higher intelligence developed on this planet. Some neurobiologists theorize that higher intelligence may have come as an aberration, a mutation. Suddenly, early man could think. The crises, these theorists argue, of such an emergence, proved daunting for primitive man, for nothing in man's history or his emotional constitution prepared him to carry the heavy weight of a brain, the unbearable responsibility of intelligence itself. Now it struck me that I was faced with a similar burden, in a way. When I was pregnant with Walker, I had used my computer as if it were a typewriter. Yet by the time he was six months old, that same typewriter, overnight, had become a genius. The weight of the world lay in that plastic box. Many nights, as Walker lay sleeping, I felt aware that the computer was sitting there, seeming to quietly hum—to seethe and boil with information. (We had been on-line just two weeks when we discovered Walker was ill.) It was a magic mirror, waiting to be charmed into speaking. Yet something stayed my hands. I knew I wasn't necessarily ready for some of the information I would find. Still, on that night I found that I couldn't look away.

I punched in keywords: "Infant," "disease," "neurological." Names of pathologies of every stripe flashed on the screen, chains of Latinate verbiage, an opaque cryptology.

I came first to the metabolic diseases of storage. PKU, or phenylketonuria, metachromatic leukodystrophy; Krabbe's disease; Canavan disease. A malfunctioning enzyme could wreak havoc with a baby's entire body, including brain development. In such metabolic diseases the brain deteriorates. Prognosis: death within a few years. I came to tuberous sclerosis, a disease in which tumors appear on the heart, the kidneys, the brain. The description said that TS often looks like autism and could be the cause of sudden kidney failure. I read about Fragile X syndrome, so named because of a "fragile site" on the X chromosome. Fragile X could also look like autism, mental retardation. There was even something called maple syrup disease in which the urine of the child smells mysteriously like maple syrup.

That night, when I closed down the computer, the room suddenly became dark except for the glow from the streetlights creeping through the shades; I sat in the near dark for a long time, thinking. Arlene made it clear that it would take weeks or months to sort out exactly what was wrong with Walker. Any of those diseases might be responsible for his behavior. We would need to wait for the results of blood tests, possible brain scans. I climbed upstairs, bent down and sniffed at Walker's diaper. But maple syrup was not our problem. Of course, I knew what word to go down and type in. I hesitated.

The World Is Too Much

MORNINGS WITH WALKER on the rug with Arlene. Walker's face is blotched with purple, because he rolled onto the rug. Just touching it makes his cheeks look bruised. His eyes have large circles around them, almost black and blue. The world seems to be an assault. Am I speaking too loudly?

More than twenty years ago, A. Jean Ayres, an occupational therapist, found a key to what makes people with sensory integration withdraw from the world into what can be an autistic retreat: Often they are not out of tune with this world, she declared, but, ironically, far too aware of it. The world is too much with them, and because they are excruciatingly sensitive, they're forced to retreat. Reading about S.I. dysfunction deepened my understanding of what Arlene was already telling me. The corners were filling in. I began looking back over perplexing moments with new insight. I realized, for example, that Walker wasn't necessarily unaware of the pediatrician's presence when he became distant in the examining room—he was simply overstimulated.

Imagine your sensory world scrambled and unregulated, your auditory intake an incessant rock station—or worse, mere static—blasting in your ears. Imagine your kitchen light as bright as a searchlight, boring into your cornea every time you turn it on. Imagine yourself in clothes so irritating that they seem lined with metal scraping brushes. Imagine walking past a woman wearing a spritz of Chanel No. 5 that leaves you disoriented and dizzy. Imagine entering a restaurant and encountering fumes so overpowering to your eyes that you think the cook must be boiling Mace. This can be the world of sensory integration dysfunction.

Understanding the enigmatic and contradictory world of sensory dysfunction, I learned, is the task of S.I. experts. Most S.I. experts initially trained as occupational therapists or physical therapists. It's also the task of parents and can seem like a sojourn in the world of Lewis Carroll. Understanding a child through his senses requires close detective work—intimate, hair-splitting observation—because each person who suffers from sensory challenges is unique.

Children with S.I. problems can also be hyposensitive (undersensitive) in one or more areas, even within the same area. I learned that certain frequencies may drive someone crazy with their intensity, while others are hard to hear. Or a person may have oversensitive hearing yet be undersensitive visually. A tactilely hyposensitive child might need to throw himself against a wall just to know he exists, just to feel himself in space. Walker flailed in space because his sense of the location of his limbs, his body parts, and even the boundaries of his own being wasn't working well. Arlene delicately pointed me toward understanding that Walker was spending most of his energy trying to figure out where he was.

In her visits, Arlene continued to stay for two or three hours. At one session, she brought the accordion tube. She sat with her legs crossed in front of her and continued to teach Walker the craft of learning to "attend," trying to move to a finer alchemy, the art of mixing attention with tolerance for faces. Perhaps Walker could one day learn to gaze into the eyes of a woman. It wouldn't be an easy task, might not work at all. Still, she explained that her intention was to reveal herself to Walker slowly. She would began with objects. She presented the tube. He grabbed it. She grabbed it back. After a few minutes he turned away. We could see what the effort was costing Walker, and I could see what it was costing Arlene. She strained at the work of keeping his attention. He often fell suddenly into a deep sleep. His mouth hung open like a fish, in the way that the weary and exhausted have of sucking in air intently, as if oxygen were scarce.

While Walker slept, Arlene and I talked.

"This is not environmental," she said.

"Environmental?"

"It's not your fault."

One day in late May, when Cliff was able to take time off work, Arlene began educating Cliff and me to further refinements in the science that was Walker. She spoke often of the risks associated with Walker's condition. It was not just a problem of what objects the baby would be willing to look at or touch. If that were Walker's problem, it would have been simpler. She kept driving home the message that Walker's sensitivity threatened the very development of his brain. If he was too sensitive to look, he couldn't give his attention to the things that mattered for brain development. He wouldn't learn. He might retreat, and retreating would mean lost brain cells. One didn't want to risk lost brain cells. They would never come back. We must try to do whatever we could to keep him sheltered from too much stimulation.

"It's probably best not to take him in the car," she said, "but if you do, put a blanket over him.

"Why a blanket?" said Cliff.

"You want to turn off his visual. Visual input," she explained, "represents only one of several systems he needs to regulate along with all others. When he's in the car, he's using many systems—his hearing, proprioception, vestibular (his sense of movement). It's a good idea to turn off at least one of the senses, so he can focus on the others, so he isn't overstimulated."

"But how will we know if he becomes overstimulated?" I asked.

"You're going to have to learn to read his cues."

Cues. Read. I had taken literature and art courses in college. There I had learned how to read the obscure text, to interpret beyond the apparent, to look for patterns across a broad and painted tapestry.

So I was going to have to interpret Walker, read him.

"You'll learn," she said. "But notice now, how calm his body is, not twisted or turned to the side. If you can keep him this way, he might be able to learn. Just remember to cover him in the car."

That afternoon I found myself standing in the driveway wondering how one could safely cover the face of the baby, especially on a warm day. I inspected the inside of the baby car seat, turned it upside down, looking for an attachment that would serve to shade him. Some baby car seats came with shields, but mine didn't. So much for buying bargain brands. I put Walker into the seat, buckled it into the car, but left the carrying handle up, ignoring the sign on the side of the device: "Warning, do not leave upright." I laid a plaid baby blanket over the plastic handle to make a tent for Walker. On the way to picking up Elizabeth and her friends at nursery school, I drove through downtown, our busy, bustling college town. Out in the world, stuck in traffic, I watched mothers with their babies cruising by on the sidewalk, sitting at cafés. In the bright, full light of day, I saw mothers wheeling their babies around in carriages, casually looking into their faces, playing peekaboo, whipping those carriages around in half circles that would have seemed a fun-house horror to Walker. Mothers were kissing babies' faces, laughing with them, pushing scratchy knit blankets up to their chins. I saw one mother eagerly spooning, pressing ice cream into her baby's mouth. Her friend's baby was lacing tiny fingers into her hair.

On the way out of town toward the nature sanctuary, the site of the nursery school, the car jostled over potholes and ditches, and bumped heavily over the dirt road. My tires shot out pebbles toward plants and trees rustling in the startlingly bright air. Birds cawed shrilly. Though I was trying to drive smoothly, the car seemed to me to be lurching as I added gas to climb an incline over the rattly one-lane metal bridge. I turned to see how Walker was doing, but I didn't want to upset the blanket. When we arrived at the school, I checked. Walker was staring blankly away, head cranked sideways. I knew the car ride had overwhelmed him, but *I'd had no choice. It was my turn to pick up the kids.* I took the car seat into the school, with the tent still covering Walker. The seat lurched against my leg. Inside, children laughed and screamed. I had never realized before how much motion and color and noise was in a typical school day. The room, tasteful and tame by most standards with its wood paneling and models of birds on the walls, was filled with bright pictures, paints, pencils, which suddenly seemed to me to be moving with intensity. I adjusted the blanket. Meanwhile, Elizabeth and her friends rushed over. She pulled the blanket off the car seat and affectionately buried her head in Walker's stomach, kissed his face. Walker stared. It occurred to me that someone might consider him merely tired, ready to nod off to sleep. Yet I saw that his hands were shaking.

"So here's the question," I asked Arlene the next time she came to the house. "Can I take Walker to the store?"

She looked down. "You can . . . it's just that . . ."

"Just what?"

"He won't be learning."

"You mean he won't be learning anywhere, unless he's at home in dim light, in quiet?"

She nodded.

Walker awakened that moment. He seemed relaxed, in a quiet state, looking at us from afar, from his place on a blanket in the sea of rug. An eerie sense shot through me. I motioned subtly with my head for Arlene to look over at him. He was with us in a way I hadn't felt for a long time. I could feel him there—his being pervading the room. In spite of the peculiar tendency of one eye to move after the other, I knew he saw us. Or at least seemed to. Arlene exhaled quickly as if to say, "Wow. Yes." Walker began to roll from his back to his stomach. As if he was going to move toward us. In the instant, a sound ripped through the room. It was high and shrill, as if a wasp wired for electronic sound were in our midst. Walker arched and flailed his arms as if he were trying to get his bearings.

"What *is* that?" I said, jumping up. I pulled the curtains aside and realized that someone next door had turned on a chain saw.

It sounds as if they are grinding raw steel. What are they doing, shoving a car into a leaf shredder?

Walker turned away, wouldn't eat all morning.

He had seemed so present with his vocalizations. Yet now I am beginning to see that though he was present in subtle ways, he had withdrawn from the rest of the world.

That night as I lay in bed, I tried to imagine a life we could patch together for the four of us. Elizabeth was an exuberant child, remarkably so—in love with all things bright and burning with intensity. They were like the figures in the yin-yang symbol, the two children sharing only some secret essence of the other at the core—the white paisley having a black inner circle, and the black having a white inner circle—Elizabeth and Walker. How could we give her what she needed and still give Walker what he needed?

Elizabeth could not tolerate being alone, she sought our attention at every turn, wanted us by her side when she fell asleep, longed for us to watch television with her. She wanted conversation, stimulation, pulled at us with every resource available to her—her charm (immense), her vocabulary (huge). At nursery school they said she talked as if she were just leaving a college lecture hall. She could shine for company, beg for it, laugh us into giving it to her, chide us, be sarcastic. She could dance and sing, and draw nearly better than I could, but what she couldn't do was go to her room and be alone. *If Walker drinks light, what does she drink? People?*

I would need to shield Walker from his sister. I mapped out something of a plan. I would need to find separate places for them to spend their time during the day. We could give Elizabeth the living room, which was more remote; Walker could have the dining room, easily darkened when the blinds were drawn, and I could stay closer, given the proximity of the kitchen. The next morning I caught Cliff before work and we sat down. I told him I didn't think we should take Walker out of the house at all.

"I understand," he said. "Too much for the little man." (That was Cliff's nickname for Walker from the first days in the hospital.) Yet by the following Sunday, we were arguing. "I'm not going to let you entomb us in this house," he insisted.

"But can't we go out separately?"

"Damn it, Pat, we're a family. We've got to stay together."

"I don't want him going out."

"Never?"

"Do you realize what it means for him?"

"This is so extreme. So absolute. How can we live this way?"

REACH sent a social worker. She sat with Cliff and me, Walker in my arms, in the afternoon while Elizabeth was at school and patiently tried to guide me into understanding that no family could live the way I was proposing. We would have to take Walker to the store, to dance lessons, on trips with the car pool. If that was our life, Walker would have to learn to fit in.

"But we need to find another way."

She looked at me skeptically.

So much of loving is about accommodation. Other people's needs change us. It's the stuff we weave our lives of. A lover likes a certain stew; it gets cooked more often. A child likes a certain dress; one buys more like it. A friend likes a certain subject; one discusses it. How much, I began to wonder, had we been accommodating Walker's special need for quiet, for solitude, without even realizing it? *How much had we accommodated to make him capable of even offering the small, but perhaps significant, offerings he had been capable of?* We had, for example, stood far away to reach Walker's attention.

Walker began to arch, and I put him down on a blanket.

"Why did you do that?" the social worker asked.

"What?"

"Put him down?"

"I think he was overstimulated from all the touching." She squinted her eyes skeptically, wrote something in her notes.

"What you need to do is think about the needs of your family," she said as she wrote.

"I am," I insisted, "My son is . . . well, he's . . . ill," I answered, gesturing toward Walker. What was the word? "He's not going to learn if I take him out."

"And what about you?" she queried.

"What do you mean? I'm his mother."

"This will put a strain on your family . . . on your marriage!"

"Do you realize what a strain it's going to put on our marriage, if our son doesn't learn?"

Arlene came the next day, carefully pulled some toys out of her canvas bag, and said, "I owe you an apology. I think I may have overstepped my bounds last week. If you need to drive to the store with Walker, drive him to the store."

"What are you talking about? You just told me days ago he wouldn't be learning if I took him out."

"The team had a discussion," said Arlene.

"What team?"

"Your team."

"We have a team?"

"Yes. At REACH. The team has decided it's best for you to take him wherever your family needs to go."

"But what about what you said?"

"It's important that the family stay healthy."

"Oh, I get it," I said. "The social worker put you up to this!"

"We don't want you to put your needs aside."

"If Walker doesn't get well, we'll spend the rest of our lives putting our needs aside!" I said.

"It's just that I think I made a mistake when we last spoke. You can't spend your life like this."

"So this is my life now? It's not going to change?"

Arlene didn't answer.

"Tell me, Arlene. If Walker were your son, would you take him to the store?"

She looked down at the baby sleeping, face puckered. "No," she said. "I wouldn't. I would keep him at home."

In the social worker's notes which I was able to read years later to prepare for this book, I find a strange quality of disconnection, of alienation, or perhaps I just don't like being written about this way. She writes: "Very distressed mother who . . . sees herself as having the potential to 'rescue' her son. . . . " Later, she comments on the level of connection I have with Walker, suggesting that she couldn't tell if it was me or Walker who was making our connections "fleeting."

I realize that the social worker wanted to help me, in the best way that she could. She was perhaps used to working with "distressed mothers." I could accept the concept that I needed to take care of myself. But I was having a hard time swallowing her philosophy that this was not a crisis, that this family with this ill child was life as usual. She seemed to have the opinion that Walker was ill but that we'd better get used to it. I also had the peculiar sense from her that she somehow blamed me for Walker's state. It was in her eyes, in her insinuations. Years later, I discovered that she was closely scrutinizing me to see how I was interacting with Walker, noting that our interactions were "superficial," as if she had found the great wellspring of the problem in me.

I began to wonder whether I was loving Walker too much, that my love, a mother's love, was too much for him. *Was it something particular about me? Did he see my need? Or perhaps his need, reflected in me?* I pulled away often, didn't touch him much, saw how much better he slept when not near me, even began to notice that Cliff could put Walker to sleep faster than I. *So what am I supposed to do—love him from afar? Love him as an idea? Think of him as something rare and perishable to be put on the shelf for safekeeping?* I couldn't help but pull away, for his sake. *How strange that pulling away relaxes him,* I thought. He seemed more in control of his body when he wasn't being touched.

I was learning how to hold him without moving. Arlene said that it wasn't me he recoiled against, wasn't my body, but it was movement itself that disorganized Walker. When I nursed him, I stayed as still as could be. His habit was to nurse frantically as if he were starving, then break off quickly. Perhaps he couldn't bear it—with skin touching skin, mouth touching breast. Add to the mix the sound of my breathing, the sound or the feel of my heart, the pressure to his joints, the work and the feel of sucking, the shock of sudden noises, the touch of the roof of his mouth. When he pulled away, his cheeks were red.

I sat frozen like a picture, knowing that if I moved, his body would not be able to follow my line of movement. His mind would become confused, and if his mind became confused, Arlene said, he might not continue to drink—and as she reminded me, might not look, or learn.

My friend Kyle came over occasionally, a mother of two great high school kids. She walked in the door, greeted Elizabeth warmly, and started looking around the room for his basket, with this hungry, deliciously optimistic smile on her face. She lit up when she saw him, adored every inch of him, brought him funny socks and teddy bears, fondled his legs and arms, scrubbing at them with assured affection. When she baby-sat him for an hour, she even put cream on his skin, which I couldn't imagine doing. Yet her fondling seemed to work. Why?

"Pat," Cliff said, "you're his mother. Of course your touching is going to be more intense."

I swallowed hard at the statement.

How to make my touching less overwhelming?

If there's too much information in the average face, how much information is in a mother's face?

Reciprocity

"YOU MUST TRY FOR RECIPROCITY," Darleen Corbett had said. "Try to get him to imitate you. Try to imitate him," Arlene suggested.

Every day after I worked with Walker, trying to gain his attention, I left him alone on a blanket in the dining room. I went into the kitchen to the ease of washing dishes in warm water, to the small comfort of moving sponge over porcelain, and looked out at the house across the way, a large, friendly looking, brick Victorian with over twenty windows, like eyes, all flashing at me, returning my gaze. Every few dishes I found myself stealing back into the dining room to check on Walker. Often he used the technique he had found to roll onto his back. One day when he was about seven and a half months old, I found him that way, striking the backward C shape, arching toward some unreachable spot in the galaxy, head bent backward, that otherness in the eyes, and I remember being filled with the strangeness of him. It rose in me like water filling a tank from below. In the moment, I caught myself in midthought, hated myself for thinking it. Blasphemy of motherhood. You must not think this way about your own child. You must, as Darleen said, try for reciprocity. Reciprocity. They had said again and again, "Try to get him to imitate you."

"Walker," I said.
     He didn't respond.
     "Walker," I said again, raising my voice.
     Nothing.

This time I determined to lower my volume—still no response. I went back into the kitchen and rinsed my hands, gazed at the house letting hot water run over my hands, returned. I went toward him and stood three feet away.

"Walker," I whispered.

He moved his head toward mine. I lay down in front of him, tried to enter his line of vision. I had the idea that if I could imitate him and move into his purview I might be able to make a connection. Could he recognize himself in me? I bent my head backward, arching my back and neck in the backward crescent—like a ballet dancer arching impossibly. Of course, it was the wrong way, but it was his way. In that odd pose, I tried to gaze out the window, cocked my eyes sideways the way he sometimes did, and tried to see what he saw—stars in a daytime sky? Or at least, I hoped that he would see what I was up to. I turned my head back toward him, regarded him for a long while. Was he watching me? I had the sense he might be. I felt his gaze, his attention. It was eerie. I lifted my leg, slowly, put it down. Lifted it again.

He lifted his leg. Put it down.

Chills ran through me. . . . It was uncanny, impossible somehow—that eerie moment in the science fiction movie when the protagonist realizes he's in the company of extraordinarily intelligent life. Ghosts were a scary thought, but in that moment I had the sudden sense that we were both ghosts, Walker and I, that all of us are ghosts. My heart was thumping madly and I wanted to say, "You're a genius," but I was afraid to break the spell, concerned that I had only imagined he was imitating me.

I lifted my arm instead.

He lifted his. I put mine down, waited for him to follow. Just then an ambulance screeched by, rising to a shrill, the shrill high point of the Doppler scale, until it seemed it was driving in from the kitchen. Within seconds it receded. Walker arched and looked away, the otherness returning to his eyes. All engagement was gone.

It didn't matter. I got off the floor and went to the phone, called Cliff. "He imitated me, Cliff," I said. "I got him to do it!" I was speaking into his answering machine. Cliff knew that Walker could imitate from far away; we'd seen him do it, waving his hands if we did. But what we'd never seen was any consistency.

When Cliff arrived home with Elizabeth, who had been visiting friends, I jumped down onto the floor with Walker to demonstrate to them what he could do. Elizabeth ran to the center of the room and danced. I asked her to stop and watch. Cliff took her onto his lap on the floor, had to hold her back, and they waited. I positioned my body seven feet from Walker. I waited for him to notice me and eventually raised my leg.

Nothing. No reaction.

"Wait a minute," I said. I rushed to him and changed his position to the salutary C shape. "Now maybe he'll do it. Just watch this," I said.

He didn't put his leg up.

I tried again, but still he did nothing.

"Come on," I urged in soothing tones. "He did it before, you guys, I swear."

"We believe you," said Cliff cheerfully, and we went into the kitchen for dinner.

The next morning, Cliff called me from work to tell me he had made an appointment for Walker with our chiropractor-nutritionist, Gary Lasneski. Lasneski was a maverick in our town. Rumors abounded about his unusual powers, that he was able to successfully treat diseases that no one else could; he was rumored to have appreciably helped someone with Lyme disease in an advanced stage, said to have relieved a woman of Graves disease, a serious condition of the thyroid. Lasneski had correctly diagnosed Cliff with an iron deficiency, a problem unusual for a man. He was so popular that his patients were on a three-month waiting list. But I had my own reasons for wanting to see Lasneski. He had a master's degree in nutrition. When I was in college I was deeply impressed by Norman Cousins's *Anatomy of an Illness As Perceived by the Patient,* in which vitamin C plays a major role in Cousins's successful fight against a rare terminal disease.

When Cliff told Lasneski our story, he insisted he needed to see Walker right away.

Walker and I were barely in the examining room when Lasneski said, "He has an eye lag."

"What's an eye lag? No doctor has mentioned this," I said, putting Walker's car seat down.

"The eyes don't move together," said Lasneski.

I asked him what that meant.

"It means," said Lasneski, "he may not be seeing us." Lasneski looked over at his assistant, Mindy, who smiled at me weakly. "It may mean he only sees flashing lights, may be experiencing storms in the brain. I suggest we give him supplements. Are you nursing?"

I nodded.

"We'll give *you* supplements."

Lasneski pulled a plastic bottle off a shelf and shook it. It rattled.

He talked quickly, urgently. "Over 50 percent of the brain is made up of these types of fatty acids. You know how people used to give babies fish oil? Well, that's essentially what we're going to give him, but there's a designer version out now, free of metallic pollutants. DHA. We're going to stuff these into him. You'll take six of them a day. Very expensive. But worth it. We'll also give him taurine for the retina. Babies can't make enough taurine. Neither can cats. If cats don't get enough of this stuff they lose their ability to see at night. The baby will need taurine to make bile salts to absorb fats. We'll also give him biotin to help regulate nerve firing in his brain. (Research later indicated that his statements about taurine and DHA and biotin were true.)

"Tell me . . . will you," I interrupted. "Is this brain damage?"

"That's the wrong way to conceive of the problem," said Lasneski. "A more accurate description would be faulty brain wiring."

I realize that some of what Lasneski said sounds unconventional, but I believed him. Cliff and I had seen improvement in our own health from Lasneski's supplements. In any case, nutrition had to be important, particularly for this child who was wasting away.

In the reception area, while I was writing a check, the frosted glass window slid open. A head stuck out to greet me. It was Mindy, Lasneski's assistant. "I know what the doctor means by storms in the brain," she said eagerly. "I suffered a head injury from a car accident— I had those storms in the brain from brain damage. I couldn't drive. I couldn't separate the raindrops from the road, the rain from the wind-shield. I couldn't remember anything new after the accident. My memory wasn't working. Eventually I worked to gain it back."

"But how did you do it?" I asked.

"I began with memorization," Mindy said. "I began memorizing poetry. I posted a poem. It was written before Plato about healing. I tried to remember a word. And then a second word. And a third."

Walker and I crossed the bridge over the Connecticut River—it was full to overflowing, rushing on toward points south, Connecticut and Long Island Sound—but I was in the same place, thinking about Walker, now considering Mindy's story, and something I couldn't shake that Dr. Lasneski had told me in his office.

"You're born with all the nerve cells you'll ever use, more than a bil-lion," Lasneski had said when I asked him if you could fix bad wiring. "Whatever connections aren't working right can't be fixed. The brain can't heal itself the way your hand can heal itself from a wound. Dead cells are dead cells. But the brain is an amazing organ. What's remark-able about the brain is the way it learns to compensate. Cells take over what needs to be done." Lasneski had grabbed his swivel chair and threw his leg over it. "Have you ever heard of Phineas Gage?"

"No."

"He was in charge of detonations for the railroad in New England. An explosion happened. A tamping iron was hurled right through his brain, his skull, and then hurled back out into the sky. You'd expect him to be dead, right? Miraculously he was able to live a life after that. His personality changed though—there's a lot of stuff he found diffi-cult to do. But he could still walk around town, talk to people. Other parts of the brain took over for the damaged ones."

If Mindy's brain could heal, why couldn't Walker's brain heal? But Walker's brain wasn't damaged exactly. It was more the wiring that was wrong. Perhaps brain damage was simpler to fix than faulty wiring. Less pervasive, less comprehensive? (The difference, say, between having dry rot in the basement and having it all over the house?) Still, it seemed to me that Mindy could tell me what Walker couldn't, something about his experience. I called her the second I arrived home.

"Tell me, Mindy. What did it feel like?"

"It felt like flashes of light and feeling, like noise and rockets taking off in my brain."

I paused to take it in, but she continued. "It felt like electrical storms. Nerve-wracking—too much all at once. Like every color and every sound and light all at once." I gazed down at Walker, in his car seat on the floor. His back was arched. No wonder.

"And what would you recommend I do?"

"Be gradual."

"Gradual?"

"I was just reading about the education of Tiger Woods. You know, the champion golfer, trained by his father. He said he never gave Tiger a challenge beyond his level of tolerance. He brought him up slowly, bit by bit, to higher and higher levels. Never challenge Walker beyond his level of tolerance."

I hung up the phone and handed Walker a plastic spoon. He took it.

That afternoon, Arlene and I were working in the dining room—dark, with the blinds drawn tightly, dark with the bruising burgundy rug, which left his cheeks rashy and purple. We laid blankets washed in hypoallergenic detergent, and she brought the fleece, because with the "input" from the soft blanket, he knew more about where he was in space. Walker, who was seven months old, still cranked his head around to see the bright white lines of sun between the slats, yet when we moved him further into the rooms, his eyes drew away from the window. We had the sense he might be changing his focus.

One day in early June, when Walker was seven and a half months old, Arlene handed Walker a toy. She looked up at me, cocked her eyebrow and smiled, "He's laying track."

"What do you mean, track?"

"Myelin. He's laying myelin."

I was still just as mystified.

"It means he's laying pathways in his brain. Every time he does something new, he lays pathways. The theory, as I understand it, is that as we learn, nerve cells come together. The pathways are reinforced when they're covered by thick cells called Schwann cells, which are like plastic insulation around electrical wires. This covering is called myelination and it reinforces the efficiency of the neural transmission along it."

A woman plays with a boy and suddenly nerves are myelinated?

"How has he changed?" I said. Skeptical. Hopeful. Yet I hadn't seen any difference.

"He's using his eyes differently. Did you notice that he seemed to be using his peripheral vision to see?" I looked at Walker.

"Can I have ten minutes Arlene?" I went to the computer and booted up. It was June 1997, and what I was about to learn from the Internet would change everything. But everything had already changed.

The Brain Doesn't Wait

IMAGINE A PERFECT CLOCK, tuned by a great Swiss master, every cog in place (possessing all the clichés of mechanical precision), polished and tucked away in the strongest and best of insulating materials, making its way on a ship to some harbor. Even though the clock is packed away, it has become the clock it was meant to be and just needs to be opened and dusted off a bit. Such was the image that I always naively embraced of the brain until that week in 1997 when I found myself sitting with several articles in my lap, mouth nearly hanging open in astonishment, to find that just the year before, in 1996, the year Walker was born, the entire story of the brain had virtually turned on its head.

I'd already done some research and was excited. I'd called Cliff again. He made another trip to the library (I was too busy trying to interact with Walker to leave the house). I remember him coming home, unloading the heavy pile with satisfaction. Magazines stacked neatly on our living room side table with pictures of gray matter, some looking like pickled fruit, others like wrinkled paper or oblong planets floating in a black beyond—magazines with pictures of babies with eyes so piercing and focused it looked like something in the iris could reach out and grab you. I quickly learned that it was the story of the century—perhaps even more important than the O. J. Simpson murder trial, that was spread across the pages of the magazines along with brain research stories.

Apparently, remarkably, neuroscience was beginning to go where mankind had never gone before, into the brain as it was thinking. This historic feat was made possible by sophisticated advancements in brain imaging techniques such as the PET (positron emission tomography) scan, the MRI (magnetic resonance imaging), and equipment that measures, from the outside, electrical activity in the brain, such as electroencephalograms. By 1996, the PET scan had heralded nothing short of a revolution in neuroscience. Formerly, many neuroscientists assumed that the brain developed outside of the womb largely according to genetic coding. Yet now that they were able to watch the brain as it did its work, scientists realized that the brain changes after birth in ways that few had imagined before they saw it with their own eyes. What PET scans and other imaging techniques were revealing was that the brain's very structure is subject to change, is in fact built to change. The brain is not a machine, like a clock that works according to predetermined and precise programming; rather the brain is a dynamic living organism that grows and changes as it lives.

As I read about brain development, I was surprised by the florid, dramatic images evoked by scientists themselves. They sometimes used metaphors of love, of mystery, even of passion. Indeed, how the brain develops seemed far more complicated, far more elegant, and far crazier than I ever imagined. As I read about brain development, I began to imagine one of those frantic and complicated nineteenth-century novels of manners with characters rushing around meeting each other, shooting off missives to each other, growing disillusioned, losing connections that simply don't work, and forging connections that would last forever.

The story of the brain's development begins, as all biological stories do, with the most rudimentary of characters, cells beginning to grow and divide. Around three weeks after conception, a pack of cells on what will become the embryo's back do a kind of trick similar to what happens in origami. The folding trick leads to the formation of a tube called the neural tube. Cells begin to travel through this funnel, moving from the tail to the head of the creature. Once they have reached their destinations, they are officially "neurons"—brain cells—and as such begin traveling long distances. One article I read said that the distance traveled by some neurons, given their microscopic size, would be the equivalent of a person hiking 3,000 miles, say, from New York to California, over treacherous terrain. No one knows exactly how they know where to go. Some of them are influenced by peer pressure, others seem determined to be unique. They move to certain parts of the nascent brain and begin connecting with other cells. They sprout two types of shoots—dendrites, which are short, and axons, which are long. Axons do the work of the pioneers, sometimes stretching across great distances themselves to make connections. When they connect, they don't actually touch. As if touching were too much, they connect over an empty space, an abyss, the "synapse," which turns their electrical charge into a chemical reaction, a kind of explosion, that delivers an electrical charge in the receiving cell.

Chaos is the first phase of creation, and brain development seems no exception. In this burst of creativity, the cells begin maniacally calling each other to make connections over synapses. They call each other so rapidly and intensively that one neuroscientist called the process "autodialing." Cells call and connect, call and connect. It's a creative leap on the part of the neurons and their outgoing axons. They are experimenting in their rushing outward, as if in hope, as if in passion, like teenagers rushing forth, making phone calls for dates, as one scientist described it. As wildly as they fail, they also succeed. Though the whole process sounds wild and random, there seems to be some profound wisdom in the connections that are made. The hand of nature and genetics has guided the process. The facts sounded almost supernatural in their scope: The brain as it develops produces a cosmic rate of 250,000 cells a minute. By the time of birth, the nervous system will contain all the nerve cells a brain will need for a lifetime, 100 billion neurons—as many as there are stars in the Milky Way. The existing circuits are the foundation for future wiring; they are the trunk lines of the brain's communication system and are responsible for, among other functions, controlling heartbeat, body reflexes, and the regulation of body temperature.

But the story of the brain is not over. And here is where the neuroscientists were making history in 1996. Scientists knew that the brain kept on developing after birth (vision, for instance, isn't fully formed at birth, nor is cognition or emotions or hearing). Yet most experts had assumed, as I have said, that the brain's structure was somehow in place or that its growth process would be genetically predetermined. As we all know now, they learned they were wrong, profoundly so.

"Of all the discoveries that have poured out of neuroscience labs in recent years," said *Time*, "the finding that electrical activity of brain cells changes the physical structure of the brain is perhaps the most breathtaking."

The breaking story that inspired the weekly journals to create large special editions that spring in 1997 was that the brain changed as it grew. What determined the brain's course? Some force outside the brain was causing it to wire in special and distinct ways. But what? The resounding answer came as neuroscientists watched the brain work: Experience made the brain shape itself into what it would become.

I read late into the night to understand why experience was important. By three o'clock that morning in late May, I had the framework of an answer it would take years to flesh out.

After birth, cells reach out and make connections over synapses where electrical charges shift, turn to chemicals over the abyss, and turn back to electrical charges—the same process that it had used to form early connections, but the story changes dramatically in this second phase. What determines how the cells connect has something to do with genetics, of course, but some striking facts suggested to me that the brain changes and builds itself more after birth than before. Eighty-three percent of dendritic growth happens after birth. Up to the age of two, 1.8 synapses per second continue to grow. The key has to do with the senses, with stimulation.

Stimulation. It was a hard word to see on the page. I cringed when I read it the first time, and I read it over and over again. *Brain development has less to do with genetic determination, more to do with the world beyond, outside, than I ever imagined.* After birth, the brain wires itself to fit the world that the child will inhabit because it is wired by experience. No wonder humans are so miraculously adaptable! The brain is created to perfectly suit the needs of the individual's personal universe. (Not that the environment solely shapes the brain; rather, one scientist explained, it's more a very complicated dance between genetics and environment.) I began to envision the brain differently, no longer as a clock ticking away on a shelf but more as a customized computer that gets programmed every day of its existence to suit the demands and special lifestyle—the smell and touch and breath—of its owner. Imagine touching the keys of a computer and having it change sheerly by the precise feel of your own unique hand.

But "stimulation" as a key to brain development after birth? It was hard to believe that stimulation could be a dominating factor. It sounded almost quaint—strange, illogical, curious to my ears. And for Walker, as damning as a prison sentence. The very element that Walker couldn't handle, his Achilles' heel, was a key mechanism by which his brain would grow and shape itself. Arlene had been telling me that Walker wouldn't learn if he was too sensitive—I had somehow assumed she meant "learn" in a more limited sense, as if she were talking about acquiring bits of knowledge. Yet now I knew she meant something far more fundamental. Stimulation was Walker's kryptonite. Did that mean he couldn't grow in any way? Articles were full of information about how the senses carry information to the brain centers, how these centers react to the stimulation they provide, how the ensuing electrical reactions produce and strengthen connections that are responsible for ability and intelligence. Yet the force of brain development is propelled and shaped by what enters. If you come into a musical family, for instance, and are surrounded by music, the brain will develop the musical centers more. If you're surrounded by rich language, your language centers will develop more, and so on.

It was a marvelous revelation. And perhaps, I considered, the breakthrough we needed—this amazing and wondrous fact that the brain is created to create itself after birth—brain development as a *conversation*. Brain development as a *response*.

I went into Walker's room and watched him. He slept deeply, breathing with difficulty, head bent back as if straining for comfort.

Yet there was a darker side to the truth of the brain's plasticity. Hidden behind the plasticity of gray matter lay a deadline: Cinderella's midnight.

Time was of the essence. Even though Walker was only seven months old, we were running out of time. Scientists talked of "critical periods," "time limits," "windows" of opportunity that opened and closed relatively quickly for a growing brain. Certain functions in the brain, centers responsible for discrete brain functions, such as the visual, or the auditory, or the cognitive, come into being at fixed points in a baby's chronological life. Like time bombs, these parts burst forth in great explosions of connection called synapse overproduction. A relatively short interval after the riot of neural connections begins, the development starts to wane.

In my naive thinking, when the therapists began suggesting that the brain was less plastic after time, I imagined the brain to be something like a pool of Jell-O, about to set within months. Later I began to see the process as being even more dramatic, a calculated and draconian piece of nature at its most efficient. There was cutting involved.

Cells in this next phase got killed off if they weren't used. It was either beautiful or horrible. The brain was trying to sculpt itself. Scientists casually called this process "pruning." As with, say, an overgrown bush, the brain refines, kills off, discards those connections that aren't useful or are sitting idle. Clearly some of the most important pruning phases, beginning in early months of development, were coming on fast for Walker, and when each phase was over, his brain would never have such opportunities again. Two researchers, Torsten Wiesel and David Hubel, were able to illustrate pruning by sewing shut the eye of a kitten shortly after birth. The kitten's brain didn't get the wiring information it needed from the senses. So few neurons connected from the eye to the visual cortex that the kitten was forever blind in the deprived eye—not blind in the eye but blind in the brain—even once the eye was opened. As surely as if the doors of a school had been chained shut, this kitten's access to visual learning was closed off simply by depriving him of stimulation—light.

Visual cortex: the term reverberated again and again through the literature. Apparently much was known about the development of the visual centers. Researchers asserted that the visual processing cortex of the brain began its wiring frenzy in the first two to four months. By six to eight months, it would begin killing off the cells that hadn't made good connections or hadn't made connections at all. That meant Walker's visual system was either in or approaching the pruning phase, the killing phase. I went into his room early the next morning. He was awake but impassive, staring off into what seemed to be an imaginary world, nearly laughing at some personal joke. Was he actually using his visual system this very moment? He seemed to be looking at angels somewhere, or dust motes in the air. Would he become functionally blind, like the kitten who hadn't received visual signals to the brain? He turned, then passed over my face. I had the sense he was looking at my aura somehow—the sense that he was there, that he knew I was there as well—but how to position himself to find me?

I called Arlene and asked her if she would come twice a week. She said yes.

The Game

We had dragged our desk chairs, squeaking across the old linoleum floor, into a circle. Each of us had come to spend this evening under fluorescent lights in a school classroom, away from our children with problems of known and "unknown etiologies," away from our children with "mental challenges," with autism, with Fragile X syndrome, with unknown maladies. We were gathering to share resources; I was a novice. I wanted to learn about state funding for therapies that insurance won't pay for; I was there to learn about our options. But I immediately found myself searching the faces around the circle. Mostly women—two men attended with their wives. These faces seemed drawn, world weary, but then most people in the evening under fluorescent lights appear so—these lights catch something about the hardness of the day. The meeting facilitator passed out forms so that the regulars, the parents who had been coming to these gatherings for years, could be reimbursed for their baby-sitter's fees for the evening. Qualifying families who came to three such meetings would receive up to $1,000 a year in reimbursements for their children's special health care or educational needs.

I listened intently, but much of the information was a blur. I had a hard time taking in the facts: instructions about applications for grants, informational resources, web sites. What I found myself listening to intently were the scraps of stories, lives that came real to me sometimes just from listening to a mother ask a question or answer a question. Two women did speak at length about their sons. There was nothing dramatic about their stories, yet I was haunted by the specter of time in these stories; something about the slowness of the unfolding. An older woman spoke of her daughter, a teenager, who was now living in a group home; another spoke of her son, now eleven, who somehow hadn't progressed as other children had. At school they had not given any labels until late in his ninth year. After the meeting, I found myself compelled to turn to a woman whose son lived in an institution, a grandmotherly woman sitting near me, and ask what her life had been like.

"In some ways, it's easier," she said.

"Easier?"

"There are trade-offs. Certain things I don't have to contend with."

"Trade-offs?"

"There was a boy at the local school: athlete, popular. I used to envy his parents. Yet he killed himself. At least I know my son is safe, and he's happy."

A tall blond woman with large features and big teeth, who had come late, began talking animatedly to someone across the room. She spoke of her son with Asperger's syndrome, a high-functioning form of autism. Though someone else might have been annoyed by her loud and incessant talking, I found myself wanting to hear everything she said. The room was emptying, but I stayed and pretended to be looking at pamphlets.

"Did you hear the latest?" she called out, gathering up her things. "Now my son wants to take over Ohio. No kidding. It's an obsession. It's all he talks about."

Arlene had once told me that the parents at REACH eventually, in years, reach a calm, an acceptance of their children's illness. Is that what it looked like?

Was I one of these women now? I asked myself this question under the cool hard lights of the classroom all night long. If I was, I wondered how I could ever muster such humor.

⌒

When Arlene's supervisor, Darleen Corbett, suggested that I needed to have a "reciprocal" relationship with Walker, she didn't suggest many ideas about how I could achieve it. *What was reciprocity? A con-*

versation? A shared understanding? A game? Surely a game was the only possibility. Still, how could one play a game without words or shared logic? I tried to think of the simplest game I could. What came to mind was catch. It was reciprocal, in any case. But Walker's eyes didn't seem to focus well. He wasn't going to be able to play catch. Anyway, what seven-month-old could play catch?

One morning about two weeks after Arlene began working with him, I was feeding Walker in the kitchen. He was looking at me, though not exactly seeing. *Why, on this particular morning, wasn't he wrenched sideways staring out the window?* I tried to make my face as impassive as I could, fearful I might scare him away, cooing softly, "Come on." At that moment, a sound ripped through the kitchen. *ERRRRRRRR. Errrreishhhhhh.* Walker jerked his head back toward the window. The nerve-grinding saw had started up next door. *What are they cutting? Raw steel? Not even 9 A.M. and there's the sound as if they are slicing a car in two and cramming it into a leaf grinder.*

I went to the window but saw nothing; all the noise was emanating from behind the fence in the yard. I returned and offered Walker another spoonful, but as the grinding and sawing persisted, he remained facing to the side of the room, toward the window and would take nothing. I brought him upstairs, but noise from the front windows was just as loud—someone was blowing leaves with a machine I thought must have a motorcycle engine. I brought Walker's basket into the bathroom and sat down in front of him. His head was still sideways, cranked away from mine. I tried to gently turn the basket so he would face me, but no matter how I moved him, his head remained in the same direction: away.

"Want to play a game, little man?" I asked. I held Walker's favorite toy, the rubbery wire sphere in front of him. I knew he would clasp it, he was good at clasping objects, but how to make this a game? He grabbed it. Quickly, I took it away.

"There, now," I said. "It's mine. Now you're going to have to fight to get it back."

Nothing. No reaction.

I placed the toy in his hand.

"Now it's my turn, give it here," I coaxed. Nothing.

I took it back myself and waved the sphere in front of Walker. He grabbed the toy; I pulled it away again. *Does he realize this is supposed to be a game? Is he just grabbing what's in sight?* Perhaps I needed to make my actions more distinct. This time, I moved my arm in a broad, sweeping motion and handed him the sphere.

"Here you go, little guy," I said, in a singsongy voice. He reached.

"Now, I want it, little man. Give it to me!" Walker held the colored toy in his hand, clinging to one of its plastic-covered wires. I thought he might be trying to give it to me, but instead, his hand, still grasping the toy, fell to his stomach. *Is it too heavy for him?*

"Now don't be greedy," I said. "Give it to me!" I put my hand out, just beyond his reach. His hand began to move, it jerked to the left, to the right, and suddenly ejected the sphere out of the basket. It occurred to me he might be trying to hand off the toy, but the exercise could just as easily have been meaningless.

"Let's try again," I said.

I picked up the shiny sphere, holding it from one of the yellow wires, and waved it in Walker's face, swung it toward his hand. He grabbed it. But had he grabbed it merely because it was there?

I clapped a bit, a gesture Arlene had taught me to encourage Walker with, and waited with my hand outstretched.

"Now it's my turn, little man. Give me the toy." Walker jerked his head quickly to the opposite side. His hand lurched with the motion of his head. The toy flew toward my feet.

Was he trying to play? I think he might have been.

The next day, Cliff was home from work to view a session with Arlene. At the end of the hour, I found the courage to ask if they wanted to see a game Walker and I might be playing. Arlene looked at me quizzically. "A game?" She was holding a rubber duck.

"Can I borrow that?" I asked. I handed the duck to Walker. "Now, give it back," I said in cooing tones. "Give it here. Let's play the game." Walker didn't move. I took it out of his hand and made an exaggerated motion of giving him the toy.

"Now give it back," I coaxed, holding my hand open near his reach. Walker's head jerked to the right; his arm moved to the left. The duck fell on his leg.

"No, really, wait," I said.

I tried again. This time the duck came right back into my hand.

Cliff jumped up onto his knees. "Wow," he said.

Arlene stared at me. *This can't be happening,* her face said. *It's not supposed to happen.*

"Do you know? I do believe he's trying to give it to you."

A smile spread across her face, a broad, amazing smile. The first I'd seen from her.

Darleen Corbett came one day to help me renegotiate my "service plan." It was clear Arlene had alerted her to the severity of Walker's problem. As we sat at my kitchen table, she confessed that she, too, had had a special needs child. She reached her hand to mine and said, "I don't tell all my clients this, but I wanted you to know." I wasn't sure how to interpret her offering. I was grateful, but the gratitude was tinged with fear. Were we special, special for even the special needs class? Darleen said, "I think you should have something for yourself. Get a job." It sounded strange to my ears, yet she was voicing a truth that I immediately understood that not many people in our culture utter—she was vocalizing wisdom that perhaps working men had always understood, that working away from the home can be a refuge for an adult, a way of clearing space.

I was, at that time, contracted to teach a college prep writing course in the upcoming August but was planning to cancel it. Now I decided not to cancel it. I would teach. I would ask my friend, Kyle, who was between jobs, to watch Walker in the morning. I'm not sure why I made this decision, but I know that in part, I felt inept with Walker. I secretly suspected that other people knew how to draw him in. Perhaps it would be best for him if I weren't with him for twelve hours each day. Teaching would mean I would be away for four hours each weekday for three weeks.

I went to my teaching file and pulled out my assignments from the previous year. Inside was a notebook.

When I taught writing, I usually asked the students to parody a story by Lorrie Moore, a contemporary short story writer who had a dry comic edge that I admired. The piece I asked the class to parody was called "How to Be an Other Woman," a story in which the narrator gives directions in the second person to the reader about how to mess up a perfectly good life by becoming the lover of a married man.

While Walker napped, I found myself scratching my own parody into my teaching notebook. As I read it now, I realize that it is arch, angry. I'm not sure such an edge was driven by anger in me or by the form itself, which somehow calls upon the writer to be dry, cynical. Here is what I wrote:

June 1997

Directions for a Typical Day:

7:30 A.M. Awaken. Lie in bed with your son. Note that he arches backward. Think: This is bad for him. Take his body and change the shape to the crescent moon shape. Coo gently to get his attention. Note that he doesn't notice you. Close shades.

8:00 A.M. Say good-bye as Cliff takes Elizabeth to your mother's hotel where she has agreed to watch her all day. He will drive to work. Miss your daughter, even before she is out the door. Repeat a line from poetry or two, something overdramatic and sappy like: "She gave away the dearest thing she ow'[n]ed, as 't'were a careless trifle."

8:00–9:00 A.M. Place your son in the car seat on top of the table. Note that he stares at the window. Try to play a game with him where you hand him a toy. Begin trying to put food into him. If he throws up, begin again. Note again that he's not looking at you. Remember that the last time you visited the supermarket, the automatic door did not open for you.

9:00 A.M. Bring your son into the dining room, draw the shades, and begin working to gain his attention. Play "the game" over and over, in the darkened room, handing the wiry toy back and forth. Remember that Arlene, the therapist, has told you that you mustn't become monotonous. You must be ever pressing forward. Think: How can such a game possibly be expanded?

10:00–12:00 Arlene arrives. Watch intently while she works to entice Walker to roll over. Watch her hold down his legs so he will roll from the shoulder. If Walker throws up, clean it up. If the phone rings, run to it, talk briefly, and return. If it is a doctor calling back, make motions to Arlene that you can't watch right now. Try not to remember that Arlene has told you

that it is her purpose to be showing you, instructing you. Hope
that you're not wasting her time.

12:00 or 1:00 Feed Walker more powdered cereal with
water. If he looks away, use your voice to keep him engaged.
Sing with him. He likes sounds. If time is tight, make meaningful faces toward Walker as he looks away while you make phone
calls to doctors and specialists. Ask the receptionist on the other
end of the line: Would an allergist see Walker? Would an
endocrinologist see him? Tell the nurses: Time is running thin.
He is losing weight. If he vomits, clean him up and begin again.

1:00–2:00 Go to a doctor's appointment or to the hospital so
blood can be drawn for tests. Go for adenoid X-rays. Explain to
the nurses that no, he hasn't been in and out of the hospital his
entire life even though he looks it. No, he hasn't had heart sur-
gery. Sit in the pediatrician's office as he soberly tells you that
there are over 500 metabolic diseases. "They're discovering new
ones every day," he says. Return to the darkened room. Play
"the game" for an hour.

2:00–4:00 Put Walker down to sleep. Note that he arches
backward like someone in pain, like something breaking away,
like part of a vegetable being peeled away from itself. Feel
sweaty. Call your neighbor who is a doctor. Call an old neighbor who is also a doctor. Call anyone. Talk about who is a good
pediatrician in town, talk about good questions to ask doctors,
talk about why doctors sometimes won't tell you what they're
thinking. Talk about everything except: What is really wrong
here. Be secretly convinced that someone somewhere knows the
truth but is keeping something from you. Get on the Internet.
Do laundry. Clean kitchen. Call your sister while she listens
attentively and asks questions. Feel a guilty sense of gratitude
when she cries in sympathy.

4:00–5:00 Return to the darkened room. Or, meet with
Vicki, REACH's nutritionist. Hold Walker in your arms while
you talk to her. If the phone rings, make more hand motions of
apology while talking to doctors about more doctors that you
might try. Discuss with Vicki your conviction that Walker has
allergies. Note that, unlike several doctors you spoke with, Vicki

takes you seriously. She encourages you to move on your allergy suspicion. But do you really want to go on a macrobiotic diet to rid your milk of all allergens? That's what it would take.

4:42 Receive phone call from friend whom you have unwittingly stood up. Look at the calendar. Squint. There are so many markings on the calendar that you hadn't noticed the friend's name squeezed in. Apologize. Try to explain. She is waiting at the park. Leave Vicki. Rush away with your son in the baby seat, covered with a blanket. The car seat bangs against your leg. Try to hold it steady while you run. Arrive at park. Sit on a bench.

5:20 Leave your friend. Drive to The Inn at Northampton to pick up Elizabeth. Note that she is happy, oblivious. She has had Danish for breakfast, chicken fingers for lunch. Her hair is wet and she has been sitting deliciously in your mother's cigarette-smoke–filled room watching cartoon sit-coms.

5:40 Return home. Place Walker on the floor in the dining room, bring Elizabeth into the kitchen. Cook with her. If she refuses, put her in front of the TV in the living room and make dinner.

6:00 Greet your husband. Feed Walker for an hour while Cliff talks to Elizabeth.

7:00–8:00 Eat dinner with Elizabeth and Cliff. Try to talk about a neutral subject, but find yourself recounting conversations with doctors. They are testing. More blood next week. No diagnosis yet. Explain to Elizabeth what diagnosis means.

7:00 Note that Cliff gives Elizabeth a bath, puts her to bed. Find yourself drawn, maniacally, obsessively, to the living room, where you place Walker on a blanket. Play the game for as long as you can stand it. Play for an hour, play for two. Play for three. One evening, near Walker's bedtime, note that he won't surrender the toy. Instead, he mouths it passionately, obsessively. Decide to pull it away with your mouth, shaking it the way you pull a slipper from the jaws of a puppy. Watch him smile. Think: Was that really a smile? Give the toy back with your mouth. Note: It was a smile. He smiles again. You have found a new game.

8:00 Put Walker to sleep. Get on the phone. Call anyone you know. Call anyone who is awake. Remember it is still early in California.

Afterward, I remembered that I always told the students to include a list in their parody. The Moore story included lists. I made my own. It was all true.

THOUGHTS FROM FAMILY AND FRIENDS

"Damn it Patsy, you'd better do something for that kid and do something now; he's wasting away. Don't listen to these goddamn charlatans. Find another doctor."

"Have the baby checked for thyroid condition. I know a family whose kid has autism and it could have been prevented. It was all thyroid."

"I know he's lost weight but can't you feed him more?"

(Overheard) "She's just obsessed with that baby. I don't know why he's in bed with them. Doesn't she realize her husband has needs?"

"I have made a pact with God. If your son gets better, I will sacrifice my hopes of having a second child."

"So your son has hypersensitivities. You realize that's autism, don't you?"

"I looked up Walker's symptoms in a book at the bookstore. I think he has tuberous sclerosis, but don't look it up yourself. You don't want to know what it says."

"No I don't know what you do all day. But I've seen your house." (Read: mess.)

"He's fine. You worry too much."

The Body Is a Map

"CAN WE TAKE A WALK SOMETIME?" asked my friend Lynn over the phone.

Lynn is a massage therapist and a bodyworker, though not an ordinary one. In her work, she is not particularly interested in helping clients relax in spas under her restoring hands (Lynn often rails against the client who wants to "disappear during a session"); rather, she is interested in challenging them, in helping them make better decisions, in changing their lives. For her, the psyche is connected to the body. Though I'm not sure I understand how. Yet I have learned over the years that Lynn knows about healing in ways that elude most of us. She has contemplated the body and its connection to the mind through Eastern religion and meditation, through psychotherapy, through study and the art of what she calls "touch modalities." But one evening, just a month after REACH began working with Walker, as we walked through my neighborhood, Lynn explained that when she was living in New Mexico she learned of a unique form of body-work called Body-Mind Centering from her mentors. "Body-Mind Centering is a term coined by its founder, Bonnie Bainbridge Cohen," she said.

Apparently, when Bainbridge Cohen was a young occupational therapist working with cerebral palsy patients, her boss said to her one day, "You need to start thinking about what you're doing when you work with these patients, because for some reason they're getting better." That was the beginning of a career that would eventually take Bainbridge Cohen to authorship and international fame as the founder of a unique form of bodywork, meant to directly heal neurological systems, among others.

Although Bainbridge Cohen lived not more than a half hour away from us in Northampton, Lynn explained that her methods were taught throughout the country and abroad.

"But the reason I mention Body-Mind Centering is because Bonnie Bainbridge Cohen works with babies. In fact, this is primarily her speciality. She works with babies who are not progressing."

"Really?" I said.

"Yes. I think you should see her."

I wanted to know how much it would cost us.

"Maybe $75.00," said Lynn.

I was quiet for a long time. I took a stick up off the ground and ripped it into shreds. Body-Mind Centering sounded suspect to me. I particularly didn't like the word "centering." The negative association was left over from my days going to the University of California at Santa Cruz, which was nestled in the woods overlooking Monterey Bay, a university known for its 1960s ideals. I associated centering with horoscopes and stinky herbal tea, madras skirts so long they were dripping with mud. Anyway, how could someone who rubs your body heal your brain?

"I'll pay for the first visit," said Lynn.

I had not been planning to follow through on Lynn's suggestion. Yet from that one generous gesture, something in me changed. I felt her urgency. It touched me. Besides, I argued to myself, this was another phone call I could make.

It was evening, so I made the call the next day, grateful to Lynn for the promising sight of numbers next to a name, a number to call. Yet Bainbridge Cohen was ill, the assistant explained to me. She asked for my location and said she would refer me to someone else, an expert in the practice who could help me. She was surprised to learn I was from Northampton. People called from all over the world. "This is easy," she said. She told me Bainbridge Cohen had a protégée, a senior teacher named Lenore Grubinger, who lived in Northampton.

Cliff and I sat in Lenore's office, sun slanting in through the windows. Balls of all shapes and colors stacked in the corners, tubes standing in barrels against the wall, toys on shelves. Lenore took Walker in her steady, graceful hands. She held him in that tight ball we had recently learned of, curling him inward, against his insistence on curling backward. "You must always return him to this crescent moon shape," she said. There it was again—that shape, the remedial C. I longed to ask her exactly why she thought it worked, yet I was too curious about what she saw in Walker.

"Can you just tell us . . ." I began perhaps too loudly, perhaps too urgently. She stilled me, as if to say, "Let's wait."

She continued to concentrate profoundly on something in Walker, bent over him, holding him, feeling his head, his body. Was she just feeling him? Exploring him? Or perhaps doing something more? She put her hands all over his head, moved to his chest, his stomach, his abdomen, back to his chest. Cliff and I watched for a long time, nearly forty-five minutes. For a moment, when I could forget why we were there, I realized I liked being next to Cliff. It occurred to me that this was the first time I had felt myself in harmony with a close friend in what seemed to be a very long time. There was something almost romantic in Cliff's rushing here during his lunch hour. It reminded me of our early days when we used to meet for meals and talk. He looked dapper when he showed up in his khaki linen suit—architect's clothes.

Lenore rested, moved her focus away from the baby toward us.

"Does he have brain damage?" I asked.

"This looks like toxic exposure, perhaps in the womb," Lenore's voice was certain, almost arrogant sounding. Emphatic.

I was surprised by such a firm diagnosis, yet I knew that she had worked with babies for years. Perhaps she had been trained to see what a physician might not. Anyway, her thought was not so different from my own.

"I've recently seen some babies diagnosed with uterine toxic exposure who looked like this."

My mind ran quickly to all the possible culprits during my pregnancy: a sinus infection, the blue cold medicine I took several nights in a row before I knew I was pregnant, antibiotics (the doctor insisted they were safe), exterminators coming to the yard, fumes from my station wagon when the back window broke.

"What would you call this?" I asked, a bit too nervously.

"It doesn't matter what you call it. What matters is what you can do for him now," said Lenore.

"But I need to *call* it. I keep imagining what kind of future he's going to have."

Lenore turned on me, regarded me with ferocity in her eyes. She seemed almost angry; maybe she was. It was a moment of animal aggression: one female dog facing off against another. Only in this case, we weren't marking territory but standing off over the fate of a baby.

"Look," she said. "I hear that you're afraid. But you mustn't put your fear first. Whatever you do, get help for your fear. He's going to know it. It's going to affect everything you do. And what you do now is infinitely important. You're his future. How you feel about him, what you do with him—he'll feel it; he is going to know it. It could block his progress."

"I'm not sure I can control fear."

"Oh, yes you can," she said, challenging, fierce, intense. "Meditate. Pray. Breathe. Do what you have to do. But work with your fear. It's running you. It won't help your son." Quickly she changed the subject.

"Let's concentrate on what you can do for him. He has to learn to push up while on his belly. He needs to discover his protective extension, a basic response."

"A basic response?"

"A primary reflex."

"What is protective extension?"

"It's when you fall and put out your hands to protect yourself. He doesn't do it. You'll have to teach him." (Years later, we learned that family movies of children with autism have shown that many babies eventually diagnosed with autism had not acquired protective extension in their early months.)

"Teach him?"

"I'll show you how."

"But one thing . . . about his future," I said. I had a question. It had to be answered.

"And don't focus on a negative future," insisted Lenore.

"But I do." I began to tell Lenore that just that day . . .

But she stopped me, stilled me, and said emphatically, "Then if you must think of the future, spend as much time imagining what you want for him as you do fearing for him."

Lenore put her hands on Walker's chest and stomach, and explained that Walker's "upper limbs needed to be more engaged with his intentions." She left us with a list of things to do which might help.

- Make sure Walker spends time on his stomach every day.
- Spend time at his level. Lie on your belly on the carpet while both prone.
- Slowly lower Walker to the floor, extend his arms, and place his open hands flat on the ground (as if he were an airplane coming in for a landing). Repeat often.
- Bring his shoulder blades forward.
- Keep Walker in flexion, bent forward around his belly button as much as possible. Let him arch out, then bring him back.
- Walker's left eye is more "integrated" into his system. Talk toward his left eye, especially when he is tired.
- Remember that perception makes movement happen.
- Make a list of improvements we see over the coming week.

On the way home we drove into town to the pharmacy to pick up Epsom salts and diapers.

During the drive, I tried to make sense of what Lenore had told us. For Lenore, the body seemed to be a map. On it she somehow read the workings of Walker's mind the way astronomers read time past in the stars. It seemed that for Lenore, the body and mind must be mirrored universes—it is as if the mind were the clouds and the body were the lake. When you look into the body, you see a reflection of the mind, the way clouds appear in a clear pool on a sunny afternoon. "In my training we have learned that the body and mind are one system," she told us. "If you enter into that system at any given point, you can change the whole. Change the body, change the mind."

After studying Walker, Lenore had talked with us about her philosophy and methods for twenty minutes. Much of it I didn't understand. "Muscle tone?" "Cellular activity?" Something about Walker's cerebellum, what she called "the low brain" seemed to her to be compromised. But Lenore was offering something that conventional doctors weren't. She was talking about doing something for Walker.

It was Lenore's contention that if we could keep Walker's body moving correctly—with, say, the excellent attention to form that a world-class tennis player adopts, with everything balanced, moving in toward a divine and winning "center"—we could profoundly affect his development. In a way, she was like Arlene, but with a stronger rigor and perfectionism—Arlene to the second power. Lenore felt that if we could keep Walker's body free of the strange poses I saw, free of what she described as "the positions that reinforced the disorganization of his nervous system" (arching, which Walker did nearly constantly, she insisted, was anathema to his healthy development), if we could keep him free from the "compensations" made by nerves and muscles that should be "following instead of leading," then she felt we might be able to help Walker form new and right pathways in his brain.

With her hands positioned gently, though with an intensity of concentration, on Walker's skull, she explained that she was also a "cranial sacral practitioner and instructor." She would be using such techniques to work on Walker's central nervous system as well.

Would this obscure-seeming art have an effect on our son? We would see. By now I would have woven a blanket of rabbits' feet, danced under the moon, if I thought it might have helped.

Outside the CVS drugstore, near the entryway, sat a man rocking rhythmically, holding a chain in the air, with a weight on the end. He held it near the periphery of his eyes, as if it were a talisman or a fetish, as if he could hear it sing. Driving home, we also passed the man who jogs all day in the street, the man covered in red and orange plastic. *Why red, why plastic, why jog?* These were the mysteries of the mind, of the errant mind; the mysteries of the nervous system. When I was in college I studied Sartre's *Being and Nothingness.* Frithjof Bergmann, my philosophy professor, had told us that Sartre one day walked by a man with no arm and realized, *Yes, this is the nature of life—we think that life is about what is present, but it is about what is missing.*

I try to think of a future I want, but I keep thinking of absences.

My mind went, as it had when we were with Lenore, to an incident that happened that afternoon. "I saw Lois," I said to Cliff. "Do you think she has autism?" But he didn't answer immediately.

Lois was a wealthy woman who had some kind of mental disability. She carried designer purses, lived in a nice apartment, and occasionally walked through town, usually alone. I recognized her from our old apartment building where she had lived down the hall. I remembered that when I first met Lois, though she was middle-aged she reminded me of a child, one who had been trained rigorously to be polite. I hadn't spoken to Lois in years, yet that day, for some reason as I passed her on the sidewalk, she stopped me. "Patty," she said "You used to live in 302. You left the apartment in 1994." She gestured that she wanted to hug me, but unexpectedly pulled back, as if she'd been trained to check her desires. I moved toward her and we embraced. As we hugged, she touched my arm in a strange way, as if exploring it, feeling it. Was this autism? I was beginning to suspect it might be. What else would explain her stiffness, and her odd greeting, translated into numbers, calculations associated with a neighbor's comings and goings. As she continued to touch my arm Lois felt me, or rather my arm, but seemed oddly oblivious as if she somehow missed the whole of me. What confused me even more was something like a paradox in Lois. She seemed passionate. About me? Not at all disaffected or cold. In fact, she seemed too invested. Yet I still felt she couldn't see me. She seemed so much to want to be with me, but was keeping back. Was I misdiagnosing her, or had I somehow always misunderstood autism? Being lost in your own world didn't necessarily mean you didn't want to get out of it, didn't want to reach out.

Lost in thought about Lois, I suddenly realized Cliff was talking to me.

"You haven't heard a word I've said, have you?"

We brought Walker home and put him in the car seat on the kitchen table to feed him. Cliff's parents came in through the kitchen door at the back of the house. Walker raised his arms to them, reaching upward. It was the first we'd seen of such a spontaneous gesture. *Was he taking initiative? Dare we call it a greeting? Was it merely a coincidence that we had just come from Lenore's?*

Nights with Walker. His body tense and turning still, as if he were rooting—
not as if for a nipple, but as if for something it seemed he might never find.
Back still curled inward. Fingers tight, clenched sometimes.

He slept snoring, not able to breathe well. Walker still stopped breathing in his sleep. I continued to train myself to wake up when he did. He was still slipping away. I still called the doctor, but he didn't call back, not for days.

It seemed that almost every night Cliff and I called our HMO nurses in distress. Occasionally we brought Walker in to be checked, but the doctors—always a different face—still insisted he was fine, just had a cold. I still insisted that Walker had sleep apnea, a condition I had read about wherein the sufferer stops breathing at night because of blocked respiratory passages or a sinus infection. "Babies don't have sinuses," said the doctor.

The nurses continuously directed us to take Walker into a steamy bathroom with hot water running in the shower, the way they had instructed us to do when Elizabeth had croup.

I guessed steam was supposed to clear the sinuses that didn't exist, I thought to myself, angrily.

One night when Cliff was asleep, I called the HMO. The nurses told me again to take Walker into the bathroom and turn on the shower. I looked down at his small sunken chest. He seemed to be trying to breathe, but unable. His neck strained to draw oxygen. But his chest was caving in as if drawing for air and reaching none: *Suck. Stop. Suck. Stop.* I looked over at Cliff, who was sleeping deeply, readying himself for another workday to begin in four hours. I picked up Walker, put him in the car, and drove to the hospital. It seemed he might die that night—die of respiratory disease or malnutrition. The only safe place for him had to be the hospital. The doctors left us alone on a gurney behind a curtain for most of the night, took a chest X-ray, and sent us home. The next day, Cliff was furious.

"Don't ever do something like that without me."

The next night was a similar story: Walker stopped breathing in his sleep. Since I had learned to listen for the absence of breathing, even in sleep, the sound, or lack of it, woke me up. He was as still as a tomb and not breathing. I shook Walker and quickly put him in his basket, brought him into the bathroom, and turned the knob: *SHHHH!* The water poured. Walker startled, threw his hands out, and wildly swung his head from side to side. *I got it now. It's the sound. Water crashing to the tub.* I rushed the basket outside into the hall and filled the room with steam with the door closed, turned off the water, then brought him back in his basket to the now silent bathroom. I flicked the light switch so he could breathe steam in the dark. He began to calm and I took him up into my arms and held him in the crescent moon shape. *(Was it a coincidence that Walker's ball shape was also fetal position? Was this shape to imitate or reconstruct the womb that somehow couldn't do its job right?)*

I do as Lenore advised. I consider the future I want. At first I see nothing. At first I see all of the other visitations—the crazy lady lurking around the foyer at Faces, the novelty store in town, who calls out obscenities to no one in particular; the man who only jogs; the man who sits rocking, playing with a small metal chain and weight. I empty my mind and see again. Into the picture, into the dream, appears a small boy running to me in the backyard. I am sitting on the porch stoop. Here he comes. A five-year-old, full of that lovely boy energy. He throws his arms around me and says, "Mommy I love you." For months, for years I will repeat this prayer. I will pray it and hope it and think it and hold him in the process. I don't know if it's possible to communicate prayers into a baby's body. But if there's any chance, I will take it. I will pray for the truth of prayers.

Science tells us that there are essentially two brains. They each are like crumpled pieces of paper. One part is called the cerebellum. If it were spread flat, it would be about one and a half feet square. The cerebellum is also called the lower brain, the "old brain" (this is actually a misnomer, since other parts are older). The cerebellum does the work of the old animal self, keeps rudimentary functions like balance, attention, motor control, and movement, coordinating sensory information with movement. The other brain is the cerebral cortex, the "new brain." The cortex is smaller than the cerebellum; spread out, it would be a rectangular sheet about one foot by two feet. The new brain is responsible for most of what we think of as intelligence, higher-order functioning, and reasoning. But the lower brain is responsible for functions more fundamental to a baby's development.

Lenore felt that the major part of Walker's brain that required healing was his cerebellum, the old brain. (My research corroborated that
many of the major areas of the brain associated with Walker's deficits,
particularly the emotional deficits, were in fact located in the cerebellum.) As for the condition of his cerebral cortex, we would have
to wait.

"But if the cerebellum is responsible for older functions, might
there be a way to somehow override it and just work on the cerebral cortex, the intelligence?"

"A baby's development is like building a house," she told us on
our second visit, as Walker lay on a blanket in her office a week after
we met. "It won't be a solid house unless you have a good foundation. What would happen if you built a house on mud? What kind
of a house would you have?"

"Do you see how closed his palms are, how tightly fisted his
hands?" Lenore said to Cliff and me that day. "Closed hands mean
a tight mind. Push your hands against his hands like this while he's
on his back." She pushed into his hands. "Intermittent compression
will help open them, help open his brain."

Such phrases—either surprising with profundity or shocking in
their weirdness—we were learning to accept from Lenore. Her talk
was unusual to my ears, thrilling and disturbing at once. Could we
believe what she did for Walker would work? Ultimately, it didn't
matter what we believed. What was important was that she felt we
had a shot, not a perfect shot.

"Look at where your son is in space," she said on that second
visit. "He's stuck. We have to help him get unstuck. That's why he
can't see you. It's as if you're in a different dimension. In fact, to
him, you are. We've got to help him push up into our plane."

"You mean sitting up?"

"Yes," said Lenore.

"Why can't we just put him up in his car seat? That helps him
to orient toward us."

"No," she said. "He's stuck because his brain hasn't developed.
And the brain develops with the body. When he learns to push up,
he'll really see you."

*How could that be, that sitting up could make a perceptual, a neuro-
logical difference?* "I still don't understand."

"Try entering his world," said Lenore. "Right now he's stuck in the horizontal plane. Then you'll understand." Lenore instructed both Cliff and me to spread out and place ourselves on the rug, lying on our backs, as Walker was. "Now, press your heads to the ground," she said. "Look up with only your eyes, into this room. Try to grasp the room conceptually, without moving your head. What do you see? Then you'll experience what it's like for him."

I tried to imagine I was a baby, with no preconceived ideas about what anything meant. The room turned into lines. I tried to press upward to better see, but I was stuck. I saw a collection of colored angled lines retreating off into directions beyond my visual scope.

Because I couldn't scan more than a fraction of the room, lines came abruptly into view and then inexplicably disappeared. Things I knew to be real, meaningful, and whole, as I suspended my prior awareness, lost meaning—a door frame became a skewed parallelogram, beginning nowhere. The floor seemed to be a sea, a huge encompassing plane that seemed to be intersecting the middle of my nose. Books on a shelf seemed to be floating in space by themselves without apparent support.

"How do you see the world?" Lenore asked. "How do you feel, feel about yourselves?" she continued.

"Weird," said Cliff. "I don't understand much. Everything's flat."

"I feel trapped, like the ceiling is getting taller and taller and I'm growing smaller and smaller," I said.

"Do you feel like you can engage with this world?"

Both Cliff and I spoke together. "No."

For the next month, after we began seeing Lenore, I stayed home most of the time with Walker and did whatever Arlene and Lenore told me to do. At times, their ideas were not in perfect agreement, though any disagreements I felt were just a matter of emphasis. Lenore was more concerned with form, with achieving perfect movement patterns. Arlene was deeply concerned with Walker's sensitivities. For Arlene, attaining perfect movement and form seemed crucial, but secondary to attaining Walker's attention. It was Arlene's belief that if Walker's wasn't overstimulated, he would keep from arching—sense precedes movement, in other words. Lenore felt that no matter what the stimulation, the arching needed to be stopped, however we could do it; form would affect perception and sensitivity. Regardless of their emphases, Lenore and Arlene proved, unwittingly, to be excellent complements to each other. Arlene spoke the argot of doctors, of sensory integration pioneers; Lenore spoke the language of shamans.

Arlene spoke of neural pathways, of sensory systems; Lenore emphasized the sensuality of Walker's being. We were to hum into Walker's chest, to hold our hands under his kidneys, lungs, stomach— to concentrate on our own so that he might receive some sensation from his organs, to "meet his injury in the nervous system and show him the healthy pathway." As far-fetched as some of these suggestions may seem, their purpose could not be denied, Walker needed to connect with us so that he could connect with the world, and he needed to connect with the world, so he could learn more about himself, know himself.

Both the therapists reminded us that Walker needed to be squeezed, to be pressed, and to be reminded of where he was in space, where his body began and where ours left off.

They spoke of "containment," of "compression," of "body contact," of the need to wrap, to pull together this flailing being into some kind of orderly conformity, to tame the wildness of his spirit. So Cliff and I squeezed. We pressed. Every night at bedtime, Cliff held Walker firmly in the C shape. Walker fought it. Lenore had told us that it was important for Cliff to let Walker arch, then relax, and in that moment of relaxation to curl him. Sometimes Cliff or I spent an hour or two putting Walker to sleep.

Cliff understood Lenore's language of the body better than I. He became expert in her art. He watched Walker's body carefully, altering its position. Before he went to bed, he checked on Walker; he curled the sleeping form into the perfect C.

One night I found him holding Walker in his arms in the dark, staring down at him, pensive, worried face stained with grief. Cliff looked up at me and said, "Pat, I look at him and I feel like I'm looking at myself. I had eczema, respiratory problems. And he looks exactly like me." Walker did. He was a miniature image of Cliff (though Cliff was not ill or weak). Walker had Cliff's well-proportioned features—the large head, strong chin, huge almond-shaped eyes.

I was thinking about Cliff's strengths, but when he spoke again, he said, "I was never very outgoing."

I shook my head as if to say, "It's not your fault." Still, I wondered what it was like to look into a baby's face and see your own strengths, your own frailties.

I looked at Walker's thin arms, watched him as his face lay buried in the blanket one afternoon when Arlene had come over.

"Does he have the strength to push himself up?"

"I don't know," she said. "But I have to believe he can." She, too, believed it was essential for Walker to raise himself up while prone.

"Here," she said. She placed him on his stomach and put a plastic key chain just beyond his reach.

He worked at push ups for hours in the next few days. I peeked around the corner from the kitchen and found him trying again and again. I saw the work of it in his face, saw him fight the weakness in his arms. It was a wonder he never stopped trying. At first nothing seemed to be happening. Then, his head would move slightly, sometimes falling, leaving him with mouthfuls of blanket. The only way out was to lift again—more push-ups. Continually, Walker worked at pushing and pushing and pushing, thin arms pressing against the ground, the head barely moving. Then he rested. I picked him up and we worked at eating for a while, then back to the dining room for more push-ups. Walker was working as hard—perhaps even harder—at his push-ups than I have ever seen a human being work.

Lenore referred us to a colleague of hers who was teaching Body-Mind Centering at nearby Hampshire College. She taught us to roll Walker, stomach forward, over a large ball. When he came over the top of the ball, moving headfirst toward the floor, he didn't put out his arms to protect his head. We worked with the ball over and over again, for two or three weeks. One day, I held Walker like an airplane and moved him toward the floor for a landing. His arms moved out slowly. Was he trying to protect his head? I slowed down the motion. When we neared the floor, his arms went up, bracing the fall. I tried again. Walker had protective extension. From then on, every time I flew him toward the ground, he braced himself. Walker had mastered a primary reflex.

I remember reading once in a childhood astronomy book that it would take a million Earths to make a ball as big as the sun. The sun's gravity is so much stronger than Earth's that if you weighed sixty pounds on Earth, you'd weigh 1,680 pounds on the sun. When Walker did his push-ups over the next weeks, Walker seemed to me like that earthling come to the sun, his body weighing more than 1,000 pounds. He strained against the tyranny of a gravity that seemed massive. Still he proved an able athlete in his efforts to do push-ups, full of determination, senseless of the meaning of success or failure—aware, perhaps, only of his wanting.

I came in from the kitchen one day to find that Walker had lifted his head several inches above the ground.

As the days of June passed—we'd been working with Walker for about five weeks—Walker was continuing his arduous push-ups; he was beginning to show some strength in his neck. As part of this process we were also trying to encourage him to roll over, pushing with his arms (instead of from his hips).

One day, I placed him on a blanket, stomach toward the ground as usual. A pile of Elizabeth's hair bands—large purple and red rings of satin—lay two feet away. When I came back from the kitchen a few minutes later, I found him lying on his stomach with one of Elizabeth's hair bands in his hands.

"You've done it, my boy." I leaped. Somehow he had crept or crawled to retrieve the bands.

He might have been a new species making his way out of the sea.

PART 3

The Questions That Haunted Us

DIANE ACKERMAN, in her book *A Natural History of the Senses*, emphasizes the importance of the senses for ego development when she asserts that it is by being touched that a newborn first learns the "difference between *I* and *other*." When Cliff and I were working with Walker, certain questions haunted us—what are we neurologically, psychologically, existentially, without clear sensations? What do those individuals with confused and dysfunctioning senses have of memories? How do people with unclear sensations store their memories? What kinds of bonds can be forged in the chaos of sensory confusion?

If Freud was correct, if the first templates by which we pattern love are born of our intimate moments with mother, what kind of future lies in store for a baby lost in sensory chaos or inconsistency, unable to forge a firm template for loving, for accepting love, for producing love? I read that the famous autistic engineer, Temple Grandin, claimed that she didn't "get" *Romeo and Juliet*. The baby with sensory processing disorder finds himself stuck in a world we can only imagine. What is that world? A primordial state? Or perhaps something worse—a kind of non-being where memory, meaning, a sense of spatial relations, and human interaction don't begin to happen, or happen haphazardly? I have heard stories of neurological patients who lose their sense of their bodies; they live as if they were ghosts, never have a sense of where they are in space. But what if such a disorientation were translated into the psychological realm as well as the physical? For individuals with autism, somehow the pain of the senses, the pain of distorted senses, seems to be the primary concern.

In both Temple Grandin's and Donna Williams's biographies about life lived with sensory integration dysfunction and autism, they speak often and compellingly about the life of the senses. In their worlds, there is a kind of hegemony of the senses—the life of the senses *is* life. And yet the senses can also be scrambled for a person with sensory processing disorder, scrambled as if he or she were on an LSD trip, so that some individuals have spoken of the distortions of synaesthesia, a disorder in which one sense seems to be experienced through another: one hears color, for instance, or sees music. I often wondered if Walker was experiencing synaesthesia, or some altered perceptual wash of sensation.

Temple Grandin talks in her book *Thinking in Pictures* about the strange sensory disorientation experienced by Donna Williams: "Fluorescent lighting in a kitchen with yellow walls blinded her. There were also situations in which things disappeared and lost their meaning. Donna described moving quickly through a hall: 'Perceptually the hall did not exist. I saw shapes and colors as it whooshed by.' When her visual system became completely overloaded with stimuli, all meaning in visual sensation was lost." Meaning was not just lost for Donna Williams on a perceptual plane. She explains in her book *Nobody Nowhere* that she was deeply crippled in her abilities to relate to others as a child; she spent her early years in a bizarre and solitary world, punctuated by incomplete or aborted relations.

I watched Walker sleeping at night, or as he stared away, and wondered how he felt.

One day Arlene brought me a handout describing an "experience" that some parents of grade-school age children with sensory integration dysfunction are invited to take part in, a kind of staged performance-art experience inviting them to literally enter their child's confused world. The brochure described the experience something like this:

The therapist invites you to imagine yourself a student. She ushers you into a small room. Lights flash on and off; you have difficulty finding a seat. A recording of static blasts so loudly your ears hurt. The sound recedes, only to be replaced by the noise of children laughing. A teacher enters and begins whispering. You can tell that she wants you to follow directions, but the lights flash on and off and you can't see her well. She is moving toward you. A shrill scratching sound blasts so deadly loud you feel yourself wanting to curl up. You try to listen to the teacher approaching, but now you're focusing on the pain in your ears. A light bores from behind her head. You close your eyes and curl up. "Look at me, damn it," she yells. She sends you to the principal's office for impertinence.

The process of fully fathoming what sensory processing is about—the ways that our senses inform our personalities and our experience—took me months, years to understand, and of course, I'm not finished.

When I began working with Arlene, I quickly learned that there exist far more than five senses. Vision, hearing, touch, taste and smell: These are the obvious senses. Yet while Arlene slowly moved Walker through the air or held him firmly in her hands, she began to delineate for me the myriad realms of other, more mysterious senses, the ones not often spoken about. There is the felt knowledge of one's own internal organs, of one's limbs, a sense of time passing, gravitational security or insecurity (the sense of how one relates to gravity). Arlene taught me about the *proprioceptive* sense (the sense of where one is in space), that within this sense there exist myriad abilities, strengths, deficits.

If we close our eyes, do we know where our hands lie or move? Our kidneys? Our toes? Some individuals don't. I have often wondered what a profound proprioceptive deficit feels like—a kind of swimming, a floating world, where the self evades itself, like water through a sieve.

Within the proprioceptive sense there exists a sense of one's relationship to moving bodies—the particular sense of one body's relationship to another body in space. Thus, the proprioceptive sense determines, in some sense, the negotiation of relationships as well. Arlene explained that Walker was spending so much time trying to figure out where he was—a sense that comes to us through the joints and muscles—that he couldn't quite know where *we* were.

I learned about the *vestibular* sense (the sense of one's body in motion or in a vehicle in motion) and, within this sense, a plethora of fine distinctions regarding directions and types of movement to which the body responds differently: swinging up and down; swinging in a plane running parallel to the ground, spinning in various postures, running, riding in a car. Each of these affects the neurological system differently. Arlene devised games we could play with Walker to give him vestibular stimulation. She put him on a blanket and dragged it around the house—this challenged him on several levels—to the extent that he was challenged to balance his body, his little hands and arms came up into the air as he tried to right himself. We swung him often, rolled him up in the carpet, unrolled him. His vestibular sense was challenged in the tumbling, yet he was given firm proprioceptive input from the hard and squeezing rug, which helped him accept the tumbling. We often bounced Walker on our knees and spoke, or sang, while we stimulated the vestibular sense, the sense of motion, making cooing noises, laughing with his laughs. Arlene had a song she often sang: *Trot, trot to Boston/Trot, trot to Lynn/Look out Walker/You're gonna' fall in*. At first he looked terrified. Eventually he came to like such games.

Over time we began using a laundry basket to pull him around the house, to acclimate him to unusual and unexpected movements.

It was hard to understand exactly why Walker behaved in many ways as if he were blind. The pediatrician at our HMO who examined Walker suggested he be tested for blindness.

"But how can you measure that?" Cliff asked.

"The eye shows an eye doctor how it can focus, regardless of what a baby can express," he explained. "When the eye doctor asks you, 'Can you see this better or that better?' he already knows. He's just entertaining you by asking." The doctor laughed. Perhaps he was joking. "We won't be requiring a response from your son."

I had always imagined that when I looked out of my eyes, I saw a view that was standard—perhaps more in focus than some who required glasses, since I don't wear glasses, but standard. Yet what I have learned about vision has changed that naive view. We don't all see the same world. (For some reason, traditional eye doctors either don't acknowledge this fact or don't care to make much of it.) According to recent theorists in sensory processing, there is a universe of stimuli to which we each respond differently: shapes, "directionality," spatial relationships. Each of us interprets what comes in visually and we construct a world based on that information. Yet we don't necessarily perceive the same world. I began to wonder if there might be visual frequencies the way that there are acoustic frequencies that we perceive differently.

Eye doctors who can measure, and sometimes correct for, many of these differences are called behavioral optometrists and view sight as a neurological function, a process of perceptual interpretation. They test for "eye tracking," "teaming" (integration of the information coming into the two eyes), "visual focusing" (one eye's ability to focus in tandem with the other eye), depth perception and visual perceptual skills, which affect balance and how the body moves. We, all of us, possess varying abilities to perceive visual information..One boy I read about was reported by a behavioral optometrist to see twice as much detail as the average person. The boy who saw too much had an anxiety disorder. No wonder. Another was terrified of dogs and couldn't catch balls until a behavioral optometrist caught what a traditional practitioner had been unable to: that the boy's visual "teaming" was not functioning. The first day he received corrective lenses, he caught a ball and let a dog come straight up to him. Such stories were a revelation to me about the connection between perception and behavior.

I struggled to understand Walker's visual sensitivity, which Arlene made clear was profound—the worst of his sensitivities. She said he was probably not using his eyesight much of the time.

What does light have that a mother doesn't? Answer? A boy's attention.

One day we asked our day-care provider to take care of Walker so we could attend a concert in which our friend's daughter was singing a solo. It was in an old neoclassical building on the Smith College campus. On the southwestern wall stood huge banks of leaded windows, thirty feet high. The afternoon sun poured into the windows, making a glow so intense it became a haze, a headachy bright intrusion that I tried to avoid. Yet for some reason I was drawn to the light, pulled into it, in spite of the fact that the light was thoroughly unpleasant. Is this some kind of instinct? I felt impressionable, unfocused, irritated. Still I couldn't look away. In that instant, I thought I might understand what was motivating Walker—a reflex? A response to intensity. What took yards and yards and yards of glaring light to make me react, took for him only a household window and the normal light of day.

The tactile system is another important sense in the world of sensory dysfunction, as it is for all of us, though we may not realize it. Arlene explained to me that she was "tactilely sensitive" herself and could barely bring herself to help Walker eat certain foods, particularly if they were gooey.

I came to realize that there is no touch like human touch. It is the most stimulating, perhaps, of all sensations. "That's why it's hard for Walker to be touched by you," she said. "The skin is an extreme source of stimulation because it was designed to be so. It's meant to give neurological messages." I began to suspect, by the both positive and negative and dramatic reactions Walker had to being held or touched, that human skin is perhaps unlike anything else in nature. Consider his reaction to nursing. He had to force himself to do it. Now I know it must have been a vortex—the mouth including a major nerve, so much skin touching skin. Was satisfaction itself stimulating to the nervous system? Certain touches organized Walker; certain touches disorganized him. But did I quite understand which did which?

The sense of smell, though it may be less talked about than the other senses, is an important one. It is neurologically closely connected to memory functions. Perhaps this is why autistic individuals, with highly sensitized noses, are reported to have often powerful memories.

Yet a strong sense of smell, I learned, could drive an autistic person mad with irritation. I understood this fact from having been pregnant, as many woman do. Both times, when I was pregnant, I could smell the butcher's department the second I walked into the supermarket, even though it was at the far end. The smell of dead flesh was often so overpowering I had to leave, gagging, and was often literally sick from it. Yet even those heightened sensations seemed tame compared to what I learned can happen in severe sensory integration disorder. I read about one boy who could identify the smell of all different kinds of animal manure—cow, sheep, horse, and even other varieties. I read about people who could not bear being in public because of smells.

One day in midsummer, my friend Mark sent me an e-mail explaining that he had a friend who lived in Norway whose baby was very ill. The infant had no sense of hunger, had received several operations, was failing to thrive. It suddenly occurred to me that the baby in question might be having sensory problems. Wasn't hunger a sense? An internal regulatory function whereby the body decided how much input one needed? It didn't take me more than another step to wonder, for the first time, if Walker's eating problems weren't largely sensory. Arlene expected his mouth was sensitive, and she had some success stimulating his mouth to help him eat better, yet still we hadn't been able to do much to stimulate appetite. Arlene felt he was often too overwhelmed to be hungry.

Perhaps the area of greatest competence for Walker was his sense of hearing. He was indeed sensitive to sound, yet he could also be responsive to our sounds. He also sometimes made noises when the radio was on, as if he might be singing. Perhaps auditory strength explains why in the early months he seemed to be imitating us, saying "Ah ew eh," for I love you. *But why had he then lost that ability?*

As soon as I began to understand the hidden senses, and the ones I thought I knew about, I had to face another fact: that perhaps the most important aspect of any sense in the nervous system may be its relationship to another sense. Arlene blithely spoke about the mysteries of the nervous system.

"The vestibular and auditory are housed next door to each other in the brain. They share the same fluid. Sound gives you a sense of space," said Arlene.

The mouth was connected to the brain and other senses in ways I would never before have imagined.

"The mouth is where we begin in the world," Arlene said.

"Begin?"

"The mouth is the center of the body. It brings together the two sides of the brain, organizing us around a midpoint. The mouth is connected to the limbic system (the emotional system), sucking brings the eyes together."

The brain I could see as a complex system, but *the mouth*? "Have you ever found yourself biting a pen while you were thinking?" asked Arlene. "That's why."

If the senses formed a rich neurological matrix, the fear was that Walker's experience might be a broken mosaic, some mesmerizing chips of illogic or color, only vaguely reflecting the themes of reality. The idea was to always create a full and whole, lived experience for Walker.

The way out was synergy. Arlene and Lenore, each in their separate languages, emphasized the same truth about the nervous system: The senses "speak" through each other; they can "learn" from each other. The senses can work to complement, distract, instruct, or inform one another. I was astounded to learn that some non-speaking children, remarkably, learn to do so first by reading, whereas other children who can't perform the visual operation of reading, learn to do so through touch, by feeling letters made of sandpaper.

We needed to talk while we touched Walker, to give sounds to actions, to name feelings, to use words to render sense to gestures, to touch, touch, touch and talk, talk, talk. Cliff and Elizabeth and I made up songs and dances. Walker at times was beginning to watch. But where was the point of overstimulation? What was the trigger that sent him reeling away from us into the internal landscape? That was always the challenge, the paradox, the danger—that the treatment could also be the poison.

If we were going to help Walker live in our world, we would have to enter his. So while Arlene and I studied the small creature on the rug, I learned to be aware of the subtle annoying noises, the harsh lights, the wound of certain textures. I tried to hear the wind outside, the scratching of branches on the window, felt, almost viscerally, the multipitched, high and airy, low and humming insult of traffic outside. I began to feel the zing of the ambulance screaming, the shrill electric whine of the saws working on our neighbor's house addition; I alerted myself to the intrusion of the *crick, crick, crick* made by the squeaky crumpling of a plastic bag. I hoped, if I could feel any of these feelings before he felt them, I could pull him away, could prevent his head from flying side to side or his eyes from moving toward those blasted bright window lights. If I could learn what he felt, I could keep him with us.

My memory of Walker's first summer is distorted, skewed. It seemed to last for years. Time was stretching, yawning. The sun was always hanging in the sky—exalting like a kid showing off. Sometimes the sun was so strong it seemed to be bending the windows to its will, especially in the bedroom or the kitchen on the south sides of the house where the blinds seemed nearly useless. Light flooded like water through the slats. It was as if noontime seemed to be all time that summer, though Walker and I were always hiding away from it in the darkness like one of the creatures in children's stories that die from light. Not until nearly nine did the sun finally give way, long past Elizabeth's "witching hour," when she seemed to lose her nerves somehow. Like many children her age, she sometimes lost self-control before dinner, crying, yelling, lashing out. We were all frayed, all "sensory defensive," overstimulated, frazzled. Still, we played with Walker every chance we found. We played the game with the wire sphere. We said his name. *Walker.* We held him in a tight ball. We jumped up and down to attract his attention—we were having to work hard to keep his attention. The electric saws droned on and on next door, but one day I realized that Walker was able to play with me for ten minutes without losing his concentration, even as the saws buzzed wildly.

Every day, on the floor with Walker, at the kitchen table, we tried to put some food into him, and we tried to understand. Yet if trying to understand Walker was difficult, trying to explain was even harder.

The Fourth of July weekend Cliff's sister, Susan, came with her daughter to nearby Springfield to visit her parents and to see us. Susan invited us to join the family in Springfield for a backyard picnic. Cliff declined. Susan called me later that day. "Can't you just come for a couple of hours?" she wanted to know. I can well imagine what she must have been feeling, after flying up to visit. She must have thought we were all going mad or were overprotective.

"It's hard to explain," I tried to tell her.

"I know," she said, patiently. "You said he's sensitive. But we'll just be in the backyard. In nature. It will be very calm and peaceful. We're not going to have loud music or fireworks."

How could I explain? The last thing in the world we wanted to do was offend Cliff's kind sister and family. So we went. As we ate, Cliff and I watched Walker.

"Look," someone said. "See, he's looking up at the trees."

But we knew that he wasn't looking at the trees at all. His gaze was lost somewhere. As it often was. While Walker stared above us into the white-blue space, I wondered how much time we were losing. What had it cost him to be gone from us for two hours? For three? For four?

New Clues

A WOMAN—Therese, a mother from Arcadia, Elizabeth's nursery school—called me one day when I had been working with REACH for about a month. She was pregnant when I was, gave birth to her daughter, Emily, a month before Walker was born. She called because she was concerned about us, had heard through the grapevine that Walker was ill. It may have been one of the most important phone calls of Walker's life, though its roots were peculiar, disturbing. Years later, Therese confessed to me that another mother from the nursery school had called her to talk about Walker (she won't reveal to me who it was, and I'm grateful). The mother, however, was apparently convinced that I wasn't feeding Walker enough. I'm still not sure why she never asked me what I was doing, or perhaps she had, but the answer didn't mean much to her. All she saw was a baby who looked like a starving child from the drought land of East Africa—ribs that pressed beyond skin and flesh, almost exoskeletal bones, arms as skinny as a hose, distended stomach, a starved look around the eyes. I can see how a mother would think that Walker's was the look of hunger. And it may well have been. We knew Walker was starving to death in a way, sliding into a shadow world. I had called the pediatrician, even sent him an emergency fax, when days before I'd tried to tell him that Walker was losing weight quickly (seven ounces in just a few days), losing in spite of how much rice cereal I pressed between his dispassionate lips.

I suppose we could be angry that someone might have thought we weren't doing enough, but the irony is that whoever called Therese had called the right person.

She called Therese because she knew Therese had experience with social services, yet what she may not have known about Therese is that she had a lifetime's experience with allergies.

When Therese received the call, she was frightened. She knew from having worked in the system that social services had a history of making fatal mistakes—taking children from their homes because of misunderstandings. She urged the other mother to resist making the call, to talk to me, and after they hung up, she immediately called me.

When I told her I thought Walker might have allergies, she believed me, embraced my theory. How could she not? She had lived with allergies her entire life. Allergies had eaten her. She had a special air filter installed in her air conditioner. She intentionally lived near the hospital.

"Look," she said. "I'm highly allergic. I've been in anaphylaxis. I need to get up twice a night to take inhaler for asthma. If my husband eats fish and kisses me, my cheeks swell. I can't visit people with dogs or cats."

I told her my own story.

When I was in college in California, I moved into the most beautiful house I had ever lived in—it was a house near the sea that had been hand-built by the owners of the local hardware store. It was Tudor style, with imported Italian tiles, leaded windows, arches. Yet from the first day living there, I was ravaged with feelings of discomfort. Tears rolled down my eyes as I sat in bed trying to read. I tore the place apart with a vacuum cleaner, but it didn't help. Eventually I visited an allergist who told me that I needed to get away from that house. He suspected mold in the walls, since I showed high allergic responses to mold on my skin tests. At that time I began reading as much as I could about allergies. Several books insisted that severe allergies can change your personality, can deeply affect the ability to concentrate, to work, to attend.

Now, here was my baby, writhing, covered with eczema, barely able to breathe, rashy after nursing. How could I not believe that something in his environment was causing such discomfort? Yet I didn't understand why any doctors wouldn't attend to this point. "The pediatrician at our HMO claims babies don't really have allergies," I told her. "Can that be true?"

"No." said Therese. Only Dr. Lasneski, the chiropractor-nutrition-ist who gave us supplements, would engage with the question. He said that Walker's eczema was decidedly an allergic response.

"After we nurse," I continued, "his cheeks are red. I want to wean him, to fill him full of only pure ingredients. The pediatrician says breast milk is the best. But I don't believe it. Not for this child. I see him rolling, writhing with discomfort, and I think I know that discomfort. Red cheeks, swollen. Tell me, Therese, do you think allergies could be so bad they could affect brain development?" I asked.

"Oh, yes," she said, "I'm sure of it. When I have bad reactions, I feel raw all over. If I eat the wrong things, they'll kill me, why wouldn't they also possibly affect someone's brain?"

She vowed to research the subject on the Internet, to call me back. She knew I was busy working with Walker.

What is he allergic to that I'm eating, or is it just me and my milk?

Therese and I agreed to meet in a park; we could talk while her children played. She brought some information. On the Internet, she had discovered that there is a phenomenon called "brain allergies." She said the subject was controversial; she had the impression that people concerned with how diet affects behavior were particularly interested in the subject. She had found that the Feingold Association asserted that diet affected the brain and that at Johns Hopkins University they had advocated a diet called the Ketogenic diet, which seems to have dramatically curtailed seizures in some epileptics.

"If Walker's nervous system is sensitive to natural levels of stimulation," I argued to Therese, "what kind of sensitivities are there in his internal system?" What kind of havoc were the chemicals in certain foods wreaking with Walker's sensitivities, abrading him, twisting him inward, damaging his ability to give us his attention?

As Therese talked, I looked down and noticed that I was wearing two different shoes, mismatched, a tennis shoe and a black leather one. We laughed. I went home and researched some more after the children slept.

What was this connection between allergies and neurological dysfunction? I felt certain they were related. I watched Walker closely. If his system were profoundly compromised by some substance, what might be the invader?

I had a clue several nights later when I went to a parents' meeting. There a woman spoke of her quest for a cure for her daughter's autism. She felt certain the problem was largely dietary. She recommended removing wheat and dairy.

Two days later, I was talking to Therese on the phone and I decided that for certain I would put Walker on hypoallergenic formula. Even Vicki, REACH's nutritionist, agreed it was a worthwhile move. I hung up quickly, drove to the pharmacy, and bought hypoallergenic formula. I drove fast. Cliff and I also called the doctor and insisted the doctor try a round of antibiotics. Something must be done for Walker's breathing.

Results came in from the X-ray of Walker's adenoids. They were inflamed. He agreed antibiotics were in order.

Is it difficult taking my baby away from the breast, Therese wants to know? No, it isn't. It's one of the easiest things I've ever done, holding Walker in my arms while he cries now from a hunger that must be overwhelming. We sit in the rocker, but I barely move—not much, not too much motion. It's one of the few things I can give him, this taking away.

I shut my ears to the cries. After several hours of having no food, he took the bottle thirstily. Therese wanted to know if it hurts me somehow that my own milk isn't good for my baby. Why take it personally? If machine oil was best for him, I'd buy a case.

Yet that night—his first off of breast milk—we noticed a difference. Walker seemed to be resting for the first night of his life. Now, a week after we had begun the supplement therapy with Dr. Lasneski, and two days after I had weaned him, the eczema was almost gone.

The next day, we made another change.

We found a new pediatrician, Dr. Cochrane, a polite man, handsome, sandy hair, and an old-world formality. He shook our hands with unusually soft fingers and studied Walker. He turned from Walker, bore his eyes into mine, looked almost frightened with the effort of it, and said, "I certainly share your concern for your son,

Ma'am." We liked him because he seemed unusually intelligent and returned our phone calls, returned them with chilling efficiency, as if we were in the hospital. He wouldn't say what was wrong for sure, but he did say, "The first thing that comes to mind is certainly autism."

Think of the future you want.

Walker was now on two brands of hypoallergenic formula made of some milk product, though with the allergens removed. I still don't fully understand how such a process is possible—to remove some aspect of the milk's protein without depriving it of its usefulness, but I always imagined it to be something like decaffeinating coffee (flyers said the protein was "predigested"). Whatever the process was, it must have been complex, because the formulas were expensive. Cliff and I estimated that keeping Walker on the formulas would cost us between $600 and $950 per month.

Cliff was growing more and more anxious about money. He began calling me from work to say he felt we should move, that no one with a baby like Walker could afford to live in a large 150-year-old house in the Historic District, at least not in one that was as needy of repairs as ours. He called me while I was supervising Walker's push-ups.

"I've called an agent. She's going to show me some houses during lunch."

"What are you talking about?" I said.

"We've got to move, Pat."

"There is no way we're moving now. Our son needs us, needs everything we've got to give."

"The supplements are costing us about $150 a month; Lenore costs $80 a week, and now this formula is costing $600 a month. That's a mortgage for some people right there, and the insurance company won't pay for a dime of any of it."

"So we'll go in debt. We'll use credit cards."

"We already are. This is no way to live."

"You can look at all the houses you want, Cliff, but I'm not moving." I hung up the phone.

I called our insurance company. They gave me a list of diagnoses that would qualify us for insurance to pay for hypoallergenic formula.

"You mean insurance won't cover hypoallergenic formulas for children with allergies?"

"No," said the woman on the other end.

I took the list and called our doctor. He called me back quickly.

"Is there something here that you can legitimately say that Walker has?" I read a list of foreign medical terms. Colitis. Malabsorption.

"No."

"Can't you say he has this gastroesophageal reflux?"

"No," said the doctor. "It's a very specific problem."

Later, when Walker was napping, I called Darleen Corbett at REACH and asked her if there was any way we could receive help for Walker's expenses. She referred me to Marianne Beach with the Department of Public Health.

Within two days, Marianne Beach was at our door, making a home visit, customary when she took on cases.

She sat on the couch and waited while I ran upstairs to retrieve Walker from the crib. It was about his time to wake up, and she wanted to meet him. I stood in the doorway for a few seconds to catch my breath. I didn't know what I'd find. Sound emanating from the room was emptiness, a void, and I had that fear that I always had that perhaps he had died in his sleep. I began to speak, hoping my voice would make him stir, but when I reached the crib I saw that he was awake already. Awake, but not awake perhaps. Walker was lying in the crib with his head curled far upward, backward. I knew what this was now, it was called "extension." His eyes were open, yet he seemed somehow frozen. "Walker," I said. No reaction. "Walker!" Nothing. I shook him a little, but he remained frozen. I'm not even sure he was blinking. I picked him up, brought him into the correct form that Arlene and Lenore insisted he needed to always be in, the perfect C, curled in toward his center. He fell into my arms like a dead weight. Head heavy, rubbery-seeming. Moving through the somewhat dimmer light of the stairwell, I tried to bring his attention around to me. I didn't speak but strained to make as blank and loving a face as I could. Was it my imagination or did he seem a little more aware in the C shape? I brought him downstairs and into the room where Marianne sat and crossed my legs on the floor.

"Is that some special thing you're doing?" she asked.

"Yes. We're to keep him in a perfect circle or C shape."

"Really—he needs to be in a shape?"

"Yes," I said. "It encourages proper brain development."

"Really?"

"Yes."

"I've never heard of that," she said.

"I know," I agreed. "It sounds superstitious."

"Actually, I think I may have had one boy, mentally retarded, whose parents did something like that." As she spoke, Walker grew agitated.

Was it the new voice, or too much holding? I lay him on the floor in the ball, making small adjustments, as my ballet teacher used to do to me to make sure I positioned myself properly, got the curve just right. I lay down close to him with our heads near each other.

I sighed. "Retarded people don't have problems with loving, do they?"

She looked at me gently as if to say, "Everybody has problems with loving, don't they?"

"It's not like with autism; was the retarded child affectionate?"

I looked down at Walker.

"So they suspect autism, do they?" said Marianne.

"Nothing official yet, but we sort of do."

"I have a lot of clients whose children have autism. One family, in the Berkshires with triplets. All three autistic."

"Wow," was all I could say.

I lay on the floor while Marianne told me something about herself and her brother with cancer, about her special interest in special needs children, about some of the strange situations she encounters.

"Once I was called in on a suspected child-abuse charge," she explained. "A doctor had examined a baby with duct tape around his diaper. When I came to the home I immediately knew what the problem was. The kid was a wild man. No wonder the mother needed to use duct tape on his diaper, he was tearing at everything in sight."

"Sounds more like the baby was abusing the parents," I said. We both laughed.

"By the way," she added, "this is backtracking, but were you ever given a drug called terbutaline?"

"Terbutaline?"

"It's given to mothers who go into labor early."

"No," I said. "I didn't go into premature labor."

"Are you sure?"

"Yes I'm sure. Why?"

"My family in the Berkshires has been doing some research with an autism expert in Boston. They believe the terbutaline she was given is responsible for their children's autism. The doctor figured it this way: Why would three fraternal—you know, non-identical—triplets all have the same disease? How could genetics factor for that? What were the genetic odds? It must have been something postconception that caused the autism. The mother was given terbutaline. Seems they've found other terbutaline women with autistic children."

"Wow."

Later in the interview, we got down to the basics. I explained to Marianne that we needed financial assistance for Walker. She explained that a program called Mass Health might cover a lot of Walker's needs and might also fill in for what insurance companies don't pay for. She looked around our house and said, "I'm not sure you'll qualify, but perhaps I can help you in another way."

The next morning at 8:30 A.M. she came to the door. Was she wearing a trench coat, or do I just imagine it?

"Come here," she said in a tone of conspiracy. We walked to her car on the street; she opened the trunk and began pulling plastic bags out of it.

"What is this?" I asked.

"Hypoallergenic formula," she said. "You said you needed some. I know a family that doesn't need this anymore."

"Is this part of your job?"

She looked at me sideways. "Well, it's not written into my job description or anything. In fact, don't mention it to my boss."

That night I was lying in bed, the day settling heavily, a leaded sediment, sleep coming fast. My body was grabbing sleep, claiming it, the sinking water pulling me, when ideas began to tumble: *babies in duct tape, retarded client, triplets with autism in the Berkshires. The oddness of three. No one child for solace. . . . And what was this drug? Tribute? Tribune . . . ?*

Walker on the floor last week, bumped his head and no response, and suddenly I saw a hypodermic needle.

I thought back to Walker's birth.

Back to a moment, the scene in the hospital flooded my awareness.

I am lying on a table, lightning entering my body: Back labor. (The famous back labor they talked about in the labor classes with dread.) All bets were off with that kind of labor—too much pressure on the spine; it seemed only a masochist would try it without pain medication. They said it would move like evil through the body, the legs, and they were right. The baby seemed to be exploding out of my nervous system rather than the womb. Electric shock.

Tired, jaded doctors—one yelling at me, the other flirting with the nurse, talking incessantly, incessantly about Steven King novels, the wicked car, the doctor's maniacal laugh.

C-section was inevitable, but the doctors weren't ready . . .

and the needle . . .

"But is it safe?" I asked.

"Honey, it's what they give asthma patients," said the nurse.

"But I'm pregnant."

"We do it all the time, honey."

I ran downstairs and went through my files for the birth records. I found the yellow sheet with its smudgy carbon writing—the word "terbutaline" written three times in separate places across the record.

First thing the next morning, I called a friend in the medical field.

"You'll never know why," she said. "What about your other concerns—the blue cold medicine, the antibiotics, genetics? And besides. Even if you feel sure you know the reason, you'll never prove it."

A Walk Around the Driveway

A WEEK AFTER WE MET with Marianne Beach, I was scheduled to teach the morning writing intensive—every weekday for three hours. My friend Kyle agreed to baby-sit for an impossibly low sum. I felt ashamed asking her. I wanted to say I knew that women were often asked or even expected to do things for reasons different than money, and I was sorry I was relying on her affections for my son, but I didn't. Instead, I said, "Could you possibly watch Walker for $4.00 an hour?" She said she might be able to do it for $5.00. I knew that Kyle was the ideal choice to spend mornings with Walker. In many ways, she had more to give him than I. She was filled with affection, caressed his body firmly, rubbed his little feet to warm them, and dressed him thoughtfully, creatively, using his berets and the new socks she had bought. She was attentive to his eating (now that he was on hypoallergenic formula, he wasn't vomiting as much). What I wasn't fully prepared for, however, was Kyle's attention to me.

Each morning as she waited for me to leave, Kyle watched me rush around the house looking for last-minute items: "Where is that *Reader's Encyclopedia* I promised to share with the students?" "Where is the notebook I was writing in last night?" "Where are my keys?" I was a bit shaky, scattered. When it was time to close the door, I leaned around it and gave a final look toward Walker. "Good-bye honey," I said. Walker didn't often look my way.

One morning Kyle arrived with a piece of paper. She handed it to me shyly. On it was a poem she had written to me with a veiled hint I might want to take antidepressants.

In anticipation of my teaching, Arlene, who had been seeing Walker for about two months, began coming in the afternoon so she could work with me and Walker when I would be home. Walker was nine months old. Most babies at that age are vigorously crawling, babbling, looking at people every moment. Giving and taking with the world is their way of learning. They do it naturally, grabbing at life. With Walker, it still took considerable effort to reach his attention. One afternoon during this period, I sat above him and lifted a small teddy bear to my eyes. He smiled and looked up. Awareness pierced through me. I could swear that he was looking right into my eyes. We held the gaze for a moment, and then he looked away.

I had the odd electric charge, a raw and slightly alarming sensation.

"Arlene," I said, "did you see that? He was looking into my eyes. I could swear it. Do you think he was?"

"Yes," she said. "You know, I have an idea. Let's take him outside."

"Are you kidding? For real? I'm not sure we should. Two weeks ago, on the Fourth of July he was outside for two or three hours and he just stared into space."

"Let's see how he does," she said. "Just for a while. He's doing a little bit better every time I see him."

We planned that on the following week for her next visit, we would take a walk.

All that weekend, I looked forward to the day that Arlene would come for our stroll with Walker. I had romantic images of Arlene and Walker and me strolling through the park, two women and a baby, enjoying the afternoon. It would be quaint, an old-fashioned comfort. I was starving for stimulation myself, but it was more than that—not so much that my senses wanted something, but more that I wanted something for me. Teaching was helpful, and was helping, but it was so much in a different world. A walk, a talk, two adults and a baby— I hungered for such a life with Walker. Arlene was one of the few adults I spoke with during the day. (Cliff and I were too busy at home to talk to each other; he had taken on a freelance job to pay for therapies.) Arlene's concern for me and for Walker gave me a focus, not just for him but for me. Even though I was home alone many hours doing the therapy, it was Arlene's and my shared work that I was doing.

When she arrived, she began to do her normal therapy but I reminded her that we had planned an outing. She looked at her watch. "Well, there's not much time, but we'll give it a try." I picked up Walker and took him out to the back porch. Arlene followed.

"Where shall we go?"

"Not far," said Arlene. "There isn't much time." Walker was squirming in my arms, arching.

"Let's put him down," she suggested. "Do you have a stroller?"

"Yes." I scrambled to pull my stroller out of the garage, where it was kept, waiting to be useful. I placed a blanket on it, and Arlene adjusted it so Walker could be inclined enough to see out.

Then we began to walk.

"Wait," said Arlene. She bent down near Walker's face, not too closely, and tried to attract his attention. He looked up at her. "Good," she said. "Now let's just take a walk around the driveway."

"Around the driveway?"

"Yes. That may be more than enough for him."

"Is that as far as we get to go?"

"It's miles for him."

I pushed the stroller. Every few feet Arlene tried to get Walker's attention. Once around the car and Walker could still look up at us, could still give us his attention. By the middle of the second trip, we had lost him. He was gazing away.

The stroll had been too much for him.

We brought him into the house and tried to work with him, but the stroller trip had overloaded his vestibular system, Arlene explained. We would have to wait until he was calmer to work again.

A few days later, Arlene pulled a red plastic ball out of her bag. It was medium sized, rubbery, covered with plastic prongs that came to a point (a fun version of those metal balls that hung from chains in the middle ages). She handed it to Walker, who held it in his hand, then immediately began screaming. The screams were loud, as if he'd been pierced by pins. I snatched it out of his hand—just a gut instinct to ward off the crying. But he didn't stop. In fact, he couldn't be calmed until the ball had disappeared into Arlene's bag completely. I was shaking from the mere pitch of his hysteria.

"What do you think it was?" I queried Arlene.

She shook her head, shrugged. "I think it was just the ball," she said. "It was just too much for him."

My nerves were shot, and I was trembling. The realization of Walker's sensitivity came home to me again, this time not just as sadness that my child might not be able to socialize, but as something more visceral—*my God, a plastic ball produces hysteria?* What about jungle gyms and mud in your toes, what about birthday balloons bursting and the squeaky brakes of buses? All the sensory challenges that face children, and here was my baby in Armageddon at the touch of a knobby plastic ball.

Still, I convinced myself that Walker was improving. Hadn't he made eye contact? Couldn't he push his head up now? I rode the high curved arc of the roller coaster, thrilled with what I thought was progress—particularly the fact that he had looked in my eyes, until I saw Arlene the following Thursday. She had seemed so positive the past few weeks about Walker's progress, had looked at Walker with loving eyes. If anyone could teach my son to love, I reasoned, it was this tall, handsome woman with brown bangs and large eyes. I excitedly mentioned an invitation I'd received from REACH to bring Walker to a playgroup. It was on a bulletin board in the kitchen. I was moving toward it while we talked when I turned and saw her standing next to me, with a sober expression.

"What's the matter?"

She held out her hand as if to stop me. "I don't think you should go."

"But I got an invitation."

"I just want to . . ." She hesitated, chose her words carefully. "It's my job to protect you. I mean, I should be protecting you, too, not just Walker."

"What do you mean protect me?"

"There'll be other babies there . . . it's just that . . ."

I think I understood what she meant. What she meant was that I would compare. I would see.

Cold air into the oven—the baked goods fallen. Did she have to say it?
There had been so much compassion in her eyes. Since Walker made eye con-
tact, I had been hopeful he might be getting better, and now . . . What is she
protecting me from? She has been so good lately at hiding her concern. Indeed,
I had begun to think she might have favored Walker among her clients.

One afternoon, when Walker was asleep I had asked her if it was
difficult to work with the mothers of extremely ill children. "At
REACH," she said, "the mothers are great. And anyway, they always
seem to find someone they feel more sorry for than themselves."

Now she doesn't want me to go to the meetings. Does she suspect I would
lie at the bottom of the food chain?

"Listen," she said. "I've got someone at REACH who might want
to work with Walker. Her name is Dawn. She'd like to come and meet
him. When would be a good time?"

She didn't tell me exactly who Dawn was, nothing about her speciality or background, only that Dawn was "interested in working
with Walker."

Dawn came into the house one day, about a week later, following
Arlene. I guessed she was in her late thirties, a woman with a wide,
friendly, almost shy smile, and thick strawberry blond hair. Oddly,
Walker did what he had done when he met Arlene. He began sprinting upside down through the air with his arms and legs, his head
swinging from side to side. I remember thinking, "Oh no, now she
won't want to work with Walker," ignorantly assuming that Dawn
could choose her cases.

I spent days waiting to discover if Dawn would work with Walker.
When Arlene arrived on the following Monday, after the visit, I said,
"Does she want to?"

"Does who?"

"Dawn."

"What?"

"Want to work with Walker?"

Arlene seemed flustered. "It's not a matter of what she wants. It's a
question of what's appropriate."

"Is it appropriate?"

"Yes, I believe it is. She'll be calling you to make an appointment."

Arlene had been avoiding the word *autism* for weeks. What Arlene didn't quite have the heart to tell me, what I learned on Dawn's visit, was that Dawn was an educator who had worked for fifteen years with children with autism.

It would be years later that I would learn that she and Dawn had returned to the office, agreeing that neither had met a baby quite like Walker.

"Do you think," said Dawn to Arlene, "that moving his hands in the air is the baby version of an autistic child flapping?"

I would learn only years later that Arlene had said yes.

But there's something else gnawing at me, a feeling I've been here before, some-how. I remember how I longed to reach my mother when she was listening to her own sirens that pulled her inward. In the car, doing errands, she used to think so intensely I felt she was trying to solve the all the problems of the world in just one car ride. One day, when I was about four or five, I thought up a solution to my problem: A joke—the perfect joke, just the funniest, most hilarious joke I could think of. It worked. Suddenly Mom turned, the face coming to life, her lovely lips opening, her eyes beaming. And she was back there with me, all of us together, laughing at the very same joke. But there were never enough jokes to keep Mom with me for good. Now I wondered. Perhaps working this hard could keep my son with us for a few moments, but a few moments didn't constitute a life. Arlene had said Walker experienced "islands of warmth and relatedness." But what good was an island, floating in a sea of discon-nectedness?

The Epidemic

ELIZABETH'S MONTH with my mother was over, and now that it was mid-July, Dawn was coming. She brought props. She came, as Arlene did, though at a different time, with a large canvas bag filled with toys. I began to think of the contents of these bags as the stuff of magicians: cups and balls to hide, scarves, photographs, mirrors. She held Walker in her lap, enticed him, moved him with her eyes, her hands, laughed and hugged him.

"Why mirrors? I said.

"So he knows himself. So he knows where I begin and where he leaves off."

It would be Dawn's focus to work on Walker's social development; Arlene's to work on Walker's physical development, though, of course, their duties would overlap. (Lenore's work was close to Arlene's, though difficult to categorize.) Dawn was formally called an educator, though she specialized in autism. Arlene was formally a physical therapist, though she was well versed in sensory integration. Dawn was also to focus on Walker's cognitive relationship with the world. At times her suggestions seemed weird or unexpected. She encouraged me to plant as much of the unexpected into Walker's daily habit as possible. "Take one of these little board books that he's familiar with, for example," she said, "and paste a picture of Elizabeth inside to surprise him. Sensitive children, and children with autism," she explained, "become dependent upon the familiar to be content, because each new thing they encounter requires an adjustment to the senses, the brain."

But a baby might be able to learn to grow used to the shock of the new?

Dawn sometimes encouraged me to bring Elizabeth into the dining room to play with Walker. She talked with Elizabeth and played with her, too. Yet it was clear to all of us that Walker wasn't quite on Elizabeth's wave length. I doubt that even if he had not been born particularly sensitive, he might not have been like her—the girl who wore dramatic white dresses with petticoats to preschool, the girl who insisted on dressing as a cowgirl for picture day. When Walker napped I spent time with Elizabeth, brushing her long hair, or we sometimes cooked together—yet the phone was always ringing. Often when the therapists came, I turned the TV or videos on. I began rationalizing that Elizabeth might someday be a movie producer. She memorized lines from movies, sang the songs from the musicals for Dawn and Arlene, who sat on the floor, enchanted, but ready to move back to work. She pretend tap-danced in the kitchen, ran in to show Dawn the picture books she had stapled and illustrated. Often, when she was near, Walker turned away from us. If she got him laughing hysterically, he might even vomit. She was simply too dazzling.

Dawn, like me, was a talker. Every spare chance we had we talked. When she spoke, she spoke of autism. Whereas Arlene (whose early insight was responsible for bringing an autism expert on board) still found "autism" a difficult word to articulate, Dawn was eager to use it. Though for Arlene, the word *autism* seemed an epithet or a judgment on Walker's character, a determination of his fate, for Dawn it was a wake-up call.

"I called a consultant to talk about Walker," Dawn told me, "and she thinks Walker's condition does sound like autism, especially the way he has his good days and has bad days."

I was troubled, perplexed. "Why all the confusion? Don't you know? Haven't you worked with hundreds of cases like this?"

"No," Dawn explained. "Nobody diagnoses autism this early." Dawn had seen autism in toddlers and adults, but she had never seen the symptoms of autism in a baby this young. Usually autism becomes apparent at eighteen months or two years, when speech and social skills are slow to develop. One of the major forms of autism shows a regressive pattern—seemingly typical children might begin to speak and then lose words. Dawn knew from the research that a significant percentage of children show symptoms from birth. But parents may not know something is wrong or find useful help until the disorder is advanced.

We waited for the appointment with the neurologist, which was scheduled for August. (Walker would be ten months old. It was the earliest he could see Walker.) Dawn emboldened me to research. Now I was no longer afraid to type the word into a search engine or to read articles or books. I remember that Proust in *Remembrance of Things Past* says that love makes us into great scholars and researchers. Very quickly I became both of these.

I was astounded to learn that over the previous ten years, the number of children with autism had increased significantly. I asked a local organization, Community Resources for People with Autism, for some statistics about incidence of the disorder and was told that a report merely three months old would be out of date. California, reflecting a national trend, reported a 210-percent increase in a decade. Estimates for current incidence nationwide varied, depending on which web site I visited or which pamphlet I was able to get. Still, even the conservative estimates seemed staggering, far more than I ever imagined: One in 500 people. Some sources claimed the incidence to be as high as one in 150.

Most of the experts agree that autism has a genetic component, but genetics apparently represents only a piece of the puzzle. When I was doing my research in 1997, several experts were speculating that a relationship may exist between genetic propensity and environmental causes. The possibility that pollution from pesticides or other chemicals may be one culprit was being vigorously debated. Sometimes autism showed up in "clusters"—mysterious concentrations of children with diagnoses—in particular neighborhoods or cities.

For some unknown reason, the percentage of young children with autism had risen dramatically. Between 1965 and 1969, only 1 percent of young children had autism. Yet by 1994–1995, the figure had risen to 17 percent. Some people, particularly parent advocacy groups, felt that vaccinations might be the explanation. They considered vaccinations problematic for two reasons: Kids are given too many at one time, being exposed to as many as three diseases for each shot, and at times more than one shot is given at once; and certain viruses or diseases in particular were suspect.

I read that many parents in both the United States and England reported a temporal relationship between the onset of autism and the MMR (measles, mumps, and rubella) vaccine, given between the ages of twelve and eighteen months in the United States. Opponents of the vaccination theory suggest that some forms of the disorder simply tend to arise at this age, yet others note that since the advent of vaccinations, the kind of autism that appears at eighteen months, once considered rare, began appearing with shocking frequency as these changes in vaccination patterns occurred. Parent groups and some researchers assert that in both the United States and England, a close relationship exists between an increase in the use of the multiple vaccine and a rise in the incidence of autism, though critics seem to insist that the relevant studies were flawed.

Another possible culprit in vaccinations is mercury poisoning. At the time I was researching, mercury was used in the vaccination additive thimerosal. If a child was given more than one vaccination at a time, the mercury level, some argued, might even be dangerously high. The symptoms of mercury poisoning are hauntingly close to those of autism: sensorimotor dysfunction, delayed reaction time, developmental delays.

Another theory suggested that the symptoms of autism were exacerbated, or even caused, by food sensitivities. Though I had only heard in June 1997 of one family of parents who had removed wheat and diary products from their children's diets, by July I learned the numbers were growing. Many parents reported observing dramatically positive effects. Three years later, Karyn Seroussi was to publish *Unraveling the Mystery of Autism and Pervasive Developmental Disorder,* arguing the same point; the book would attract significant attention.

A partial explanation for the rise in incidence seemed to be that the very definition of autism was expanding. In 1943, when the term was coined, the disorder was viewed as an intractable mental disease, largely untreatable, a cousin to schizophrenia. Our understanding was being recast. Each time the *American Psychiatric Association's Diagnostic and Statistical Manual for Mental Disorders* (then, and still, in its fourth edition, *DSM-IV*) was revised, the scope of autism broadened. In common and clinical language, "autism spectrum disorder" grew to encompass everything from autism in its most virulent form (sometimes call "full-blown" or "classical" autism) to less severe forms such as pervasive developmental disorder and Asperger's syndrome. Some people put attention deficit disorder and other learning disorders in the spectrum. One school of thought saw autism as a personality type—the cliché of the classic "engineer": highly intelligent, highly visual, mechanically oriented, associative, relatively unskilled verbally and socially.

At the far end of the spectrum are people dwelling in a Dantean nightmare. They exist among us but not with us, without meaningful speech or even language comprehension; theirs is a world of objects rather than people. They may bite themselves or others, scream out for no apparent reason, have uncontrollable tantrums, thrash, bang their heads against walls, act as though in a trance, rock back and forth, or wave their hands in incomprehensible patterns. The worse cases involve severe mental retardation. Even in less severe circumstances, children with autism may refuse or be unable to look at others, or they may repeat phrases from Disney movies, for example, or fragments of commercials, without seeming to know what they've said. People with autism may engage in obsessive behaviors, focusing on one thing and refusing to let it out of their sight; they may stare at a stain on a rug and rub it incessantly. Some such behaviors can cause severe injury, and sufferers must be institutionalized or watched constantly by an aide. One woman I spoke with told me that for an entire summer, she had worked with a man with autism who lived in a residential hospital and engaged in one activity alone: He hit his ears from behind, slapping at them with both hands.

"That was my whole job," she said. "All summer . . . trying to keep him from doing it, and he never stopped. That's all he did."

"Why didn't you just let him do it?" I asked naively.

"He would have bled to death."

Dawn came once a week and worked with Walker for as much time as she could. Like Arlene, she stayed far longer than she was supposed to—lingering through her lunch hour, talking to me endlessly while Walker slept.

Dawn was a storyteller, and while Walker slept or rested, like Scheherazade she wove yarns. She spoke of her long history working with disabled and autistic children, of the odd quirky and beguiling behavior and personalities of children with autism, about the mystery of the senses, about the slowness of psychologists to understand the role that sensitivity plays in autism.

Imagine a five-year-old girl with autism sitting in a room calmly. Unexpectedly, she begins to scream. She throws her head to the ground and thrashes wildly. The teacher assumes she's having a schizophrenic episode; something in her own demented consciousness must be causing this girl's pain. Such behavior continues periodically for years. One day someone enters the boiler room next door to the classroom where our student is playing. The water heater clicks on, emitting a low hum. Immediately, the child with autism begins to scream and pull at her hair. Could the heater explain her behavior? The teacher clicks off the heater. The child stops crying. She turns it on: the child screams.

⌒

Once there was a conference during which a boy with autism was coming to speak. Dawn and the rest of the audience had been advised not to wear perfume or deodorant or to chew gum in the large conference room, lest it irritate the sensitivities of the young speaker. He was introduced and quickly came into the room, but he did not move toward the podium but instead began to move toward someone's seat in the middle of the crowd.

"Can you please take that gum out of your mouth?"

He had not seen the gum, but acute sensitivity told him in the instant it was there.

Dawn taught me to see the devastating effects of autism, not fundamentally as a disease of the spirit or the soul but as the secondary result of sensitivity and processing problems not being attended to early in infancy.

I am beginning to realize that we can only know ourselves through the eyes of another, through their reactions to us. How important it is, then, to be aware of others' reactions. When our receptors don't work, it is as if the mirror goes dim. We can't see people clearly and neither, then, can we see ourselves. Over and over if such back-and-forth messages go awry—stimulation not well interpreted, reactions distorted—we will have a child who is bound to grow mentally ill, seeing neither himself nor his world clearly. The mind might grow like a weird bonsai, not because it was meant to, or designed to, but because what it received from the world was unusual. The sun grows dim, or too stark. The plant is cut too much. It grows beautiful, but odd.

I attended a meeting on autism and heard a story. I reproduce it here as well as I can remember it.

A boy heard voices ringing in his ears, throbbing in his head, voices prattling the stuff of daily life—"I did not take your keys . . ." "Well they were on the bureau . . ." "No, give me an apple instead." He spoke about and repeated these voices, often verbatim, to his family. The boy had seen many doctors, was diagnosed with schizophrenia, given various drug therapies and sent away to an institution. One day when he was eighteen years old, living at home again, he began articulating a series of sentences. His mother, barely listening to the conversation—it had grown to be the white noise of her days—left her son in midsentence and stepped into the backyard to hang some laundry. As she approached the fence, however, she heard something extraordinary—two women were carrying on the second half of the conversation her son had begun in the house.

Doctors were called in, and the diagnosis was changed. The boy was not insane, living in an imaginary world; the voices were real. They had always been real. All these years, he'd been hearing people speak, through fences and through walls. No longer psychotic, he was now given the appellation "autistic."

When I called the presenter of this story to ask her if I could interview the boy's family, she explained that it is a composite story based on the experiences of two families of children with autism she worked with—the families were extremely sensitive about their children's disorders and she felt she needed to mask the particulars, yet she asserted that this story carries the truth of many people's experience with autism. It's not about insanity, but hypersensitivity. The boy described above was not suffering from a problem of being out of touch with the world, but quite the contrary: His "psychotic" behavior, paradoxically, derived from what we might describe as an overconcentration of the actual, too much of the real.

A young child repeating such voices in ancient times, in the middle ages, might have been presumed to be possessed by evil spirits. In the nineteenth and, indeed, most of the twentieth century, such a child would most likely have been considered irremediably disturbed, untreatable, mad. Still today, in some corners of the world such tragic miscalculations are being made all the time.

"Is there such a thing as autism without a sensory processing disorder?" I asked Dawn.

"None that I know of," she replied. I searched for an incidence of autism without sensory dysfunction and found none myself. Sensory processing disorder, the malfunctioning of the senses, was so integral to autism spectrum disorder that there seemed to be no known cases without it—though they can be present in typical individuals as well.

"What do you do to decompress?" asked the social worker. She sat on the couch opposite me and Cliff. He had come home from work specifically for the appointment. I wanted to ask her what she expected of us. "Do you think we can just pop a couple of beers," I imagined saying, "flip on some *I Love Lucy* reruns, take a toss in the hay?" But I didn't. Instead, Cliff answered. He talked wistfully about things we had done when I was pregnant with Walker, of going to the theater and taking walks in the woods, of things he'd like to do, things he thought we could do now. *Go for a walk? That would be like leaving a house when it was on fire.*

The social worker clearly seemed to be on Cliff's side. She seemed impressed by Cliff's efforts to see the bright side and was particularly pleased when Cliff said that Walker was a "great little guy." She felt we should go to the theater, that we should take walks. But when? My insistence that we were simply too busy made her distrustful of me, as if I were inventing a ploy to . . . to what? I couldn't understand. I was furious. How could Cliff seem so nonchalant? (It took me years to understand that he was trying to hold up his end, to counterbalance the uncontrollable flood of ballast I was taking on—the weight of my inwardness, the closing in of ranks, the shutting off from the world, the maniacal, obsessive need to research.) At that time it was just betrayal that I experienced from Cliff. If he wasn't with me, I reasoned, he was against me, seeming too focused on work, houses, money. The thought was too hard to look at, too white hot. I turned away and looked down at the rug.

While we talked, Walker lay on the ground, doing his push-ups.

"It's hard for me to relax when I'm worried," I said.

"Let's discuss your worries," she said.

"Arlene says we're making progress, but I'm fearful Walker will regress. There is a kind of autism in which the child regresses."

"No, there isn't," she said.

"What?" I wasn't sure I was hearing her correctly. "Of course there is. It happens at eighteen months."

"No," she said, "Autism is autism. Either you have it or you don't."

The room seemed to contract.

"What we really need is help," I said at length, changing the subject. "Could you help us?"

"What do you need help with?"

"I need help making phone calls, or even to have an extra hand with Walker while I make phone calls."

"I can see you're an excellent networker. You don't need my help. Besides that's not why I'm here."

"Why are you here?"

"I'm here to talk about how you're handling all this, to talk about your feelings."

She looked down at Walker, "Why don't you pick him up?"

"I don't want to overstimulate him." She looked at me quizzically.

Did she believe that Walker's problems were my fault—that I simply wasn't mothering him properly? Was it really possible that Walker's problem was my fault?

While the social worker spoke, my mind wandered. It seemed to me that years ago my mother had told me of an autism expert who insisted that autism was the fault of mothers. But I couldn't remember his name. All I could remember was that he had an institute in Chicago, and that years ago in the *New Yorker* I had read an article of his that I very much admired. He was a high muckety-muck among psychologists. *What was his name?*

Arlene arrived at the end of the meeting to work with Walker. After saying good-bye to the social worker, I found myself slipping away for a few minutes while Arlene took up work with Walker.

I pulled up a search engine and typed all the words I could think of: "mothers," "autism," "fault," "blame," "cause." Two names appeared in several entries, Bruno Bettelheim and Leo Kanner. Apparently the latter had publicly recanted any claims to blaming mothers. The other name I knew fairly well. My college professors in psychology used to evoke the name with reverence; intellectuals in the coffeehouses evoked it pompously. This was indeed the psychologist who had written the *New Yorker* article I had so admired. Bettelheim had been a formidable intellectual presence. I called Cliff at the University of Massachusetts where he worked and asked him to bring any relevant Bettelheim books home from the library. The one he brought was *The Empty Fortress: Infantile Autism and the Birth of the Self* (1967), which sat on the kitchen counter for days until, one morning, I began flipping through it as I sat on hold with a medical office. It seemed a mass of words, a dense philosophical tome. Paragraph after paragraph described with complexity and downright opacity the psychological intricacies of what happens when a baby sucks a breast. I flipped further and saw something about a mother's resentment, a mother's wish that her child would die. I closed the book.

For days I brooded. I had never wished Walker dead. In fact, I thought often about a concept called "Mamatoto," from the Swahili, which I'd learned about during my pregnancy. It is a concept that we Westerners don't quite possess—the notion that mother and child are one. Breathing together, feeding together. "How is Mamatoto?" Cliff sometimes said when he came home from work. Yet still, I remembered that when I was carrying Walker, everything had seemed dark. It had been that way, too, with Elizabeth. Pregnancy never seemed to agree with me. Darkness, like a cloak, seemed to fall between me and the sun. It seemed to follow me everywhere. I became fascinated by horror. The horror, I reasoned, was somehow related to my nausea, which lasted far beyond morning and through most of the pregnancy. As the nausea wore on, so did the darkness, the canopy. It moved through the summer like a black parasol, following me, dogging me. Drawn to dark worlds—mirroring my malaise?—I found myself reading Shelley's *Frankenstein* and Elie Wiesel's *Night*. Now I wondered if I had somehow hurt my son by reading Shelley and Wiesel. *Are such thoughts rational? If not, why do they feel so real to me? Why does the social worker look at me and scribble things into her notes? Does she trust me?*

The following week I found myself again in the circle of parents in the school classroom at night. Pamphlets were distributed. Same tired, worn eyes were there, though some of the faces were new. The talkative blond woman was talking quickly, loudly across the room again. I looked down at a flyer on social learning classes for children with autism while I listened to her speak. She talked about her son at school, something about a soccer game, and the next moment I heard, "Yes, he is a fraud. Didn't you know that? It came out in the press a few months ago. All that stuff about blaming mothers—hooey."

I strained to hear, to learn if she was talking about Bettelheim, but the meeting began and I couldn't bring myself to approach her afterward. *Could it be that Bettelheim had been proven a fraud?* I went back to the Internet. This time I typed in Bettelheim and fraud. First to pop on screen: Review of two new biographies.

With help from Cliff, *The Creation of Dr. B: A Biography of Bruno Bettelheim* was in my hands by nightfall.

Clearly, one of the most surprising and disturbing parts of the autism story did indeed lie with one of the twentieth century's most charismatic and powerful intellectuals. For more than thirty years, the conception and treatment of autism lay under the spell of this brilliant Austrian, who seems to have bribed his way out of a concentration camp in Germany and come to America with a compelling and fecund literary imagination. Bettelheim presented a résumé full of egregious misrepresentations—untruths that were discovered only after his suicide in 1990. He claimed, for example, to have three Ph.D.s, one in psychology, when in fact his sole doctorate was in "philosophical aesthetics." He claimed to have been caretaker for a girl named Patsy who was autistic. She was not. He claimed to have been embraced by Freud, but no evidence is available that they even met. Yet Bettelheim, who seems to have felt a resentment of Nietzschian proportions, persuaded a credulous world that he knew the cause of autism because he had seen the phenomenon in the concentration camp: people retreat in "extreme situations." As he explained in that seminal book, *The Empty Fortress*, the cause of autism was an unloving mother who wished that her child did not exist, a persecutor, a woman whose "black milk" (an image from Paul Celan's poem about the death camps) so threatened her child that he was forced into "autistic withdrawal." The term "refrigerator mother" thrived under Bettelheim. Tragically, I learned, such an explanation for autism still exists in some parts of the world.

Richard Pollak, the biography's author, explains that one of the most important books to vindicate parents was written by the father of an autistic child. In 1964, Bernard Rimland, the founder and now the director of the Autism Research Institute, wrote *Infantile Autism: The Syndrome and Its Implications for a Neural Theory of Behavior.* Bettelheim dismissed Rimland's idea that autism is biologically based, but Rimland was proved correct. I later discovered that in 1975, the neurologist Stephen Hauser, then a medical student at Harvard, and Robert DeLong, then the chief of pediatric neurology at Massachusetts General Hospital, found abnormalities in the brain ventricles of autistic subjects. In 1983, neurologists Margaret Bauman and Thomas Kemper began dissecting the brains of subjects with autism, finding abnormalities in the cerebellum and the limbic system.

After I read the biography about Bettelheim, I thought for several days about the social worker. I guess it didn't matter what she thought. I called and told her I didn't want her to come every week. We were going to change Walker's environment to suit him—of that I was certain—change it so he could learn. Even Cliff, though reluctant to give up our freedom, agreed with me that if Walker wasn't learning by being out and about, we must limit his time away from home as much as possible. *But what if Walker didn't learn? What if he proved part of the significant percentage who couldn't? Anyway, even if nothing could be done, didn't the social worker understand grief? We weren't going to be decompressing anytime soon.* In my journal, I find a cryptic line: "There are no bowling alleys on the dark side of the moon." It was the kind of bad poetry line I used to write in college, but I remember the feeling behind it. It was my way of talking about how useless seeking pleasure can be in the midst of darkness and obsession. It was my way of trying to justify the fact that I didn't want to have fun, didn't want to move to a new house, wouldn't be going to the theater or even for a walk in the woods anytime soon.

PART 4

Through a Door in the Wall

SLOWLY, IMPERCEPTIBLY, as the days of the summer passed, emotion began to show on Walker's face. He laughed more and more. The veil seemed to be lifting. He began to smile consistently, to give all of us unabashed eye contact. He seemed almost giddy, the way that teenagers sometimes can be filled with pleasure, joy, and silliness—a ticklish, slightly illicit, incurable pleasure.

"He seems so happy," I said to Arlene one day.

Arlene didn't respond right away.

"That's good, isn't it?"

Arlene nodded yes, it was good. But she looked down and swallowed in an odd way.

"What?" I said.

"With Walker's kind of regulatory disorder, there's a lack of integration of the emotions. What has happened is that the positive has come in, but only the positive has come in."

Walker lay on the floor and began looking at his hands.

"Look," I said, "this is great." I thought he was exploring himself.

"I don't know why they do that," she said.

"They?"

"Children like this."

"It's not normal to look at your hands?"

"Some people think they may be seeing streamers of light or color trailing the hand."

In her records, on June 24 (when Walker was eight and a half months old), Darleen Corbett, REACH's director, writes:

There were sustained periods of eye contact where I felt like he was drinking in my depths. . . . Although reported delight in peek-a-boo, he seems to be reacting less to discovery; less from an inner sense of pleasure, more to my animation, and it was a delayed response.

Banging surfaces, not yet at midline.

When holding something in each hand, desire to mouth; strange impulse that predominates.

Still strong pull inward.

Darleen Corbett noticed a "strange impulse" to mouth objects. Of course, most babies have such instincts, but Walker's was strange in its intensity. There were times when we would barely attract his attention he was so busy sucking. He sucked now constantly. The impulse was an obsession; it got in the way. It stood between him and his ability to move forward, stood sometimes between him and his ability to know us. If you're sucking constantly, you can't crawl, you can't walk. You certainly won't learn to talk.

Still, Dawn and Arlene and Cliff and I worked hard to entice him forward. And he worked even harder. He continued doing his daily push-ups. After a week, he could hold himself two inches from the floor. Within a month, he could hold himself up on all fours.

After ten weeks with REACH, Walker could make eye contact, he had improved upper-body tone, making it possible for him to begin using a high chair instead of the car seat on the kitchen table. He babbled, which is what most children did at his age.

Still, he was far behind the typical baby, who, at that age, was voraciously crawling around the house, grabbing, perhaps even beginning to climb; some precocious ones were even beginning to walk.

The neurologist finally met Walker. He measured Walker's head and watched him. Walker was responsive to the man, smiled, and made a little eye contact. The neurologist wasn't sure if Walker had autism or not and suggested we see a psychologist at the hospital.

We saw her a few days later. She tested Walker's motor skills, his cognitive skills. She felt he was intelligent. She held him up near a huge picture window for ten minutes, watching him intently as she turned his body in various poses, subtly differing orientations to the window.

Always, he was the compass, turning his gaze to the light. Not once did he look at her for more than a fleeting second at that close range. Eyes ever to the window.

She, too, felt it was too early to tell.

When I met with Dawn two days later, she was deeply disturbed by the clinicians' response to Walker. From her practice, she knew that waiting for symptoms to be more obvious was tantamount to poison. She didn't say this, but I sensed that she felt "waiting to see" was like letting one's baby crawl to the rooftop, "waiting" to see what would happen. Hadn't the psychologist and neurologist understood that Walker had been in intensive intervention for the past ten weeks? Of course his eye contact had improved. Gaining eye contact was the easy step. More than fifteen years of experience had taught her that even relatively subtle signs in babies and toddlers could turn into autism. She insisted ours was a fight against time. "What looks like not much in a baby could be very serious in a toddler, and devastating in a school-age child," said Dawn. "In my practice, I've seen many babies with the signs of autism go unnoticed by doctors and parents until they received very serious diagnoses, some- times even years later. Why not begin work early and possibly even pre- vent the diagnosis, or mitigate its severity?"

I wasn't completely following her. "But how would you meet such babies?"

"Siblings of my clients."

She later explained to me that, remarkably, pediatricians in America are often not adequately trained in child development to be able to suc- cessfully screen for the disorder.

"But what about the neurologist?" I said. "The man is an expert in the workings of the brain, in brain pathology."

"Unfortunately," said Dawn, "neurologists are generalists."

Dawn further explained that for a long time she had believed that the description of autism that appeared in the *DSM-IV* was a description of the disorder in its more advanced stages, failing to properly describe or even note what autism might look like in earlier stages. Still, whatever one called Walker's problem, she felt he would surely be receiving the diagnosis of autism within a year if we didn't act, and act quickly.

By fortunate coincidence Dawn was primed to do something that was out of the ordinary in her practice. Just three months before she met Walker, she had read an article by Stanley Greenspan and his colleague Serena Wieder in the journal *Zero to Three*, outlining an effective new approach for treating toddlers and babies with symptoms of autism. She was intrigued, excited.

One day she came to my house with yet another article. It was a prepublication draft of a "chart review" of Greenspan's 200 patients with autism. She explained to me that Stanley Greenspan was a child psychiatrist well known for his work in child development. He had spent sixteen years studying the subject at the National Institute of Mental Health, which led to a new philosophy of emotional development—for which he had won the Ittleson Award, the American Psychiatric Association's highest honor for research in child psychiatry. In his years at NIMH, Greenspan arrived at sophisticated criteria for understanding and defining emotional maturity and began to map out its phases. He applied recent research about how babies and toddlers "process" the vast amount of sensory information available to them each day. On the basis of his insights, Greenspan designed a therapeutic model to help children with a variety of problems. He called it D.I.R. (developmental, individual-difference, relationship-based model) or, informally, "floor time." (A year after Dawn discovered Greenspan's work through articles, he made the approach available to the public in his 1998 book, *The Child with Special Needs*.)

Floor time required parental involvement. Though it emphasized relationship, fun, joy, the method drew its power from parents' ability to entice an impaired child to perform at increasingly higher levels of attention, cognition, and motor functioning—far higher than that child would normally be disposed to. It was tailored to a child's particular deficits and strengths and was designed to grow in scope as the child climbed the developmental ladder.

The article that Dawn brought me reported results that struck me as astoundingly positive. Greenspan had been able to help over 50 percent of his 200 patients to become fully functioning children—warm, engaged, interactive, verbal, and creative. Another 30 percent made substantial progress. He helped children reach these unexpected levels of functioning by using a comprehensive program including occupational therapy, speech therapy, and floor time. The therapy required that a child be reacting to his parents or therapist in what Greenspan called "circles of communication." A circle would be opened if someone tried to engage the child and closed if someone received a response. Someone smiles and the baby smiles back: one circle. Hand a toy to the baby and the baby hands it back: two circles.

The important question for Greenspan, however, was how high could a child "with challenges" climb?

I called Greenspan, who, though notoriously difficult to see, was eager to work with Walker because Walker was so young—by that time, nine months old. Two months later, I received a call from Greenspan's assistant, Sarah.

"I have a cancellation," said Sarah.

"But I thought there was a year waiting list."

"It's open for you. You can have three or four sessions," she said.

"Three or four?"

"Because you live so far away, it will take three hours for Dr. Greenspan to evaluate your son."

I hung up the phone, discouraged. There was no way we could afford three or four sessions with a famous psychiatrist. Besides, the trip to his office in Bethesda, Maryland, including air fare and car rental, might cost up to $1,500.00. *Who were we kidding?*

Still, I somehow felt compelled to make it work. Perhaps we could borrow the money or let it become credit card debt.

Cliff was more worried than I, and I was about to cancel the appointment when I called the insurance company. To my surprise, they said we were covered. Their contribution would work out to 50 percent of Greenspan's fees.

We drove up to Greenspan's large property on a gravel drive encircling a grove of oaks, walked around the back of the house near the tennis courts, and waited in an enclosed porch. He invited us into a large, comfortable room with threadbare rugs, old chairs and couches, stacked with papers and books, and littered with toys.

Greenspan leaned over Walker's records and studied them close-ly, holding his glasses as if they were a magnifying glass. He asked questions and took copious notes, leaning over the paper. He looked up occasionally and studied the baby on the floor. I watched him closely, ever anxious to see reflected in someone's eyes a window into Walker. I could not read anything about Walker in Greenspan's eyes, but I liked what I saw in this doctor. He was a tall, middle-aged man, balding slightly, wearing a blue sport shirt and chinos. There was a softness in his facial skin and a gentleness in the eyes, as if he'd just woken up. I had the impression of a person somehow softened by years instead of the familiar reverse. Greenspan stood up and disap-peared through a hardwood door that at first seemed hidden, as if it were part of the paneled wall. I looked at Cliff, then studied Walker. We'd come a long way since May, had managed to lure Walker, at times, from those enticing sirens that beckoned him inward.

With little appetite, Walker was frail, but he was learning to move. First he had crept, then crawled. Elizabeth and I had found empty boxes at a dumpster at nearby Smith College and made obstacle courses for him. He crept through one box into the next. When he had become slightly stronger, we put pillows in the boxes, surfaces of varying tex-tures, stuffed animals, balls, and blankets to negotiate. Cliff's sister, Susan, had given Walker some plastic stacking cups. Elizabeth, Cliff, and I made towers and enticed Walker to move toward them. He had learned the joy of demolition—crept toward the towers and destroyed them. The crashing sound was not a bother. *Was he becoming less sensitive?*

Cliff and I were buoyant on the day we came to suburban Washington, D.C. to meet Greenspan. The morning before we came, we had visited a café, where Walker hung over my shoulder, looking at a woman at the next table, smiling at her. We were proud that Walker could smile at people, that he could at last crawl, that we'd been able to teach him some simple games. Walker didn't stare at light much anymore. Yet I saw now in Greenspan's office, in this new room, that he was struggling to keep himself together. A baby nearly a year old (by now he was eleven months) would typically explore a new space, yet he didn't. There seemed to be little room in his mind or awareness for the new, for the toy or the window or the loose paper. Instead, he was just trying to manage the massive weight of the new-ness, trying to find out where he was in space. He rocked his head back and forth, back and forth; struggled to control his body, his arms flailed. A thin pattern of light fell across the oriental carpets, though he looked at neither the light nor the rug.

Greenspan reappeared through the hidden door in the wall, seated himself, picked up a video camera, loaded it with a new cartridge, and gently suggested one of us get down on the floor.

"Dad?" He looked at Cliff.

Cliff got down on the floor and began to play with Walker. Cliff began trying to interact with him, yet Walker stayed largely mired in his own world. He picked up a block, knocked it against Cliff's block, and crawled away to play on his own. After a few minutes of Cliff trying to somehow catch up, Walker began frantically creeping toward the ends of the oriental carpets that lay across Greenspan's floor. At the sides of the rugs lay long white strings, unraveled parts of the rug. He flew to the strings, grabbed them, sucked his thumb.

"Mom," said Greenspan, inviting me down. I went to the floor, eager to show what Arlene and Dawn had taught me. Yet Walker was difficult to reach.

I worked hard to entice him away from the oriental rug strings. But the more tired Walker grew, the more hungrily he pulled at the strings, which he rubbed in his palm like a rosary and flicked against his upper lip.

Still, Walker and I made some progress. Together he and I played "row, row, row your boat." Back and forth we rocked in front of Greenspan, and I, as Arlene had taught me, stopped my motion after each cycle, until Walker began to rock again to show me he wanted more.

Dr. Greenspan was happy to see that Walker was somewhat engaged, that he could creep across the floor to knock down our standard tower of plastic cups, but he wanted more. He steered us toward understanding that Walker's problem-solving needed to be not so much with toys, but with people. Walker needed to be constantly looking, laughing. "There are several levels from which we need to approach this. You want to get a level of juiciness into your play. Make it fun, joyful. But you also want to get the rhythm faster," he said. "We don't want him spacing out." Greenspan explained that we needed to keep Walker in a constant flow. If we made a sound, he must make a sound—that's one circle. We laugh, he laughs, that's another circle.

The point was: It wasn't just about reacting and staying focused. *It had to be about people.* It had to be about *us* first.

"NO, no no!" Greenspan called out to me, "Now you've lost him."

Cliff came to the floor again, and appeared to think for a moment about this concept . . . play *through* people . . . people being more important than things . . . and then lay down on the floor and put the plastic cups on his eyes.

"Now say, 'I bet you can't get them' to Walker," said Greenspan.

I chimed in enthusiastically like someone at a horse race, "Go get them, Walker."

Greenspan turned to me. He was still the gentle man with the slightly sleepy eyes, yet somehow I saw something fierce and unrelenting there. He grew sober, serious, admonishing, and made it clear that I must never do that. Never. I must be careful not to tell Walker what to do. "Instead inspire him. No one tells a novelist what to write—they need to inspire you. Right?" he said.

Cliff hid himself behind a piece of cardboard. Walker smiled. Cliff peeked out.

"Now make him work for it!" called out Greenspan somewhat whimsically. "Make him pull the cardboard away!" Walker pulled. Cliff hid behind again. Walker pulled it. Cliff put a dinosaur in his mouth. Walker grabbed it back.

"Hide it in your hand," directed Greenspan, quickly. "Ask him, 'Where's the dinosaur?'"

Walker looked around; Cliff made an enticing clicking sound to catch his attention. Walker grabbed the dinosaur.

"Now hide it again. 'Where's the dinosaur?'" encouraged Greenspan.

Cliff quickly hid the dinosaur under his legs.

"Now hide it in one hand and pretend it's in the other."

Walker found the dinosaur quickly.

"Now you're cookin'," said Greenspan.

The three-hour-long appointment went like that. Each time Walker proved he could do something, Greenspan made us sweat to make him go a step further.

When it was my turn again, I found even the old games, the "tower game" to be a challenge. It seemed to me that Walker was tired, obsessed with finding comfort. I was consistently thwarted by the bedeviling oriental rug strings. Walker grabbed and sucked and seemed to pull himself into a vortex, a private world that we were no part of. There seemed no reaching him. It was clear to me that Walker was exhausted, perhaps more than I'd ever seen him. Arlene had taught me to read the signs, yet now Greenspan seemed to be ignoring them.

Still, he could see that Walker was tired because he said, "Say, 'You tired buddy?' (He gave his voice the tenor of a cartoon mouse.) 'I'm going to lie on your tummy.'"

I said it, I said what the doctor said, in the cartoon voice, and I lay on Walker's tummy. Walker began pushing me. I came back. He pushed me again—this time he was laughing. I was laughing, too.

"Oh, you're a good kicker," I said, finding myself lost in a moment of joy with Walker, pushing at his legs and laughing. Walker laughed again, kicked me, and pulled my hair. All of a sudden, he pulled himself up at complete attention, his posture firm and reaching upward. I had thought he was too tired, too sensitive. Now, he seemed a different child, ready for action.

"You see that," said Greenspan. "You take a simple thing like him tuning out, lying down passive, and turn it into a game, and see what he does? He pulls up and wants to play some more." I'd seen Walker laughing maniacally, yet there was a joyousness to him now that seemed unfamiliar.

After two hours, Cliff and I were exhausted, but what we'd accomplished wasn't enough for Greenspan. He wanted Walker to make choices with me. He'd noticed that Walker had enjoyed it when I took his hands and swung them back and forth.

"Mom, why don't you sit in front of Walker," he suggested. "Now show him your hands; hold them up. Tell him this one will be a 'back-and-forth' game. (He indicated his right hand and swung his head back and forth.) And tell him this one will be 'a kiss.'" (He indicated his left hand.) "Which game does Walker want? Now try to make it juicy and make it fun." Greenspan prompted me, with the elevated tone of a clown at a child's birthday party: "Touch my hand, buddy. Which one do you want?"

(*At eleven months old he's got to make choices?* I thought to myself.)

Walker began touching my hands, yet I didn't have the feeling he completely got the rules of the game. I was working harder than I'd ever worked in my life, kissing him if he touched one hand, prompting him to keep up the game, whipping his arms back and forth, his body gleefully moving with them. I wasn't sure he knew he was making choices at all. Still, he was with me.

The evening after the appointment, Cliff and I were sitting in a restaurant with Walker. Greenspan had told us that we would need to make Walker work for what he wanted. "You must become the button that makes anything he wants happen."

"I'll give you this cup," I said, "if you squeeze my finger." Walker didn't react. We weren't sure he was even intelligent enough to understand. I said it again.

The boy who had previously never responded to a verbal request put his hand up to mine and squeezed.

A Challenge, a Game,
a Vocation, a Sentence

WE FLEW INTO HARTFORD, picked up Elizabeth at her grandparents', and drove home the same day. By ten the next morning, Dawn arrived. She was eager to see the videotape of the meeting with Greenspan.

We watched some of it together, Dawn laughing, watching me frantically working to make Walker "choose" a hand for a game. After a few minutes, I suggested I teach her "floor time," Greenspan-style. For weeks Dawn had been teaching me everything I knew. Now it was my turn. Dawn held a knobby plastic ball over Walker.

"No," I barked out. "Too close. Hold it higher!"

"Do you want this?" she asked him.

"Make your voice more exciting," I said. "Gear it up!" She got on her knees, revved.

"Do you want this, you want it?" she asked, raising her voice. Walker began to come to life. I encouraged Dawn to speed up her reaction time, not to let a second go without forcing forward, enticing, inviting, squeaking with delight and allure. Walker and Dawn kept up a continuous flow of interaction for several minutes. After five minutes of floor time, Dawn looked up at me, her hair disheveled. "God," she said, laughing heartily—there seemed no need to protect Walker from our volume anymore. It was as if Walker's sensory system had changed from that one appointment. He seemed, suddenly, hyposensitive in certain areas, hungry for stimulation and able to receive it (though I knew that in many areas he remained a hypersensitive child). "What would happen if you did this with a typical kid?" asked Dawn, still puffing at her bangs. "He'd be at Harvard by the age of twelve!"

It was a powerful moment for me. Dawn and I were together, trying something new. It felt queer, though—*I was training her*—but Dawn made it easy with her humor. It all seemed ridiculous, but also miraculous. So *this* is it? *This* is what floor time is about. Dawn had been enticing kids away from their internal landscapes for fifteen years, helping them to function, to interact more capably. She had made good progress with many kids (I suspect she had a natural gift for it—empathy, intellectual curiosity, childlike humor, and charm), but she had always bumped up against kids' limitations. The question had always been how to push past those limitations. It just hadn't seemed possible to reach light speed with them. Many kids with autism had a deep sense of intimacy with their own parents, but that's often where the intimacy left off—the rest of the world was left out, as if the kids had grown up learning a different language, a private language.

Dawn had known from articles and books that floor time could be fully successful with about half the children in Greenspan's caseload; she had known that floor time was "intensive" and that it needed to be comprehensive, efficient, wrapping up into a tight ball all the needs of the child at once—his need to move, to feel, to speak. What she hadn't quite known, couldn't have gleaned from the books, was the spirit of floor time, the sheer speed and energy of it. We both understood now that we would need to push harder than we'd imagined. I'd been too tentative. I was too reluctant, too scared of Walker's sensitivities to get in there. But I had to. We had placed the bar too low. We hadn't gotten the rhythm. Arlene and Dawn had taught me that floor time needed to be as soft as a slow dance—indeed, it had to be so when Walker was six months old. Yet in the past few weeks, without my realizing it, we had stepped up the pace. We had begun to "dance" more with Walker, waltzing our way through the give-and-take. Yet now I understood the muscle of floor time, the push of it, the constant experiment of it to try and try new things—new frequencies, new speeds, new angles. Floor time for Walker wasn't a waltz. Floor time for Walker was swing, it was rap. It was rap with a fireworks display.

I looked down at Dawn, who was playing with Walker's feet, playing an impromptu game that seemed to have him captivated. Dawn was encouraging him, daring him to show he wanted more. I jumped down to join them on the floor, found I couldn't keep away. I held up an electronic toy filled with colorful buttons. "You want this, buddy?" I said, playfully mocking Greenspan, "Well, you're gonna' have to squeeze my finger."

Walker did nothing.

I raised the level of excitement in my voice. "Want it? Want it?," I squeaked quickly.

Walker reached up and squeezed. Dawn moved in and worked Walker up into a frenzy of joy and connection, making faces, insisting he respond quickly, encouraging him to move his body and getting him to be an equal partner in the dance, and enticing him to keep asking for more.

We were seeing parts of Walker we had only glimpsed, parts that had always somehow slammed the door in our faces before. Now the door was opening. We saw Walker's sense of humor, his intelligence, in the spontaneous expression of joy back and forth.

After half an hour, we fell onto the floor laughing.

"Man, the guy's a slave driver!" said Dawn, blowing on her bangs.

"You don't know the half of it," I said, standing up. I motioned for her to follow me to watch more of the office visit with Greenspan, fast-forwarding to the end, when Greenspan gave his summing up, prognosis, and prescription.

I brought Walker into the room with us and laid him on a blanket. He sucked his thumb, fingered his blanket strings hungrily, retreated more intensely than I'd seen in a long time, whipping his head back and forth occasionally as if to shake it all off.

Dawn watched the tape as Greenspan gave an overview and summing up. Usually he audio-taped his formal assessment and recommendations, but Cliff and I had asked him if we could videotape him so Dawn and Arlene could see him. In the summing up, he fed us an extraordinary amount of information. He spoke about us, about our need to change our attitude. He revealed the myriad ways in which we showed him and, unfortunately, Walker that we had unwittingly developed diminished expectations for our son's performance. He insisted we not move Walker's body. "Let him move. Don't do the work for him."

I looked on, realizing that this man was seeing my son, but seeing through different eyes—seeing with an extraordinarily sophisticated level of detail, laying out a description of Walker in terms of all of his processing modalities: his visual, auditory, tactile, vestibular, proprioceptive senses. He analyzed Walker's level of affect, measured quantifiably Walker's ability for sustained attention, described qualitatively his ability for richness of emotional expression. The facts came flying like sleet at a speeding car. I could see that Dawn was overwhelmed. She took copious notes, asked if she could study the tape at home.

"Wait one minute. Can you just answer one question for me?" I asked Dawn as she was about to leave.

"Yes?"

"There's something I don't get. Why is it that all these weeks we've been protecting Walker from stimulation and now Greenspan seems to want to intensify stimulation?"

She studied the floor for a long time and then answered. "I don't think he's intensifying stimulation. What he's intensifying are engagement and intimacy. He's asking you to get in closer."

"But we're working so hard, so fast. I'm worried we'll overstimulate Walker."

"Yeah, I know. It seems crazy, but it works with Walker. Besides, we're not always going fast. Remember when he had you lie down with Walker? He's got you slowing down, too, moving into his mood. I don't think this will overstimulate him. The theory here—and I believe this is the cornerstone of floor time itself—is that by keeping him interacting, you are protecting him. You're offering the greatest protection of all—communication."

Dawn turned, waved good-bye to Walker, and Walker did an extraordinary thing. He waved good-bye back. It wasn't just the vague imitations we had seen in the past; he really seemed to know what he was doing.

The feeling was exciting, overwhelming. Now I sat on the floor and stared ahead for several minutes. It had been so good to be laughing with Dawn. How long had it been since I'd laughed like that—as an adult with an adult, tears rolling down our cheeks? Dawn and I had been flying, racing at warp speed to keep Walker relating. But she was gone now. What was I supposed to do? Was I supposed to start it up again? I looked at my boy. The head was flying from side to side again (I hadn't seen that for some time). I still worried that floor time might be too much stress for him. As I stared at Walker, the whole weight of what was expected of me became clear. I reviewed the regimen. Greenspan had insisted Walker needed two sessions a week of sensory-based physical therapy (Arlene), an educator performing floor time twice a week (Dawn), and as for me and Cliff: eight to ten twenty-to-thirty-minute sessions of floor time per day. *Eight to ten sessions a day.* And that didn't even count going to Lenore's, which we did now once every two weeks, and going to doctors' appointments.

I sat staring for a long time, brooding. I was like Walker, driving hard into my obsession, but there seemed no way out: Floor time was a challenge, a game, a vocation, a prison sentence. How on earth could I do eight to ten sessions a day, take care of Elizabeth, myself, and a house? Suddenly, now the problem wasn't Walker anymore and what he could and couldn't do. It was me, my limitations. Human limitations.

In Greenspan's office, when Walker was pulling my hair he was also laughing in a way I'd never seen or heard him laugh. I'd observed a maniacal laugh, an intense, almost otherworldly laugh. Yet I had never heard a lighthearted or serene laugh from Walker, the kind that comes from the gut.

"Tell me, when your son is like this, do you still worry about his diagnosis? Do you worry about autism?" Greenspan had asked.

I had laughed a nervous laugh and said no. But I can't say I was telling the truth. I knew, though, that I'd never framed the question of Walker's health in terms of moments. I'd been too focused on the future to begin to think about moments. I was too focused on diagnosis—looking for a static statement of Walker's identity, as if destiny were indelibly written on the cranium. Yet in that question, Greenspan was presenting us with a different philosophy. A philosophy about moments—a new philosophy of disability? Of mental illness? Or at least a philosophy of *this* illness: that if we keep our son having healthy moments, we might make a healthy future, and if we let him have unhealthy moments, we might make an unhealthy future. The question was rhetorical, Socratic, asked as a way of teaching, asked as a way of implying an answer: *Did we understand that we could help our son by changing ourselves? Did we understand that we could help ourselves by changing* our *moments with our son?*

Still, I knew from that question what the philosophy meant for us. It meant we were far more responsible for what could happen than I had ever realized. There was an elation, a magic, a queer, eerie feeling, as if we were in a science fiction movie and what we did or didn't do would determine the fate of the human race.

Yet how would it be possible? Even with one child, for the past few years as a mother, I had often felt stretched. Motherhood had, from the minute I'd fallen into it, seemed to me to be a profession with a deceptive job description, a poorly designed job. Someone had failed to include the other three people necessary for the work.

Now, how to stretch time? Could I really muster that much charm on a daily basis?

At the next visit, I cornered Dawn. I needed her now more than Walker did.

I showered Dawn with questions, with information I'd pulled up on the net, with stuff I'd heard from acquaintances, at meetings, from friends of friends.

Did Greenspan's method really "cure" autism?

"Nobody in the autism world likes to the use the word *cure,*" said Dawn. She felt it evoked images of biological reverses that simply don't exist in neurological treatment.

"But Dawn, some people with autism, or those once labeled autistic, are leading independent, fulfilling lives. I reminded her of cases she already knew about. Some of the stars of the autism world—who were thriving. Raun K. Kaufman, for example, the subject of the 1977 book *Son Rise,* was given a diagnosis of severe autism at eighteen months. Treated by his pioneering parents, who invented their own intensive therapy, he emerged from autism at five and went forward to graduate from Brown University in 1995. "He's now a writer and teacher and I hear he is 'charismatic,' 'funny,' 'witty,' and 'deeply caring.' Tell me, Dawn, isn't Greenspan suggesting the theory that through therapy it's possible to move along the spectrum or possibly even off it to a full, happy life? That explanation would explain why broadly differing levels exist even among the highest of functioning."

"I think he might be," said Dawn. (I cornered her at my dining room table while Walker crawled into the living room and offered her a cup of tea.)

"Kaufman considers himself 'rehabilitated,' 'completely recovered'—off the 'spectrum,'" I said.

"How do you know that?"

"I called the publicity department of his parents' institute and asked them. When I asked what his personality was like, the woman giggled a little bit. I had a feeling she had a crush on him."

"Temple Grandin doesn't consider herself off the spectrum," said Dawn. By then I knew about Grandin. It was hard not to. Her name was everywhere in the literature. I knew she was leading an active life as a professor of animal sciences at Colorado State University, working as an engineer, writing and lecturing about her experience with the disorder.

"Grandin emphasizes the benefits of her autism," continued Dawn. "Intelligence, clarity of thought, the ability to visualize whole systems in three dimensions—yet she speaks eloquently about her continuing challenges: sensitivity, difficulty reading people's faces and emotions, and anxiety."

"But Dawn, it is possible to get beyond autism, isn't it?"

"I'm not sure," said Dawn. "It would appear so, but it's . . . it's not as easy as it seems. It's not like a disease that you leave behind. Still, Greenspan believes it's eminently treatable, and his results, if they're true, are impressive."

"What distinguishes autism that is treatable from autism that isn't?" I asked.

"No one knows," she said. "But 12 to 19 percent of people with autism have proved resistant to treatment; 22 to 29 percent can be helped moderately. Some school studies suggest that the vast majority of children with autism cannot be helped appreciably. What really counts is what kind of treatment one has. Intensity of treatment is crucial. Programs that give hours of one-on-one therapy each day have better outcomes than programs treating many children at once. Another factor that may be very important is time."

"I know," I said. Dawn had gently led me toward the theory that the very definition of autism may in fact be the secondary effect of autism—the result of letting the disorder go untreated.

I knew Walker needed therapy—that it had to be intensive—but what I couldn't handle was the idea that it all had to be me, or mostly me, since Cliff was gone ten hours a day at work.

"Dawn," I said, "I read something in a web site last night from a mother whose child was in an intensive interactive program. She said she wasn't her son's therapist, that a mother shouldn't have to be her son's therapist. She said her son had a troop of people who did it all. The problem is they're doing a different kind of therapy. It's—" I was about to name it when she interrupted,

"ABA."

"Yes, exactly, but why didn't you tell me about it before?" *Did it really matter if we did floor time, as long as we got help?* "Look at this," I said to Dawn, rushing to my desk for some information.

I read, "Thirty years ago, something happened in Los Angeles that changed the landscape of autism forever."

I recounted the groundbreaking history to Dawn, though at the time I didn't realize there was little need to.

Dr. Ivar Lovaas began experimenting at UCLA, using behavior modification techniques on children with the diagnosis. Eventually, in 1987, he published a landmark study, proving for the first time that the devastating symptoms of autism could be ameliorated, even removed.

In his experiment, Lovaas separated thirty-eight preschool-age children with autism into two groups of nineteen. The first group was given an average of forty hours per week of intensive behavioral intervention, also called applied behavioral analysis (ABA). The therapies involved repetitive exercises in behavior modification. The children sat in a chair and received a request: "Put this cube in a bucket," the therapist might say. If a child reacted appropriately, he was rewarded with positive reinforcement—a cookie, something he liked. If not, the request was repeated, again and again. Lovaas theorized that if a child participated in a constant series of these exchanges called "discrete trials," he would, by the laws of behaviorism, adopt more socially correct behaviors, which would be consistently reinforced.

Lovaas's results were unprecedented in his field; for the first time in history, someone in the scientific community had proven that autism was treatable—not just in a discrete case, but in several. The children receiving intensive intervention enjoyed an average IQ point increase of thirty points. Nine of the nineteen children went on to attend "typical" preschools. Children in the second, or control, group of Lovaas's study, who had received merely five to ten hours per week of behavioral therapy, reacted as if they hadn't been treated at all: not one was eventually placed in a typical class nor did any of them show an increase in IQ.

"Dawn, so why didn't you tell me about this?" I asked. "In fact, there's a book that a mother told me I should read . . ."

"Yes, I know,' said Dawn.

"Why didn't you suggest I read it?"

"I don't recommend you read it," said Dawn.

"But why?"

"It'll scare you."

"What could possibly be scary? Other mothers have read it."

"It begins with the children screaming in therapy."

"Oh." I put the sheet down.

"I know this is disappointing. It would be easier having a therapist do all the work, but the behaviorist approach is not one I recommend. I'm not alone. Some parent groups are critical of Lovaas because in the early days he recommended 'aversive" techniques— spanking, showing anger, looking away, yelling—as means of coercing children to behave differently."

"But surely they don't do that any more."

"It's true, they don't."

"But I heard that his techniques have been evolving for thirty years." I read from a printout: "'Lovaas has been able to refine his techniques to find more effective means of positive reinforcement, removing aversive techniques and adding a social component to his program: playgroups and peer playdates with facilitators.' Besides, look at this," I said to Dawn. "They were able to cure 49 percent of patients."

"Cure?" said Dawn. "I don't think that's what they're claiming."

I looked at her quizzically, then reached back for the sheet of paper.

"The therapists are trained in very rote methods," said Dawn, putting down her cup. "I've watched them work. I don't recommend it. Some states believe that Lovaas's program is the only one that works. They believe his research is definitive. But I know a bit more about that research. First of all, they handpicked their subjects. They wouldn't take anyone over three and a half years old, with one exception: If a child showed strengths in language skills, they would take him or her up to the age of five. It's true the subjects made progress, and Lovaas does deserve credit for being the first researcher to prove that autism is treatable. I use Lovaas's method with kids who have serious problems with imitating. But I have always been uncomfortable with their claims. They claim to produce students indistinguishable from their peers. I haven't seen that. Certainly in a classroom situation a teacher might not notice any significant problems, but autism doesn't necessarily have to do with the classroom. The therapy doesn't address emotional development. I've seen some of these kids. At best they can be shy, but they can also act strangely. They're trained to look people in the eye, so they'll come in a room and stare you down. Even with kids who come out seeming very normal there tend to be some social problems."

"But one mother wrote she was able to convince the state of New York to pay for behavioral therapy. Do you realize what that would mean for us? Do you think Massachusetts would pay therapists to do floor time?

Dawn stood up and moved toward the living room where Walker was lying. "No one's ever done it that I know of."

I followed. "I know what we could do!" I said. "We'll get the state to pay for a behavioral trainer and ask her to clean my kitchen. Then I can do the floor time myself all day."

Dawn laughed. We both laughed. Dawn moved to find her canvas bag.

"But," I said, following her back out of the room, "they raised the kids' IQ."

Dawn looked down shyly and didn't answer immediately. It's clear there was little left for her to say. As for me, I was twisting in the wind now and I knew it. I knew what she would say—that autism had little to do with intelligence, and she did. She mentioned that many people on the spectrum are quite cognitively gifted. "They might be able to swim through MIT, but they won't be able to hold down a job—won't be able to talk to clients, bosses, people at the water cooler."

"There's no doubt, Pat," she said. "Lovaas made a breakthrough. But there's so much more you can do, especially for a baby. This stuff with Greenspan is new, but it's convincing to me, and the results, if they're true, are very exciting. You want your son to be emotionally healthy."

Yes, I wanted to say. *But what did it mean for my emotional development? How I dreamed of having a professional at the door with a briefcase and a bag of toys for every hour of the day, working with Walker minute by minute.*

"I'm not his therapist," the phrase from the woman in New York stuck in my head. "I'm his mother," she had said.

What was all this fuss about emotional development?

Begin with Desire

CLIFF CAME HOME each night during that summer and ate dinner with me and Elizabeth. He listened intently while I talked about what I'd learned that day, what Walker did or didn't do. Cliff smiled, chewed, offered thoughts. Yet as summer moved into Indian summer, he seemed to grow less interested, to grow weary of my constant discussions, weary of having to be the one to keep loose ends together, weary of having to bring the groceries home. After dinner, he disappeared into Walker's bedroom for the two-hour ritual of putting him to sleep, tightening his large arms to contain a baby's reeling, struggling body. I disappeared into Elizabeth's room.

Emotional development. The words stuck in my craw as I noticed the days got lonelier and longer. I looked forward to the visits from Dawn and Arlene. They would be my companions, could perhaps answer the bigger questions. There was so much I didn't understand.

I was still struggling in some internal world to fathom this notion of emotional development versus cognitive development, which I had for so long assumed was the more important part of the self. *At school or in college, who ever talked about emotional development?* What seemed important at school was success and IQ.

Yet a few days after Dawn and I discussed Lovaas, I received a note that made me think hard about this new subject.

One night at about 1 A.M. during one of my late-night research marathons, I received an e-mail from Beth, an old high school friend. After eight years of silence, Beth was looking for me.

I dashed off a quick greeting and included a phrase mentioning my long-standing admiration for her. How I wished I'd been more like

Beth as we were growing up. In my note I mentioned briefly that I regretted not having taken my high school courses more seriously, as she had done. Beth had been an academic star at school, a gifted writer. After she graduated from college, Beth moved to an island in the Pacific Northwest where she worked in nonprofit fund-raising. Yet something happened to Beth at that job that changed her. Her boss was replaced; the man who replaced her was, to Beth's mind, not particularly competent. Beth found it difficult to show her full respect and support. To her utter shock, he fired her. Now, jobless in a jobless market, she stayed at home making pies, taking care of her garden, and watching herons take flight from her pond.

When I mentioned that I wished I'd taken school more seriously, Beth wrote back a most surprising reply:

> *Dear Pat,*
>
> *I don't agree with you that you wasted your years in high school. You didn't waste them at all. Perhaps I wasted mine. One thing I always admired about you was that you always knew how to hang out with friends. Hanging out was a skill I never learned. I was brought up to think of myself as different, as separate, as better than other people. Now I've changed my focus. Lately, I've been thinking about working in groups, and functioning in organizations, about teamwork. Don't berate yourself for not taking high school seriously. How seriously should anyone have taken it? And don't underrate your ability to hang out with people. It's a gift.*
>
> *Love, Beth*

A few months later, I would attend a conference given by Greenspan, who would explain a similar idea, though in a very different way.

In recent years, Greenspan and his associates had discovered something peculiar. They could teach children with autism certain cognitive and living skills through an intensive regime, as Lovaas had, but for some reason the children became stuck when they were asked to do anything imaginative or conceptually abstract. Even autistic children who were geniuses at mathematics and music had difficulty making certain simple connections between their reality and the world of abstractions. Psychologists and researchers noted a similar problem with social development: Children with autism could not seem to wrap their minds around the idea that other people have feelings and make judgments. Often autistic people don't seem to feel sympathy for others or have an understanding of others' thought processes. At an early age, when most children are detecting how the minds of their parents and peers work, scheming to get what they want out of their social environment, many children with autism can't understand the simplest pun or conceive of how anyone could detect a lie, though some might be able to calculate in a matter of seconds how many of their birthdays will fall on a Tuesday. They seem hopelessly mired in the literal.

Psychologists and researchers in autism have coined the term "theory of mind" to describe the ability to understand how other people reason as they do. Greenspan and his associates asked themselves: Why do many people with autism lack theory of mind? And why can't children with autism make the leap into abstractions? Why couldn't they do higher-order math or talk in a meaningful way about the meaning of good and evil? From a traditional developmental point of view, there was no reason to assume that children with autism would have trouble conceptualizing abstractions. The pioneering Swiss psychologist Jean Piaget had established long ago that abstractions are born when a child operates on his environment (pull a string, a bell rings: causality). But Greenspan was convinced that some part of development must be missing in an autistic baby's mind. What was it? The answer was staring him right in the face. Or rather, the answer was in all those young faces that simply couldn't look him in the eye. Greenspan and his colleagues made a leap; these children, they suddenly realized, wouldn't understand abstractions *until they understood their own emotions.* Already celebrated for his work in developmental psychiatry, Greenspan had come to a turning point in his understanding of human cognitive development through studying the dysfunction of autistic children. He understood that as a child is developing, everything he does and thinks is largely because of his emotions.

The emotional function is not just the part of the brain we associate with soap operas or crying children, or even merely that part we associate with loss and grief, with joy and lust; rather, the emotions represent a complex system for ordering the individual's entire universe. The emotions allow a child and an adult to sort material. Knowledge, wisdom, experience, information: Each of these are brought into complex networks in the brain, into endless and surprising categories, all finding their place in the emotions, which compose the human ability to ascribe meaning. It is for this reason, Greenspan understood, that the efforts being made to date in the realm of artificial intelligence to duplicate higher reasoning have failed. Even quite young children are capable of cognitive abstractions and refinements beyond what machines can accomplish; machines lack emotions.

Children apply what they learn emotionally to the physical world, not the reverse, as Piaget thought. "The first lesson in causality," Greenspan says, "is not in pulling the string to ring the bell. The first lesson in causality happens months earlier—pulling your mother's heartstring with a smile in order to receive one back." Furthermore, he says, the earliest concepts of math are nothing but reasoning driven by emotion. "For instance, when a child is learning concepts of quantity, he doesn't understand conceptually, he understands emotionally, in terms of his affective universe. What is 'a lot' to a toddler? It's more than you expect. What is 'a little'? It's less than you want."

First we "get it" from our personal experience, and then we abstract. What was missing from the autistic child's experience was a clear understanding of himself—a connection between feelings, actions, and ideas. He couldn't abstract into a conceptual world beyond himself because he didn't "get" himself.

The path to combating autism was clear to Greenspan. A therapist alone couldn't teach a child with autism to come out of his world; the parents (or someone else with an emotional connection to the child) would have to be involved.

The foundation of cognitive development would need to be laid at home. This emphasis on emotional development separated Greenspan dramatically from the behaviorist tradition in treating autism. He argued that the brain and the mind would be developed only by "wooing"—enticing the child into an emotional relationship.

One of the elements of Walker's experience most confusing to me was his tolerance for stimulation. Arlene had been teaching me to treat him gingerly. Yet over time, she was also teaching me to draw Walker out. Greenspan showed Cliff and me that Walker could tolerate much more than we imagined he could. But how could we gauge if we were giving him too much or too little?

The answer to how we could regulate Walker's sensory intake was the same answer for how best to approach him: Desire—his appetite for how much play he wanted—was the moderator between self and nervous system. Ultimately, during play, it didn't fully matter if Walker had a tendency to reel against a certain kind of touch while craving another kind, or whether he recoiled at certain frequencies or was responsive to a few. For in the moment, what really mattered *was what he wanted*. His wanting, and his ability to show what he wanted, would tell us what his nervous system was prepared for, could tolerate at any given point. The mind may not always know what the body can handle—so floor time seemed to suggest—but the emotional system somehow knows what the body needs. *Perhaps the gut knows the nervous system best of all.*

Three years later, Cliff and I heard this same idea expressed by Daniel Goleman, author of *Emotional Intelligence*, during a talk he gave at the University of Massachusetts. Goleman noted that a cancer patient who had lost a major emotional center in the brain when a tumor was removed had lost his job, his home, his wife. Yet no one could figure out exactly what had gone wrong. He didn't seem much changed. Goleman asserted that the emotions are in fact the executive center, the place where we actually make our final decisions. One day the patient's neurologist realized that the man couldn't make a simple decision about when to meet next. Having lost his emotional center, he had lost his sense of meaning. "A significant force in shaping our values is our emotions," said Goleman. "Ethical decisions are made not just by the rational parts of the brain but by those centers that drive the emotions."

Floor time, then, was about two things, about building tolerance and about building humanity. We would work with Walker in an emotionally rich atmosphere. What we were trying to teach—a skill, say, like crawling or sitting up—was secondary in importance to relationships, secondary to *us*. If Walker was interested in a chain of measuring spoons, we would use that interest to make ourselves interesting. (You want the measuring spoons? Well, I'm going to take them. I take the spoons and put them near my face and laugh. You want them? I'll wait for a smile and then I'll give them back.)

Walker's desire was not, however, a goal in itself. It was only the means to the goal. To let desire run rampant might mean to lose him, to let his will wander too deeply to an internal place. As long as Walker was "with us," as long as he was attending to our world, was learning to be increasingly interactive, we followed his lead.

And so desire became the sweet spot where Walker met the world because he was ready for it. Wanting connection, he moved toward it. He was free in desire, free to control himself, free to respond as he chose. In desire, Walker was able to shape his world, and shape himself in relation to it. He was teaching his teachers.

Tyranny of Attention

I HAD SOMETIMES FELT PERPLEXED when I looked in the mirror during those four and a half years before Walker was born. Elizabeth and I were so close, it was as if I half expected to see her face in the glass instead of my own. We had gone everywhere together. I had kept her, a large smiling baby in a sling, by my side. Our togetherness had been sometimes more than even I could handle. After she was born, I was in bliss most of the time; then I might sink into despair, exhaustion. Walker, on the other hand, was obviously her opposite. If Walker drank light, Elizabeth drank color, vibrance; he recoiled from the shine of her. Hunger for intimacy made her desperate with him at times, overbearing, as if she wanted to reach in and pull something right out of him. She was grasping for communion, but he withered in her hands.

Lenore insisted that Walker needed to be more like Elizabeth, more outgoing, more outwardly directed, less inward in his gaze, but she also believed that Elizabeth needed to be more like Walker (though of course, not to the degree of urgency). Elizabeth could benefit from learning to be more inward-moving, more introspective; she could benefit from learning to be comfortable with solitude. Ultimately the issue was a question of temperament. She was the ultimate extrovert, he the ultimate introvert. So it might be good for Elizabeth if I encouraged her to be alone sometimes. Still, the contrast between their disparate needs made it continually difficult to ever find time to do anything valuable for both of them simultaneously.

Loudness, which delighted Elizabeth, scared Walker: her meat, his poison.

My relationship with Elizabeth changed overnight, over months. As I worked with Walker for hours every day, I found myself putting Elizabeth in front of the television more and more. She was often watching three hours a day of TV now that she was in kindergarten. She was passionate about movies, loved musicals: *Mary Poppins, The Sound of Music.* Disney. Disney. Disney. I introduced her to Charlie Chaplin, the Marx Brothers, The Three Stooges, Our Gang, Woody Allen. She would have a great repertoire of movies under her belt, but I felt sad and sickened about it most of the time, the hazy blue-gray flickering light emanating from the living room.

That fall that Walker turned one, Elizabeth developed a particular obsession for a film called *Fly Away Home,* a fictionalized story of a girl's heroism as she flies an ultralight plane to lead a motherless flock of geese on a successful migration. The movie begins as a thirteen-year-old girl named Amy loses her mother in a car crash in the rain. Over and over Elizabeth watched the accident; over and over she watched Amy step into the role of mother to save some geese.

So here's the question I still don't know the answer to. Was it about her and me? Was it about my absence? Elizabeth now insisted that we call her Amy. She asked her friends to call her Amy. She embroidered a goose on burlap during her kindergarten class, worked on it furiously. They took it away and put it in a children's art exhibit at the Smith College museum. She signed the work "Amy."

Occasionally, we went into the world together, Elizabeth and I. I clung to her interest in this universe. Time with her was rich. I longed to be there with her, laughing in pizza parlors, attending dance concerts, but our time together was short—stolen for an hour or two here or there. (I did have the pleasure of spending an hour reading to her most nights while Cliff was with Walker). Friends were generously inviting Elizabeth over. One friend, Jonathan, sent dinner invitations written in crayon. They held hands in kindergarten. The teacher seemed to take a special interest in Elizabeth, and her grandparents took her out to dinner and shopping often. During dinners, Cliff and I still talked about Walker's day; a once-demanding child was becoming uncharacteristically patient, she listened quietly. I was determined to make a special afternoon that would belong to us alone—but how would it be possible? Perhaps I could hire a sitter, train her in floor time? When friends came to bring Elizabeth to playdates, I often felt a stripe of gratitude, and the queerest sense they'd come to steal something from me.

Circles of communication. We went round and round them.

Doing floor time, I often felt I was performing a desperate sort of stand-up comedy to save my son's life. Not only were the sessions exhausting—we found ourselves clapping, jumping up and down, singing, egging Walker on to move or to knock down blocks—but floor time required that our voices be ever livelier, the games more enticing, the joke funnier. Our energy and focus toward Walker had to be at the highest levels possible. Children like Walker, we understood all too clearly, were inclined to recede to internal landscapes that were far more seductive than the "real world." Greenspan assured us that we must not only maintain Walker's attention but also actually "build" Walker, or help him build himself, block by block so to speak, through each phase of development. We made up songs. One involved a dance called "the bottle dance": "Bot-tle bot-tle bot-tle bot-tle bot-tle bot. Bot-tle bot-tle bot. Yeah."

While Elizabeth and I sang this song, one of us held Walker's bottle in the air. We moved from left foot to right, back to left. Actually, we looked more like cheerleaders than dancers. The idea was to keep all the senses trained on one event, drinking. Mom and Elizabeth dance and sing and the bottle sways through the air, and afterward, I drink. If we could keep him listening and "drinking in" all these events, not only could we keep him with us, but we could teach him logical sequences, the logic of life lived outside the imagination.

Greenspan had said Walker was capable of only two or three circles—not much for a child nearly one year old. But now we were supposed to move him up to twenty or thirty.

Cliff and I did the math. Greenspan prescribed eight to ten floor times a day (each session twenty to thirty minutes long). We figured that eight was the most we could manage. If Dawn or Arlene came on Tuesday, Thursday, and Friday, on those days they could cover two, three, maybe even four, but they only came three times a week. That meant that three days of the week Cliff and I would be responsible for only four floor-time sessions, but four days of the week, Cliff and I would be responsible for eight sessions. Two of those days, I would need to work solo with Walker; Cliff couldn't do any sessions after work. He needed to eat, and afterward, he held Walker in a ball for a long time, in the "crescent moon" shape, trying to relax him for sleep.

I was required to pick up Elizabeth from school, take her to dance lessons and playdates, to shop, cook, clean, and do research (having taken hold of research, I couldn't let it go). The problem was often one of energy. How much, after the buzz of daily life, was left for floor time?

Cliff agreed to take on shopping and to do errands on his way home from work, yet his time for floor time was limited; he was instinctively spending increasing amounts of time with Elizabeth on weekends.

Here was our math:

Walker's Time Not in Floor Time
    4 hours feeding
    1 hour: changing diapers, bathing, etc.
    12 hours sleeping
    2 hours napping
5 Hours Left for Floor Time

Conclusion: any time Walker was not sleeping, bathing, being diapered, eating, or drinking, he should be doing floor time.

"I think you might need to take some time off work," I said to Cliff.

"What do you mean?"

"Walker needs us now. I've read personal accounts of men taking time off work or restructuring their time so they could be with their children."

"I'm already taking time off. I don't . . . Pat, there's something you don't understand. This whole show of ours is riding on a boat. I support this family, and if I lose my job, that boat goes down."

"Who said anything about you losing your job?"

"Pat," his voice rose. "Don't you see? This thing is devouring us. We were in debt going into this. How far in the hole can we get? What do you do when you hit rock bottom? Sell the car? The house?"

"We can't think about money now."

"*You* can't think about money. It's your luxury—worry about Walker. You're free to be as obsessed as you want. He's your universe. I've got to worry about the rest of us." *That's his luxury.*

⟿

The house got messier and messier. A large brown box arrived via UPS from a friend I'll call Victoria. It sat in the entryway untouched for days. When she called *(Was she hurt? Irritated? How had I done such a poor job explaining?)* to ask if we'd received the parcel, I was embarrassed, sheepish. Of course I would open it. *But when?* I didn't have the guts to tell her there was no time to open a simple present. Victoria was a sensitive person. She would take my stalling as a reflection on my regard for her—yet I couldn't find time to open the box. I was afraid of that box. I knew there would be paper to put away, thank-you notes to write; she told me there was something from her mother inside as well. (Opening the presents, looking at them, admiring them, putting things away: one floor time session.)

I eventually opened the parcel and found inside a large stuffed dragon puppet, some charming Halloween bibs, and a spectacular girl's dress: a green calico dirndl that might have been worn in the 1830s, or up in the Swiss Alps, with a large sash and a separate eyelet lace apron. It was one of the most beautiful handmade girls' dresses I had ever seen, made by a woman whom I had never met, Victoria's mother.

Now as I write these words I have the perspective to fully appreciate the dress. Yet at the time, I found it hard to accept it comfortably. The dress continues to be the crown jewel of Elizabeth's closet, and she wore it for years after she received it. (Now she hopes to start a business with a friend renting Halloween costumes; the dress is among her best offerings.) One couldn't help but appreciate the time, the generosity, the creativity of my friend's mother—but at the time I wasn't ready. The world had changed, the axis of the world had slid. There were no balls or functions in our world. The dress, as achingly beautiful as it was, made me feel guilty, exposed. I could barely look at it without feeling uncomfortable. Mostly what I worried about was having the time to properly thank Victoria and her mother.

I called Victoria, thanked her with floor-time energy, and asked for her mother's address in the Midwest.

It took me weeks to finally find the time to write the note. It kept slipping out of my mind.

Victoria called me a couple of weeks later. She said she understood I was busy but wanted to know if I could send her a picture of Elizabeth in the dress, and one to her mother. (Buying film, processing film, addressing letters: one and a half floor-time sessions.) A few months later Victoria sent another large package. I don't remember if I ever did send her the photos, but I will never forget the pain I caused when I eventually called to ask her to send no more gifts. The friendship grew thin and strained, and I mark this event as the major wound in a relationship that didn't survive. The rift in our friendship was my fault. I stopped calling. I had always been attracted to profoundly sensitive people; now I simply didn't have any more to give to an other person's sensitivities. Yet I still miss Victoria's wit, her intelligence, her stories.

A few days after I spoke with Dawn about Greenspan and Lovaas, I called Cliff at work. Cliff and I rarely if ever had time to talk at home, and now that Walker was asleep I wanted to discuss the pros and cons of Lovaas and Greenspan, the relative advantages of doing the therapy yourself and having someone do it for you. His answering machine picked up. I knew it might be a long time before Cliff checked his messages. I found the number of one of the secretaries in his office, called and asked if she knew where he was. She put me on hold. While I waited, I thought intently about what I wanted to discuss with Cliff; I fell into a reverie.

I knew that Greenspan was the answer, that Dawn believed in him and he believed in Walker, yet I was wrestling with a yawning hunger to be free from this burden.

Most of all, I was eager to ask Cliff his impressions about Walker—was he less sensitive recently? I was struggling to understand the nature of "oversensitivity" and "undersensitivity." Walker's sensory orientations at times seemed to me as changeable as moods, as elusive as other people's thoughts.

It seemed to me that the child who was too sensitive was now, at least in some respects, hungering for sensation. *But when did this change occur? After our visit to Greenspan? During our visit to Greenspan?* He longed to grab my hair and laughed on occasion. At times, Walker seemed more overexcited than lost in his own world. Was this the same phenomenon? Its opposite? Was overexcitability the next phase of development? (First go into yourself and then come at the world full bore?) I had read that overstimulation could look like understimulation—one could either retreat if the world was too overstimulating or, ironically, be excitable for the same reason. It seemed a maddening science. We had to give our son constant attention, yet w*asn't our purpose to guard Walker's sensitivity?* There were signs that our attention was too much for him. He would sink inward, and I could see him flailing against it all, brushing us off as if we were a swarm of irritating insects. His head flew, his legs kicked. Dawn called this "stimming" (self-stimulation). It is what drove Walker in Greenspan's office to seek the ends of the carpets, to suck furiously, to rub the beguiling strings against his lips. *Where was Cliff anyway? One thing I know,* I thought, *I detest the word* stimming. *It suggests something slightly unseemly, slightly sexual. What you're supposed to teach your children not to do in public.*

Older children with severe sensory problems apparently flapped their hands like birds when they were overstimulated. I saw a girl excessively self-stimulating herself one Saturday when I was at the park with Elizabeth (neurological aberration was everywhere now). The girl was sitting on the top of the play structure, not playing or hanging or jumping or sliding the way all the other kids were; she was curled into herself, sitting cross-legged, handling a rubber ball (the size of a tennis ball) with thousands of rubbery tentacles hanging. She was feeling them with an intensity that can only be called sexual. The world seemed to have fallen away for her and what remained was pure sensation. She seemed to me to be in a state of bliss. I wondered if children with sensory integration difficulties might not know something about sensation that we don't. *Do they feel* more *than we do? Might bliss somehow be hidden in string—in the unraveling of carpets and the rubber strands of Koosh Balls?*

The questions pulled at me so tightly that for a split second I forgot what I was waiting for—who was I on hold with? When the unfamiliar voice returned and said, "He's at the Faculty Club," I said, "Who?"

"Cliff."

The Faculty Club? Cliff wasn't a professor. He was an architect, a university planner. They were planning a large integrated science building, a new nursing school. Of course he would spend time with the faculty at the club, but something in me scattered like buckshot. It had somehow never occurred to me that Cliff was leading a normal life away from the house. Dimensions had changed, the world tilted and stretched. How could he dine out? Somehow I imagined he was as harried and absorbed as I. Yet now I saw that his life had not changed as much as mine. He had a lunch hour. He was spending time with people, talking about things. *He might even be laughing.*

By the time Cliff came home, I was furious with him. He hadn't done anything wrong, but . . . . I angrily chopped vegetables, hiding behind my hair while I prepared dinner. I didn't speak much during the meal. Finally I said, "So what's this with the Faculty Club?"

"What about it?"

"Nothing," I answered.

For several days we passed each other in the hall with our eyes down. Cliff still put his attentions into Elizabeth. Or at night, he spent an hour with Walker after dinner, holding him in the ball shape until Walker fell asleep. I spent time reading pamphlets and books, making calls, or on the Internet or collapsed in bed. There wasn't time to talk. A few days later, he called from work.

"I've been wanting to talk to you, and I know you want to talk to me," the voice was warm, inviting. I took it as an introduction to discuss Walker and launched into a long soliloquy about Lovaas and Greenspan and did parents really have to be their kids' therapists, but he stopped me. "I can't talk long," he said. "But I wanted to tell you. I've driven by some houses in Amherst. Some good deals."

Did I really do this, or do I imagine that I did it? In a scene in my mind, I hung up on Cliff. I hung up on him a hundred times. I slammed the phone into its plastic cradle.

Weeks passed. On the weekends, Cliff still put his energy into Elizabeth. Sometimes he didn't do the floor times that Greenspan recommended he do. I knew he was challenged by floor time. He seemed more confident helping Walker work on body movement. It was as if he had taken over the physical and I the emotional.

We lived in separate worlds.

I knew we were a marked race. I had read the statistics on divorces in families with special needs kids—staggeringly high. Cliff was doing more than any man I knew—superhuman things after a day's work—grocery shopping, a lot of the laundry. He took time off work to attend appointments; we had cut back with Lenore to about once a month, but he occasionally left work to meet with Arlene or Dawn. Yet now I was in the trenches; he wasn't. Worse, he seemed to be slipping away. Once eager to learn, to know more, to be at meetings, he now seemed distant, inaccessible, disappearing. If I wanted to spend time with him, it was somehow my job to call the baby-sitter. I couldn't bear the resentment.

Dawn called me in the fall, about a month after we returned from Greenspan's.

Mysteriously, after years of never having seen a baby with Walker's problems, now, inexplicably, a new baby "presenting in a similar way" appeared in her caseload—low upper tone, poor affect, gaze aversion. Could she give the parents our number?

Cliff and I agreed to take the kids and visit the parents, Dan and Marina, and their eleven-month-old son, Luca. One Sunday we drove out Route 66 into the country past Knightville with Elizabeth and Walker. The leaves were stunning again, bright as fire, the way they were the fall a year before, when Walker was born. Dan and Marina had rented a large cabin near a lake so they could enjoy peak season. Dan drove to work in Amherst, about an hour away, during the weekdays while Marina and her baby, Luca, stayed at the cabin with her Italian mother and aunt. We drove up the drive, the car crunching on leaves. The road dead-ended at the house; beyond was the lake. Cliff pulled the emergency brake. Yellow and orange and burnished red leaves underfoot; I was nervous. We were greeted by the older Italian matrons who let us in the kitchen door. They were sweet, deferential, a bit shy, shuffling around a kitchen the size of a closet, almost whispering to each other in Italian. The rest of the cabin was large, two stories with mysterious doors in the paneled living room leading who knows where. Marina was wearing jeans and a tight, rust-colored T-shirt. She was strong, sensual, determined, and sexy, her stomach slightly showing. Her husband was gentle, sweet; an intellectual. Their baby, Luca, a month younger than Walker, did not connect well. He looked to the side, wouldn't reach out to the world. He sat in a baby seat or the women held him while we ate. The meal was huge and luxurious—chicken and wine and pasta and bread and salad. I could feel the closeness of these people, and yet concern, family panic, a new order developing. I found myself recounting a story I had recently heard about a boy who was institutionalized for insanity. Within days of institutionalization, he became normal. When I got to the punch line, I realized I'd made a terrible mistake. "The boy was Italian," I said, falteringly. "When he was away from tomatoes and tomato sauce, he was fine." I looked down at the spaghetti and said something stupid like "Er . . . that's what I heard." Still, I tried to convince Marina and Dan that Walker's behavior improved when I removed wheat and dairy. I could tell they thought the idea was foolish. Besides, Luca was growing well. After lunch I got down on the floor and pulled out Walker's favorite toy, a white plastic box with a button that makes the box play music. (This was in a category that REACH called "cause and effect toys"—baby pushes, music plays.)

I held Luca's hand over the button and pushed several times, trying to up the emotional ante to inspire him to push the button on his own, but he didn't seem to want to. I moved across the room, raised the tenor of my voice, went into the high Mickey Mouse, and tried to inspire Luca to crawl toward me, but he seemed uninterested, or tired. I returned to the music toy. After some cajoling, he seemed to like it. He pushed the button a couple of times. Cliff and I suggested we leave the toy for Luca. It was the toy he liked best.

Over the next two weeks, Marina and I talked on the phone when we could. She told me in her thick, sensual accent, "The window is our enemy. Luca sleeps with us, and every day when he wakes up he stares out. We want to shut out that light." *"Yes," is all I can say, not knowing if my heart wants to leap or to fall—do there have to be two babies who stare at light?*

Marina and Dan were beginning to do floor time with Luca. Dawn visited Luca and did floor time as well.

They were, however, following traditional neurological diagnostic procedures with their son. We were not, for very specific reasons. We had expressed our anxiety to Greenspan about giving Walker an MRI, since we were concerned that he might have an adverse reaction to the anesthesia. Greenspan recommended that we ask the specialist what the practical goal of any given procedure would be before we agreed to it. Was the MRI purely academic, or could it lead to some productive treatment? The neurologist said that the odds were slim that any treatment would come from the MRI, and thus we decided to wait.

Luca was on a different diagnostic path than Walker, suffering complications that we didn't understand. Dan and Marina went to Boston to have a special EEG for Luca. For hours they sat with him and played while wires remained taped to his head. The results: They learned he was having seizures. These were described to me as storms or explosions in the brain that might be doing further damage. They were advised to give Luca medication. The medication made him drowsy. The floor time was harder to accomplish with a drowsy baby.

Marina and Dan invited us to Luca's birthday party. Later, we had them over for brunch. I sat on the floor with Walker. Cliff was in a chair. They sat on the couch. Elizabeth moved about the room. We talked about Greenspan. But having guests was hard for us. We could barely accomplish day-to-day survival tasks, and neither one of us knew if we had the energy to bond. I longed to. Cleaning, cooking, being with new people. I was ecstatic, but exhausted. It felt so new and refreshing to have guests in the house, to meet new people—it was life again, a honeymoon, an escape—but the work of it, with everything else on the docket, was like putting on a last-minute Broadway show. As they sat on the couch, Dan suggested we come over for dinner. *They want us to come over.* Cliff made a humming noise—a hemming and hawing noise. Later, he asked me to decline; he was overwhelmed by all that needed to be done.

A week later, I called Marina. She had just learned that Luca was suffering from a rare form of Down syndrome. Because it was a rare genetic configuration, the prognosis, they were told, might be good, might be better than what the average Down syndrome child could hope for. Anyway, Down was being reevaluated, reunderstood at that time. There was even a TV star who had Down. There was hope for Luca. Still, the news felt black. I couldn't help but feel Dan and Marina's grief. How to talk about it on the phone when a mother tells you her son has Down syndrome? I tried to console Marina. My words felt empty and fake. Even as I was consoling her, I felt her slipping away into another world that didn't include me. She was my one connection to another mother with my experience, and now we were as separate as I and any mother in my neighborhood.

REACH gave Dan and Marina the numbers of the Down syndrome families. I didn't hear from Marina for a long time. I saw her occasionally, through the smoky glass observation window at REACH, playing with the playgroup, laughing with the other parents.

The Down syndrome group was a tight-knit one at REACH. The parents were talented, energetic. Valle and Phil were leaders, laughers. They expressed gratitude for their charming, social son with Down syndrome, Aidan. Valle wrote for a family magazine. Phil was a playwright. He brought Aidan to the groups. He entertained the mothers and always had them chuckling. When Arlene at last told me I could begin to bring Walker to the groups, I quickly learned that they did not work for him. The parents spoke and laughed too loudly for Walker. I wanted to join in, yet with Walker, I had to draw away.

Walker was a paradox, a study in extremes. Sometimes he didn't seem to care for food; at other times, he inhaled it as if it were made of light. Yet his body didn't recognize the extremes—it seemed to override any sense of surfeit; he moved straight from eager eating to nausea. The cup filled one drop too full and he gagged, losing green avocado, white rice cereal, yellow banana, forfeiting all of the calories that might have taken as long as an hour to stoke into him. Arlene encouraged us to read his warning signs, but it was hard even for her to read the signs.

"All babies throw up," said our new pediatrician.

"Not like this," we insisted.

Finally, perhaps to get us out of his office, the pediatrician agreed to give us a referral to a pediatric gastroenterologist.

On the first visit, Cliff, Walker, and I found ourselves waiting in the gastroenterologist's office for an hour and a half. Two baby toys and a few books lay on a table near the chairs. After the first ten minutes, Walker had worked through all of them. Across the room sat a boy in a wheelchair with a large metal ring, like the model of Saturn's moons, sticking out of his shaven head. The lights were dull in there—gray, flickering, and stinging. Walker grew at first impatient, then restless, then almost desperate with his desire to escape the room. A half an hour. An hour. An hour and fifteen minutes. Cliff and I took turns chasing him while he crawled across the room, making his way to magazines, the coat rack. He clawed at the magazines. Where was everybody? The nurses worked quietly behind the booth as if they were keeping a secret. Maybe the entire office had slipped out of some secret door and left the building? Eventually a nurse called us in. She weighed Walker and left us to wait in a small cell with fluorescent lights and a *McCall's* magazine. We waited another twenty minutes, Walker wild with boredom and impatience. The doctor entered. He was a squat man with beady, bulbous eyes who didn't look at us much. He pressed on Walker's stomach briefly, stared at a chart, and insisted that Walker's vomiting was not likely to be due to allergies.

"But I know he has allergies. His skin turns black-and-blue at the touch of a carpet; he projectile vomited once when I tried to give him milk," I said.

He was unimpressed. I insisted he give a test for allergies. He finally agreed on a RAST panel, a blood test screening for standard allergies. When we visited two weeks later, he was surprised to see that Walker proved allergic to wheat, milk, and a variety of other foods.

"Astute mother," he said, flatly, seeming resentful.

We were ushered into a small office, where the nutritionist sat surrounded by display boxes of cereals, formulas, grain bars, and juices. Walker wouldn't sit still. We tag-team watched him. Mostly, Cliff chased him down the halls as he crawled around the waiting room while the nutritionist gave us ideas about what we could feed our son. She recommended we put Walker on a formula not made from dairy.

"I thought they were able to remove the allergens in that hypoallergenic formula."

"In theory they do, but it may not be possible to remove all of them. We've had good luck with Neocate.

Within a day of taking Neocate, Walker was drinking better. Soon he was vomiting much less often, only once a week instead of twice a day.

Partly Heard Song

"HE'S SO GOOD at looking at us now," I said to Arlene.

"Yes," she said. "He makes good eye contact." But her voice was flat. "It's encouraging," she continued hesitantly. "But I . . ." Her voice trailed off.

"Tell me," I said, trying to make my voice as nonchalant as possible.

She didn't answer for a long time, considered Walker's face, looked at me. "He doesn't seem to care if you leave the room. He should care. If we could make him care . . ."

<div align="center">~~~</div>

We didn't have a cake for Walker's birthday on October 17. We sat at the kitchen table feeding him hamburger, his new delight. The three of us sang "Happy Birthday." Cliff's parents invited us for dinner the following weekend. At their dinner table, Walker banged his head against their old wooden high chair much of the evening. *Did it hurt? I mean, did it hurt him?*

<div align="center">~~~</div>

Dawn and I attended a lecture given at Smith College by Harvard neurologist Margaret Bauman.

During her lecture, Bauman showed several videotapes of people with autism. One in particular fascinated me, an interview with an autistic boy. He had a chubby, friendly face, sandy-colored hair, and an impish, welcoming smile. Bauman was showing the tape to illustrate the oddities of how people with autism use language. The boy stared straight into the camera and explained in detail his own personal lexicon: "I call my sister 'the nun,' and I call my dad 'the lawyer.' I call the television 'mom,'" he said with a wry smile. We all laughed afterward at the oddity, but something else washed over me—a revelation. This was not the utterance of a disconnected person. In fact, it seemed to me that this boy was saying *more* about his experience, not less. Now I saw that this boy was talking less like an emotionally disturbed individual and sounding more like a poet. I had had this thought several times before, but I always dismissed it as a romantic fancy. Yet I was flat up against a lot of evidence that people with autism have an acute sense of awareness, not just in their senses but in their psyches. (Yet how strange that they might not understand certain jokes. Was it possible that they were just tuned in to *different* aspects of reality?) In any case, it seemed to me a brilliant commentary on contemporary life for a kid to call his television "mom."

We viewed other videotapes at the conference, saw people with autism shuffling around kitchens, awkwardly opening doors, talking stiffly without inflection like automatons. But between the lines there was something in those videotapes that one could never read in a book.

"Dawn," I said afterward, on the way home. I looked at her face. It was in flickering shadows and lights as we sped past trees and streetlights. "I always thought that people with autism talked and moved stiffly because they didn't have feelings. But is it possible they have very strong feelings, but they just don't have good motor planning skills?"

In a flash we passed a streetlight; Dawn's face was lit up, smiling— I had finally gotten it.

Dawn and I sat in her white Toyota, parked next to our house, talking for over an hour. I was nearly shaking with excitement.

I had entered that lecture hall believing that people with autism had somehow lost their humanity. Now I had an overwhelming sense that people with autism were actually experiencing the reverse: they might be even dripping with humanity, drowning in it. I had once read that the autistic mind tends toward the associative rather than the logical. Lacking logic does not necessarily mean without meaning. I had the feeling that meaning abounded for these children. They were seeing something real, expressing something personal, perhaps even the ways artists do. Now I remembered a quotation I had once found from Hans Asperger, one of the first psychologists to observe and define the characteristics of autism: "It seems that for success in science and art, a dash of autism is essential."

And I remembered that the autistic artist Jessey Park had her own personal way of saying "I don't know." Instead, Jessey said: "Partly heard song." *Is this a quirk of language, or is the language telling us more about Jessey's experience?*

Years later, I was struck with the same observation when I attended a conference at which brain researcher Eric Courchesne revealed discoveries about the brains of people with autism.

At their lab in La Jolla in the year 2001, his wife and colleague, Karen Pierce, and three colleagues discovered by using brain-imagining technology that autistic people showed no brain activity when exposed to a picture of a face. Having personal experience working with children with autism, Pierce was skeptical of such results. She redid the study, this time exposing the children with autism to the faces of their mothers. The results: The children with autism not only showed brain activity when they were looking at their mothers' faces, as the typical children had, *but they showed significantly more brain activity than the typical children* when looking at their mothers' faces.

Pierce's study may illustrate my hypothesis from a scientific view: that the emotions of children with autism run deep. It is perhaps for this very reason that the autistic brain chooses not to be responsive to a stranger's face. If faces bore into you like a brand, why expose yourself?

Why look straight into the sun?

I learned something else at Bauman's lecture. I had entered the hall believing that autistic individuals who couldn't speak could not do so because of a social deficit. Though there was some element of truth to my assumption, I now understood how much of the disability was purely mechanical. Dawn explained that though some children with

autism may be brilliant or have typical IQs, a part of their brain simply can't "sequence" the complicated chain of decisions and execu-
tions needed to use language. Language is the sine qua non of sensory-motor accomplishments. Language requires the ability to take in
long chains of words; it requires the ability to manipulate words in the
brain; it requires the ability to discern a variety of sounds; it requires
agility of the tongue; and it requires the ability to coordinate intention and motor response.

And there's timing. Each of these is not a matter of intelligence,
but of mechanics.

Some children with sensory and processing challenges simply
couldn't span all the hurdles to make it to speaking. Though some
might even be able to multiply twenty-digit numbers in their heads
or play Chopin by ear, their minds and tongues simply couldn't wrap
around speech.

Dawn often spoke of two distinct forms of language: "receptive
language," the ability to understand what is said by other people, and
its counterpart, the ability to reproduce and create language. We had
little evidence, when Walker was nearly one, for knowing whether he
had cracked our sonic-encoded messages. And anyway, even if he
proved to have the full ability to receive them, both Cliff and I
understood he might never be able to make them himself.

"If he can't talk, we'll try to teach him sign language," said Dawn. "Or
picture exchange."

"Picture exchange?"

"Yes," said Dawn. "I taught it to a local boy. He points to pictures
instead of using words. It's a new system. I made a videotape of myself
teaching it to the child. It's exciting." She looked at me brightly. "Now
he has a way of showing what he wants and what he needs."

I tried to imagine what life would be like using pictures for every interaction. I was a verbal person myself. The truth was, verbal discourse
meant more to me than . . . well . . . I could say. I was excited by the
game of language, delighted by the music of it, lulled by the cadence of
those long, delicious chains of syntactical logic: sitting in cafés, debating
at dinner, chattering on the phone with another talking head—such
experiences seemed to be all of life, defining. *What would a relationship
be, finally, without language?*

I tried to stay away from worry, but it was almost a pleasure, a nasty little habit like scratching scabs or grinding teeth. If Walker were wordless, he would probably live in an institution, or a small group home.

Language was a mysterious barrier, and Walker, by the age of one, showed few signs that would predict his future; though he was responsive at times to our requests, it was difficult to tell if he was guessing our meaning or reading our words. Dawn and Arlene were concerned, I knew. Arlene still stayed as long as she could, and now Dawn was doing the same. Thus, while Dawn worked vigilantly to lay the foundations of language, Arlene encouraged Walker to solve problems with his body, to see what he was doing as relational. Yet how relational he was remained a mystery.

Walker did have some good skills—though not the skills of his one-year-old counterparts. His body was still lost in space, and he was disoriented by touch; he was frail and could fall into his own secret realm. However, he could imitate our actions, he babbled, he enjoyed a sleeping game Dawn made up, in which they both traded off pretending to go to sleep, and he could make the sound "Hiiiiiiiiiii," though we weren't sure he knew what it meant.

I focused on what worked. I often found myself repeating over and over the moment of exquisite triumph when Walker had squeezed my finger in the restaurant near Greenspan's office. I repeated variations of it ad nauseam: "I'll give you this toy; I'll give you this spoon." Dawn encouraged me to move further. She wanted me to put flexibility, spontaneity into the relationship. But how could I? I longed for a formula that would work. ABA, the therapeutic approach that Lovaas recommended, depended upon formulas, repetition, but Dawn insisted that with floor time, the idea was to challenge Walker's brain at every turn, to train it toward the human and its infinite variety.

Dawn also warned Cliff and me against being too focused on what she called "splinter skills"—small milestones such as stacking blocks that in other therapies were goals in themselves. Dawn said that by working in the constantly interactive environment, we were teaching Walker how to learn. "If he can learn how to learn, he can learn anything."

Dawn was eager to see if we could teach Walker to point.

"Point? Why?" I asked. "Isn't that a splinter skill?"

"Not at all," said Dawn. "Far from it. I mean pointing as a shared experience. It's fundamental." Dawn explained to me that recent researchers had been able to identify a lack of pointing as among the earliest signs of autism—one of its hallmarks. Long after the time that their typical peers have been jumping up and down pointing at sky-writing in the air, at dogs and babies in carriages, at candy in the market, laughing with other children, autistic children failed to point as if to say, "Look at that, you guys!"

Pointing was a significant milestone in emotional maturity, and even in learning speech.

One day shortly after Walker's birthday, Dawn and I sat next to Walker, flanking him on either side, while he sat rocking back and forth with excitement, waving his hands. Dawn put a flashy merry-go-round toy on the floor and pointed. She held Walker's head so it would follow the line of her finger gesturing toward the toy. For several days, Walker had trouble following the line. His eyes seemed incapable of the necessary focus. *What was this woman putting her finger in the air for?* Dawn began taking Walker's own finger and pointing it. She pulled the small digit out from among the other fingers—it seemed curled in with them, as though they were attached at the knuckle. Pointing, for Walker, might be motorically difficult in its own right. She straightened the finger and aimed it toward the toy. She talked excitedly about the merry-go-round and leaned in toward it while he pointed. Still, Walker looked around the room aimlessly, confused, as if the gesture meant nothing.

One day, Dawn and Arlene and I were all again on the floor with Walker. We had taught him to crawl by ten months, but he still couldn't sit up by himself (a skill his peers had mastered at six months). Seeing that he was trying to make it up, we cheered him on. He succeeded—vertical on his own for the first time. We all clapped. This primarily physical leap spurred a social one as well—he looked from Dawn to me to Arlene, as if to say, "Hey you guys, did you see me?"

"Look what he just did!" Arlene exclaimed. "He looked from one of us to the other and back again. He's never done that before!" Walker had performed a sophisticated form of social referencing.

From that day on, Walker always looked at us to see if we were impressed with accomplishments.

Within a week of his birthday, Walker was pointing.

Words

AS RECENTLY AS THE 1960S, it was believed that children take a relatively passive role in learning language. Speech and language professionals largely believed that babies learn to speak because they simply hear words and pick them up out of the environment. They thought that language acquisition was somehow unrelated to other skills that babies acquired.

How could babies make such a great leap from not speaking to speaking? Was learning language the miraculous and solitary "moment" in the child's development it was always thought to be?

As neuroscience began to assert that babies' brains are active far earlier than was previously realized and that the brain is constantly "remodeling itself," theorists began wondering if there wasn't some process taking place in a baby's brain before language, heralding that great avalanche of word flow that occurs so suddenly with typical infants.

What researchers uncovered proved to be revolutionary in the field. They learned that the use of the spoken word is only a blip, albeit a dramatic one, the next point on a continuum that reaches far back into a baby's history, earlier than even his first intimations of speech comprehension, earlier, even, than his ability to point at a birthday balloon floating through the air.

In the 1980s, several researchers began questioning how babies learn and communicate, specifically how babies gather information from their caregivers. Simon Baron-Cohen, T. Berry Brazelton, Robert Emde, Daniel Stern, Stanley Greenspan, and Peter Mundy, to name a few, were involved in finding out what heralded a baby's ability to communicate. Looking specifically at how babies gather information from their caregivers, they observed that babies learn from being part of a process, not from being passive conduits of information or knowledge. Observing the very active form of communication taking place between a healthy baby and his caregiver, some began using the term "joint attention," a term that would come to define a new field of inquiry into the developing baby's mind.

A baby taking part in "joint attention" might, for instance, watch his mother subtly nod, and then he would react accordingly, or he would look to his caregiver when something in his environment surprised him.

Now researchers had a springboard for making great leaps of understanding about how babies learn speech. Language doesn't begin when a child speaks—that is in some ways *the middle of a process*. Language begins in its most nascent form when a child begins to care about Mom and Dad, care about what they are doing, looking at, or saying.

How can a baby learn the arcane language of Mom and Dad's desires, intentions, expectations? At first, researchers assumed that infants learned to pay attention to Mom and Dad simply because it was rewarding. But such an assumption left a lot of questions unanswered.

A baby, for example, may be able to learn the word "apple" if Mom picks one up and points to it, but such direct explication represents only a very small percentage of how a baby acquires a vocabulary. A baby couldn't possibly learn all the words there are to learn even if he sat in a room with Mom watching her pick up apples and pillows and pencils for hours. How many parents have time to name the world over and again for a baby?

In the 1990s, Dare Baldwin realized that there must be another way a baby learns, and learns so quickly. The answer: a reference point. When a mother pushes a baby in a baby carriage down the avenue, effusing about the burgeoning crocuses peeping out of the grass, how does a baby know, for instance, to look at the tiny flowers emerging from the lawn? Why isn't he gazing at the squirrels peeking out from behind trees or watching the sun peeking out from a cloud cover? Nature's deeper intentions are hidden within this simple human instinct: Mom and Dad and siblings have to count, whether or not a baby realizes it, for Mom and Dad and whoever is close are going to be the key that will unlock the great beyond, including the great beyond of language. Because the baby cares about what Mom thinks, the baby seeks her focus of attention. She is the still point in his turning world. If the baby learns to see the world first through Mom's eyes, then he will learn massive amounts of language in a short time. *Mom looks at the flowers, I look at the flowers. Mom looks at the sky, I look at the sky.*

The gift of "joint attention" (or a slightly more sophisticated version, sometimes called "shared attention") is not only the basis of all language acquisition but is most likely the source of our most important learning. In the mid-1980s, researchers Roger Bakeman and Lauren Adamson discovered that the longer the sustained shared attention and focus, the more a child will learn.

In 1990, Peter Mundy, Marian Sigman, and Connie Kasari applied the study of joint attention to children with autism. They discovered that joint attention, which normally occurs in early infancy around the age of six or eight months, was severely lacking in children with autism. It would prove to be a seminal piece of research, an investigation that began to change the field of autism.

The woman who set me on the path to learning about the history of speech acquisition was a student at Smith College. By the time I met her in the fall of 1997, Amy was already a senior in college.

One day in early September, as she later told me, Amy was sitting in a classroom at Smith College around a large oak table with twenty or so other students when her clinical psychology professor read aloud a plea from "a family in the neighborhood of Smith" whose young son was ill with neurological problems and symptoms of autism. They were looking for student volunteers to work with Walker. Perhaps Amy heard something like the ring of fate in that plea, which I had written, or maybe she just thought she'd like to help, but she also knew more than a little about autism.

Working in Mississippi at a state hospital while she was in high school, Amy had been given the assignment of caring for a man who spent his days acting out repetitive self-abusive behaviors; he hit himself so often that he was in threat of mortal injury. There was little hope of reaching the man, or of offering a way out of his Dantean world of craving what hurts. Yet she thought she might be able to improve the quality of his life in some small way. Understanding that his compulsion to hit himself was largely sensory based, Amy brought stimulating balls and objects for her patient to play with. Thus, he would not be compelled to "stim," self-stimulate with his own body. Her idea worked. She was buoyant until the next time she came back to the hospital. The toys and objects were missing. In their place was the standard restraining equipment. The hospital staff, underpaid and not well educated, had preferred the easier customary solution of using restraining equipment. Her second experience with autism was altogether different. Still in high school, Amy worked with a nonverbal child with autism in a kindergarten class. Amy was able, through one-on-one work, to begin to teach the child his alphabet. The experience was thrilling and led her to consider pursuing studies in psychology at college.

The minute her clinical psychology class was dismissed, Amy ran out of the hall, across the quad to the nearest phone booth, and left a charmingly breathless message on our machine:

"I hope nobody has called before me," she said with the generous vowels of a Mississippi accent. I could tell at once, she was young, eager. I had just come home from the store—where I had had to take Walker with me. Arlene was waiting when I arrived. I apologized to Arlene and asked her once again if she could work with Walker alone for a few minutes while I put the groceries away. Afterward, I stood in front of my answering machine, my brow furrowed with a quizzical surprise. I really hadn't expected anyone to answer. I called Amy and invited her to come over right away.

I had been alone working with Walker much of the past few weeks during the day before Elizabeth came home, and it was somehow peculiar having an adult other than Dawn or Arlene standing in the living room. Yet particularly this young adult, Amy. She was a presence—wearing black, high, thick-soled shoes, a white pullover, and a leather coat. Something about Amy reminded me of a 1940s starlet. Simply put, she was beautiful. She came into my messy kitchen shortly after Arlene left and approached Walker with an animated face. She beamed a smile worthy of a toothpaste commercial and drew him out immediately. I didn't realize at the time what a coup even this fact alone was—the fact that Walker was attracted to this stranger showed that he was learning some sensory tolerance, that he could have a taste for the things that shine in this world. She was a walking version of floor time.

Amy explained that she was required to choose a subject of study for her course project in a seminar on developmental psychology. She hoped her professor, Peter Pufall, would let her work with Walker.

We were grateful she wanted Walker to be a project. I was very ill at ease with the idea of accepting charity for its own sake.

After meeting us, as she told me later, Amy went straight to Pufall's office to discuss working with Walker.

He was skeptical. There were ethical problems. What if we wanted Amy to use methods that compromised her ideas? What if Walker became attached to her? Might he be hurt by her pulling away after the end of the semester? Did she want to make such a big commitment? Smith students usually worked with children at the college's laboratory school, the Smith College Campus School, largely populated with typical children of professors and professionals. Part of the elementary school's admissions process included signing a waiver, allowing the children to be participants in student psychology and education studies. No liabilities. But Amy didn't want to work with that population. "They don't need me," she said. "The work won't be as important."

She went back to Pufall, but he was adamant. Working with Walker would be a mistake. He wanted Amy to be analyzing a group of several subjects so she could learn statistical calculations, to analyze large quantities of data. "An intervention study on one child is different from a study of twenty children," he insisted. "This baby is just a case study."

"I know that's important," said Amy. "In fact I hope to focus on those studies in the future, but I can't let go of this now. Besides, I *would be* analyzing facts and information," Amy insisted. "I will use videotapes, and collect data daily on Walker."

A few days later, she appeared in his office, soaking wet—she had walked in her leather jacket straight from our house in the rain. "I'm going to work with Walker anyway, no matter what you decide," she told him.

Pufall looked at Amy, saw her dripping with water and determination, and suddenly something in him softened. "I'll tell you something," he said. "I'm nearing the end of my career, I'll be retiring soon. I've been doing book studies and group studies for too long. It might be good to get back close to working with just one child again. Something can happen with this kind of work. It can be very rewarding. I may regret it, but I'm going to say yes."

"How much time will you be needing me?" asked Amy when she came to tell me the news.

I was shy to tell her just how much attention floor time required, particularly since I knew what Smith students were up against—chem labs, swim meets, all-nighters, and those elaborate, formal Friday afternoon teas.

"How about if I come every weekday," she said. "For two hours?"

I wasn't sure she could handle it. "How can you do that?"

"No . . . no, really," she insisted, "I'd like to."

I left the room to hide my tears.

And she came—Amy came every weekday, from 4 to 6. While she worked I made phone calls, cooked or cleaned, or spent time with Elizabeth, making up for lost time. Elizabeth and I baked popovers together, read. We even took some walks together.

One morning that fall, I received a call from the school that Elizabeth had contracted lice there. All of the kids with eggs in their hair would be sent home. When I came to retrieve Elizabeth from school that Friday morning, the nurse said, "Well, I guess you'll be watching a lot of videos this weekend."

"What?"

"It'll take hours to comb all those eggs out of her hair. There's only one way to keep a kindergartner still—rent some videos." *More videos?* I thought. The nurse gave me explicit directions for buying a shampoo formula that promised to kill lice and their eggs. She informed me that I would need to bag up and seal every stuffed animal, every hat, every scarf, every pillow and cushion in our house, and if possible, Elizabeth's mattress, for ten days.

Elizabeth and I took Walker in his covered car seat to the store. I was still reluctant to take him out of the house for long periods, besides the occasional walk in a stroller around the car in the drive-way for a small dose of vestibular stimulation, but this was a trip he would have to take. We bought the pesticide shampoo, three boxes of trash bags, special combs. We went to the video store and chose four movies: Disney's *Pocahontas*, Woody Allen's *Sleeper*, a collection of the Our Gang series, and *National Velvet*. At home that afternoon we greeted Amy, who sat on the floor and took Walker up on her lap. She rolled onto her back and held Walker up in the air over her, looking him in the eye and smiling. Elizabeth and I headed for the tub. Rubbing the insect poison on Elizabeth's head, I now saw live crea-tures scurrying up and down the shafts of her hair toward her scalp. I had hoped the medication would kill the insects on contact; instead, the pesticide seemed to do little or nothing, besides perhaps scaring them out of hiding. I spent several hours afterward standing behind Elizabeth on the couch in the living room, combing lice eggs out of her waist-long hair while the creatures scurried around on the shafts. While the insects ran for their lives, Elizabeth and I talked. Elizabeth and I, both fascinated with language, laughed about all the terms we had been using without consciously realizing they were related to lice: "lousy," "fine-toothed comb," "cooties." Hour after hour I combed. She sat still—watched more Disney, more Woody Allen, more cartoon sit-coms on public television. But there was a difference now; I was in the room with her. We laughed at the movies, ate snacks. At bedtime every night, following a home remedy I read about, I cov-ered her head in olive oil. After five days of combing and bagging, we were allowed to send Elizabeth back to school. The lice were gone; however, they had merely migrated to me. In spite of the fact that Cliff and I were now going to sleep every night with olive oil on our hair, wrapped in towels, in spite of our having to cover nearly every-thing that we owned that could be considered soft in bags, Amy and her presence afforded me the pleasure of getting to know every strand of Elizabeth's hair. But there was another advantage to the lice: Cliff and I were together. He did for me as I had done for Elizabeth, combed my hair after the children were asleep. He stood over me for hours, running the comb through my hair, a brief refuge.

After her sessions with Walker, as the fall sped by, Amy often stayed to talk. She spoke of her discussions with Professor Pufall. I suspected that Pufall was catching Amy's enthusiasm for the project. (In fact, over time, I began to wonder when he found time to meet with other students.) They discussed Walker's situation at length. Walker was then a year old. While some children that age were rushing out into the world, beginning to walk and talk, eating large varieties of food, Walker had just learned to sit up on his own. He sat in a high chair now, but he trembled slightly as he worked to keep his weight steady—the instinct was to fall forward or sideways. He hunched over, and we were required to roll up a towel and wedge it beside him as support. He ate few foods, and what he did eat we had to coax him to take. And though he could look someone in the eye, he could just as easily be lost in his own world.

Meanwhile, we explained the fundamentals of floor time to Amy, but clearly, our word wasn't enough. A voracious researcher, she came often with information, with articles. Because Pufall's area of expertise was typical children's artwork, she and Pufall would be learning together. She often came by to talk to Dawn and me about the latest discoveries in child development. Amy was particularly interested in the area of speech acquisition. In her research, she discovered the work of Peter Mundy and grew fascinated by the concept of "joint attention." If joint attention predicts degrees of language acquisition in children with autism, then there had to be some way to address Walker's relatively poor joint attention skills. What was most exciting about Mundy's research to Amy was that it was the first research she found hinting at what autism might look like in early infancy. Most of the studies available only discussed how autism looked after the age of two.

Mundy found that joint attention, dramatically lacking in children with autism, was a skill that developed in normal kids between six and eight months.

Unfortunately, Amy found, no one had discovered a formal way to teach joint attention to infants. (In fact, to this day, there is still no general consensus among researchers on whether the skill can be taught, though I think that a strong argument can be made that Arlene, Dawn, Cliff, and I were able to teach joint attention to Walker in our first months with him; pointing and looking for approval are strong markers of the beginnings of joint attention.) To researchers, it seemed to be just something babies do.

Knowing that language is often the bête noire of children with autism, Amy was determined to teach Walker some skills to help him develop language.

Walker might never learn more than the few sounds he already knew, or might lose the sounds he had, but she was willing to give it a try.

Pufall led Amy to studies by a former Smith student, Susan Goldin-Meadow, and Linda Acredolo and her colleague Susan Goodwin at the University of California at Davis. They had just researched the role that preverbal behaviors have on language development—specifically gestures. Since some forms of joint attention involve gestures, she decided to try their approach. Acredolo and Goodwin's research showed that typical children develop gestures to symbolize words approximately one month before they produce words. Gestures were important because they showed that children use symbols to "communicate" actively as a phase of "joint attention," even before the tongue begins making words.

The idea was to see if Walker could first learn to make symbols and then transfer the gestural symbols to words.

Amy came over one chilly afternoon when Arlene and I were in the dining room with Walker on the floor. "I'd like to teach Walker to make a gesture for the word *duck*. Do you think it might be possible?"

Arlene looked at Amy, turned to me, and smiled. I knew that smile. It meant: "I'm going to have to disappoint you. Give me a minute to think about letting you down easy."

"It won't work unless the word means something to him," said Arlene skeptically.

I regarded Amy. I knew what we were all thinking: How can we make a word mean something to him. *Meaning? What is meaning for a baby, anyway?* She was disappointed.

Arlene brightened. "For the past weeks, Pat and Cliff and I have been talking about Walker's dietary problems. Here is a child with severe eating problems. In some ways he seems to be starving to death.

Walker throws up and we don't know why. He can barely get food down. We never know when he's hungry; he won't or can't tell us. Other times he gobbles the few foods he will or can eat too quickly, not chewing well. Then he throws up. If we could only find out when he felt full, we could help him regulate his intake—perhaps you could teach Walker to show us?"

Amy was beaming. It was decided. Food is one thing we know does mean something to this baby. Amy left the house excitedly.

The next visit, Amy arrived energetic, happy, full of ideas. She had been talking to Pufall again. They had the plan mapped out. She would come in the late afternoon to feed Walker dinner. She would feed him spoonful by spoonful, and after every bite, she would teach Walker the simplest gesture that she and Pufall could devise; she would take his hand and pound it flat on the table to indicate "more." "More, more," she would reinforce, voicing the gesture's intent.

When he looked full, she would pull the food away, and right afterward, she would gesture "no more" by making an "X" formation with her arms over Walker's high-chair tray.

All the while, Dawn and Arlene and Cliff and I would work on other forms of floor time. Dawn on cognitive and social—she would be holding him in her lap, looking into mirrors together, bringing books, playing hand games. Arlene would work on body development; she would hide toys in clear plastic boxes, hand them to Walker, and wait to see if he could figure out how to retrieve them; she would begin trying to teach him to walk by supporting him as he would pull up to a coffee table or a toy box. Cliff and I would work on all of the pieces. And so we began. On the weekends, Cliff took a special interest in Walker's physical development. He encouraged Walker to try to learn to stand with help, as Arlene taught him. He or I sat on the floor, placing toys on the couch, encouraging Walker to lift up to retrieve them. Regardless of what any of us were working on with Walker, we encouraged him to be part of an emotional moment. We would all define any activity with Walker, first and foremost, as relational.

Amy fed Walker for an hour or an hour and a half. She played with him afterward—often playing a game with Walker that Arlene and Dawn invented to help him learn more gestures. If Walker was just waking up from a nap, Amy came and stood above Walker in his crib. She lifted her arms up in the sky, brightly querying: "Up?" as if to say,

"Want to get out of here, kid? Show me your stuff." Our hope was that Walker would want so much to leave the crib that he would make the gesture.

Dawn and Arlene insisted that when Amy and Cliff and I worked with Walker, our play needed to have a flexible, spontaneous quality. Walker needed to react to *myriad situations, thousands of situations of need and desire*, not just feeding or escaping the crib. They encouraged us all to be creative.

Amy was very physical with Walker, holding him, playing with him, rolling onto her back on the floor, holding him over her face, making eye contact. Seeing Walker with other women lavishing him with affection was somehow profoundly satisfying.

We saw a different Walker every day. His behavior was all over the map. For two hours he might be able to attend without any self-absorbed behavior, then he would dive headfirst, overwhelmed in his own waters, wallowing in thumb-sucking and head moving. His excitement levels rose, and a once-sleepy baby often seemed impossible to settle down. Excitement would slip into mania, mania unreachable. I was confused—it felt at times as though we were driving him away from us, overwhelming him with too much attention, *too many people in his face.* Was he trying to shake us off?

For the first two weeks, Amy provided all the effort and intention for Walker's signs. She took his hands, with hers over his, and repeated again and again the gestures she wanted him to learn—pounding his hands on his high-chair tray for "more," and making a crossing, a "no" signal with her arms, for "no more" or "all done." She spoke the words while she made him gesture.

One day, she was mashing some banana in a bowl and Walker hit the tray hard. Had he meant to pound? She couldn't make him repeat the gesture, but the next day, he pounded on his own several times. She called from the kitchen excitedly. Elizabeth and I ran in to see. Walker was pounding. Could it mean he wanted to eat? I hoped so.

Within a week, Walker pounded every time he wanted a bite. By November, Walker used signs for "all done" and "more" consistently. He might, in fact, someday be able to talk, but there was a lot we didn't know. The questions in our minds were: Would he be able to form strings of logic, strings of syntax? Was his brain organized enough, wired well enough to plan, order, and shape words to make discourse possible? And then, there was of course the hurdle of receptive language itself. We didn't know how well Walker understood what we said.

Some afternoons I barely had time to speak to Amy. I might be rushing into the kitchen to get something for Elizabeth, or driving Elizabeth somewhere.

One day she said, "Could you keep a record of Walker's feeding behavior? You could write down if he ever pounds the table, and when."

"I'm sorry, Amy," I said. "I'm so busy, I don't think it will be possible. There are days I don't shower." I didn't like disappointing Amy. She was giving so much to Walker—I just had nothing left to give myself.

Amy, however was undaunted. The next day she appeared with a machine, an old tape recorder she had borrowed from the psychology department and asked me to speak into the machine every time Walker did something positive—showed signs of learning the gestures. The recordings are filled with excited phrases from me.

One day Dawn and I were standing in the kitchen talking about when we might be able to take Walker around the driveway again. "Should I take him outside for a minute or two?" I said to Dawn.

Walker turned 180 degrees and looked at the door.

Dawn and I looked at each other. "Did you see what I just saw?" She nodded quickly, her hair was nodding too. So much was in her eyes. She told me my son had receptive language. "October 18," I said into the tape recorder. "Walker has receptive language."

One morning while Arlene and I were working with Walker, Arlene threw a plastic yellow foot across the room. Walker crawled to grab it and bring it back to her. He smiled. She threw it again and asked him to pick it up. It was hard work for him crawling back and forth. His stamina was low—other babies may be walking by this age, but he wasn't close; movement was a struggle. Even keeping his head up was a struggle.

"Come on Walker. Don't you want to go get the foot?" Arlene encouraged.

He sat down, shook his head, and crossed his arms in front of himself vigorously, as if to say, "no more." Arlene and I stiffened in surprise.

"Do you realize what this means?" said Arlene.

"He might be able to talk?" I asked.

"He can abstract. He can generalize. He just took a symbol of an idea from eating and brought it into our play together. That's pretty smart."

"But do you think it will mean he can talk?"

She smiled.

The Specter of Loss

WALKER WAS SMART. If we didn't know this when Walker gestured "no more" during the game, we would know it within a few short weeks. As if he were one of the subjects of Acredolo and Goodwin's gestural studies on typical children, almost exactly a month after Walker learned "more," he began speaking it. By November 1997, when Walker was thirteen months old and had been working with Amy for two months and REACH for six, Walker was imitating our speech. He said "up" and "no more." By the following February, four months after Amy began her gesture study, Walker was using words, using words on his own, abstracting, and using words a lot. The gestures fell away like training wheels. Amy recorded in her notes: "First new NON-IMITATED word: 'apple sauce,' a week later: 'avocado.' A week after that eleven words: 'up,' 'all done,' 'please,' 'bottle,' 'play,' 'ball,' 'down,' 'hat,' 'hop,' 'eyes,' and 'banana.'" By late winter 1998, Amy excitedly reported to me she thought Walker might be learning language at the rate of typical children, an avalanche.

Amy gave a presentation of her work at the end of the semester. Her adviser, Peter Pufall, told me that this was one of the most exciting things that had happened at Smith in years.

One of the elements of Greenspan's "integrated program" that continued to fascinate and perplex me was the notion that skills are wrapped together. With an intellectual gain, invariably a physical one appeared as well. In Amy's log, she noted that as Walker began to speak, his body stiffened less. "When he spoke those words to me," said Amy, "he made dazzling eye contact." By the time Amy returned to Mississippi for the six-week winter break, we knew that Walker was

remarkably intelligent, that he would speak and would speak well—
that he would continue to learn words. In fact, we began to suspect
he might have an extraordinary ability for language.

What we didn't know was whether he would lose the ability.

A significant number of children with autism spectrum disorder, we
knew from research, and from what Dawn had taught us, first show
signs of the disorder when they begin, at about eighteen months, to
regress. As part of the regressive pattern, children lose some or all of the
speech they've already gained. Words start slipping out of their vocabu-
laries, disappearing mysteriously. Sometimes children who regress are
left linguistically with nothing. They might fall mute, might lose a once
easily won ability to understand spoken language. In the whir of work
and car pools and television and voices and trips to the mall, it might
take a while for the adults in a child's life to notice what's happened.

The professionals at REACH called such regression "losing milestones."

Did Walker at that point have autism spectrum disorder?
Greenspan felt you couldn't describe a baby as autistic. He hinted that
such a condition could lead to autism. But could you prevent autism?
Or was it inside the body, like a mine, embedded? No one knew. We
didn't know. All we could do was read the signs: Did Walker look like
a child with autism? Walker was struggling with a body that wouldn't
always do what he needed it to. His senses were still not functioning
well. He looked out of the periphery of his vision. (Peripheral vision
requires less-sophisticated brain functioning—a more atavistic capacity, like instinct, or reflex.) Emotion, which occasionally bloomed on
his face, could just as easily fall away, leaving him blank, retreating,
sucking his thumb, ignoring us. It was as if his emotions were suddenly hidden by a curtain, though our deeper worry was that he
wasn't feeling them at all. Such ambiguity and lost moments, the steps
backward, left us dogged by the specter of potentially lost milestones.
Dawn had no way of telling if Walker belonged to that particular
strain of the disorder that went backward and sometimes couldn't
make it forward again. So little was known about autism and infants.
Regression, the possibility of his slipping away, was always present, a
wolf hovering beyond the hedges.

And perhaps we were seeing it from time to time: Days differed so dramatically one from the next. One day Walker was up, moving and gesturing, laughing, and saying his new words, but then the next he might be congested, dark, worrying his worry beads again, unreachable, sucking at his thumb, lying on the floor as if to look and sit up and crawl were too much for him. REACH reports record that just seven weeks after his appointment with Greenspan, Walker kept engaged and related for a full two hours. The next day, however, his capacity for attention had shifted. He moved back into the shadowy realm, as if he'd been called back to the quiet, to the world within.

With the floor time, he swung his head from side to side less and less, but that winter of 1998 as his muscles grew stronger, he began banging his head with increasing vigor, frequency, and speed on the back of the high chair.

Oddly, he seemed less muted and hidden and more exaggerated in his responses. He brought his arms up into the air and moved them up and down as if he were cheering on a whole football team. The world seemed almost always exciting for him now, and he reveled in it, but it made his body a little crazy.

Still, what was beginning to peek out, and even shine, was a passion for anything we brought his way, delight, and even hunger for knowledge. Walker was growing in awareness.

At times, he was a sponge absorbing the whole of the sea. He absorbed language at a fast clip. It made sense that he'd show a little stress from the taking in of it all, but what we didn't know, couldn't know the answer to was this question: Did the head banging and all the dark brooding and the distancing mean he would always be acting strangely?

When winter break was over, Amy came over and sat with Walker, feeding him in the early evening, watching him throw his head back so hard it had to be painful. Amy often put her hand behind to buffer the blow. She never said anything, but I could see the worry in her eyes, in the subtle wincing. She knew from her research that all children bang their heads, but excessive head banging was not a good thing—if not a technical hallmark of autism, certainly one of its reddest flags. It belonged with a list of self-abusing behaviors she had seen in her time working at the state institution in her hometown in Mississippi. There she had seen people throwing themselves against walls, as if punishing themselves for some crime only they were aware of.

She never told me how much she worried about Walker until years later.

Perhaps she didn't have to. I saw it, and I was doing it myself. There was so much at stake—so much to lose, and yet there were so many moments of triumph in those early months.

He "gestured 'no more' twice today," says my recorded voice on the audiotape. "Gestured 'more' four times." "Gestured 'no more' seven times." "Spoke 'ba-ba' for bottle today." "Used several words today." "He's making eye contact more." "He's laughing more." "He's joyful today." "He said 'cado' today for 'avocado.'" "He says 'Amburger!' 'Amburger!' now all the time."

Ways to Make a Salad

THE RESULTS WERE ALMOST UNCANNY, hard to believe: What they were calling "high affect" (an exciting emotional atmosphere) actually raised Walker's muscle tone. You could see him in that rich give-and-take, growing excited, his back rising like a watered plant stem. The back lengthened, firmed, the arms reached upward. He was ready for fun.

We had been working with REACH for nine months by the time Amy's semester was over.

Walker made full eye contact. His serious, pensive face was beginning to show a sense of humor. He might laugh. Elizabeth and Cliff and I clapped when Walker did well. We clapped when he was interactive. We egged him on to move through the obstacle courses we continued to make—sometimes with tunnels of refrigerator boxes filling the living room. We clapped and cheered when he moved toward the cups he could knock down. We clapped when he retrieved toys from over pillows, from under tables. We learned to play dumb, to expect him to do as much of the work as possible. He knew we were there. He looked back at us while he performed his stunts, loved our appreciation.

There was a peculiar paradox to our experience. Even while everyone worried, even while we talked about some of the scariest possibilities, even while we discussed Walker's stormy digestive system and spent hours every day feeding him—it could feel like the best times. It might almost have been romantic. Cliff and I were often elated, alive, excited. It was as if something sharp had ripped through the everydayness of our lives, cut the haze away. I see Cliff sitting on the floor, chasing Walker around on his hands and knees, laughing, stacking cups, building towers of wooden blocks. I see Elizabeth beginning to laugh with Walker, to occasionally be able to feed him or tease him. The moments of discovery could be shimmering. If Walker was even a little better, we had cause to celebrate.

It was a time of losing old ideas. They fell away. Doing Greenspan's floor time, I was learning the new discoveries of brain development, the very foundations of intelligence. I had studied Western civilization in college and mistakenly believed that the body was somehow inferior to the mind. Yet using Greenspan's developmental approach, I quickly understood that the brain depends on the body for its breadth of knowledge. By moving through space, we integrate with the world, and thus by declaring ourselves a creature in it, we come to know it and can call ourselves intelligent beings. Movement stimulates brain function. Time and again, Arlene went straight to the body and its movements to help stimulate the nerve impulses that build mental pathways. Arlene, for example, when Walker was grabbing toys, often encouraged him to reach not just forward but crossways, "crossing mid-line," as she called it.

"What's so important about crossing mid-line?" I said.

"It connects the two parts of his brain, left and right. If he can reach across his body, he'll better be able to conceptualize an angled line, or a triangle, or one day draw an X, because he's already drawn one, with his body."

Yet still, there were other turns. Evenings, often, I lay in bed at night before Cliff came up, my body humming still with an edgy static from the hours of frantically gesturing and moving and touching and talking and endlessly, endlessly talking and touching—hours of what Greenspan was calling "rapid back and forth." Something just under my skin, and even the humming silence, seemed overwhelming, overbearing, nerve grating. I felt as if it would never dissipate, though there was no need to worry about sleep—sleep would come. What I began to worry about—over the ten or more months we'd been working with Walker—was Cliff. I worried about his coming upstairs. I had in those moments a rocking repulsion to the idea of human contact. I missed Cliff, missed all the kinds of connection we had once so easily enjoyed: humor, and debates and chitchat, scratching each other's backs—the delicacy and explosion that intimacy can be. Yet I couldn't get close to it. I couldn't stand the thought of being touched, even touched by words. I was like the old cat I had in childhood who'd died of liver disease. As he waned, he felt intense hunger but sickened at the sight of food. I sometimes found myself praying that Cliff might decide not to come upstairs at all. *Oh! To be surrounded in nothingness for an entire night!*

As if in answer to my prayer, he often stayed away.

One night I found myself uncontrollably emotional. I came downstairs where he was sitting on the couch and asked him to hold me.

He wouldn't. A shadow had fallen between us. It took me months, maybe even years to understand what had happened to us. I had for so long been assuming that Cliff was rejecting me, hiding out at work, away. He had seemed to me to be distant, evasive, skipping stones over the tops of things. I didn't understand how much like me he really was.

Now I can see the ways that Cliff was hands-on with Walker. He seemed to take a special interest in the advice given to us by Lenore. He followed Walker around the house and tucked his feet into alignment when he was learning to crawl, he kept Walker from arching, when he could, he soothed Walker with his calm, slow, low voice. Like the rest of us, he learned to feed Walker and ask him what his choices were, held him firm in his arms for hours every week. Yet why hadn't all his work added up for me? His focus on money, on moving, and the mere fact of his being gone at work ten hours a day seemed an affront, a way of escaping. Now, he admits that perhaps he was hiding out at times. What I hadn't understood—it occurred to me only recently, now five years later—was that I, too, was hiding out in my own way. I had rejected Cliff, left him months before, leaving a void. *And anyway, even if I suddenly did muster something to offer, what did he have left to give?*

One day a neighbor yelled at us about recyclables stacking up on our back porch.

"Why is she so angry?" I said to Arlene.

"Anger can mask sadness," said Arlene.

By the spring of 1998, when Walker was a year and three months old, Amy was no longer studying Walker for school; her thesis was due and she was applying to graduate school. "I realize that I've grown with Walker," she said, her eyes wet with elation. She would apply to several graduate schools in child development, to do studies on babies. When she began coming less and less often, we understood. Still, we didn't know how we could keep up Walker's intensive schedule.

Dawn and Greenspan both insisted that Walker was doing well because of all the work. Stopping could mean loss, regression. Greenspan was adamant that we had only begun.

There was nothing to do but write the director of REACH a letter outlining our needs. Cliff and I stayed up late one night composing the request. The next day, when I touched it up and printed it out, four professionals from REACH happened to simultaneously be at the house to work with Walker or observe him: Dawn, Arlene, Vicki the nutritionist, and a visiting occupational therapist. I invited them to read the letter.

"You've done it!" "Beautiful, Pat." "Elegantly argued!" They cheered me on to open the door as if it were a starting gate, to go and mail the letter. Still, I don't think any of them were surprised when the reply came back a rejection: REACH could offer no extra services for Walker. He was already receiving more services from REACH than they had ever offered a child.

Still, though Dawn worked to hide it, I could tell she was angry, frustrated. We had an opportunity, a great one, of reaching Walker. She knew that Greenspan's prescription, as unreasonable as it may have sounded, was accurate. Eight to ten sessions a day was our only chance. She also knew from research that as much as ten hours a week of intensive therapy could be ineffective, leaving kids as lost as if they'd had none.

"We need a diagnosis, don't we, Dawn?" I said. "One mother told me it's the only way the state will help with therapy."

She agreed.

"But can we get one?" I asked.

"I don't know who would diagnose a child as young as Walker. We both agreed that a diagnosis from Greenspan might be hard to come by. Not because he lacked courage, but he admirably preferred to observe children as individuals rather than use labels—not because labels were damning, but because they weren't accurate, weren't clinically useful. Trying to reduce Greenspan's assessment down to the word "autism" was like trying to get Cliff to say, "It's just a building. All buildings are alike."

To Greenspan, Walker was a complex human being, as we all are, with a web of auditory and visual and tactile and vestibular strengths and weaknesses.

Arlene insisted that autism was a "trash can" word. It was a receptacle for putting in a lot of different things, many mysteries.

I called Greenspan's office on a Wednesday. His assistant told me to call him at midnight the following night.

"Midnight?"

"Yes," she said cheerfully. "He often stays up until 4 A.M."

By the time I reached Greenspan on the phone, it was nearly 1 A.M. Still, he was generous with his time. Patient. Spoke to me at length. He reiterated that he was ill at ease with such words, but he felt that REACH needed to understand. He felt that Walker, being so young, must be described as having "pre-autistic tendencies." Almost no one diagnosed babies.

He sent a fax to REACH the next day.

Darleen Corbett, REACH's director, called a meeting to take place in our living room. Dawn, Arlene, Darleen, and Claire, REACH's clinical supervisor, and Cliff and I all sat on chairs arranged in a circle. Darleen sat with a legal pad on her lap and spoke. "We have decided, on the basis of Dr. Greenspan's assessment, to increase Walker's therapy time. We will give Walker eight hours of therapy time from Dawn and Arlene combined." Cliff and I looked at each other, smiled. Nothing had prepared us for what was to follow. In a decision unprecedented at REACH, they had been able to access funds from the Massachusetts Department of Public Health to pay a tutor to come ten hours a week to work with Walker.

REACH sent a new social worker: Debbie Roth-Howe. She came with a list of phone calls she had made, trying to help find funding assistance for someone else to help do floor time. She went back to the REACH office and made scores of other calls—to doctors, to community assistance agencies. One day, while Walker slept, Debbie was sitting at the kitchen table. I told her I didn't know how I would be able to pick Elizabeth up from school. There were appointments for Walker. I was unwittingly double-booking. I'd stood up friends, stood up professionals. I was under an avalanche; simply too much to do. She suggested that I call some neighbors. I turned to hide my emotion, and when I turned back, Debbie's eyes were welled up. She took the cup of tea I handed her, insisting I shouldn't be making her tea, and told me the story of her own fall into the snake pit: a sudden call from the elementary school, her son had not been able to stand at lunchtime to go to the cafeteria. He began saying things that didn't make sense, not recognizing his teacher. There was the wheelchair, the emergency room, learning of his brain tumor, receiving meals from neighbors.

"Is he all right?"

"Yes. Now. For now," said Debbie. "But listen to my idea. I have a teenage daughter, Leah. She needs to do a community service project." She proposed that Debbie and Leah come on Sundays. "Leah could play with Elizabeth while I do floor time with Walker."

"Sundays? You want to give up your Sundays? You can't possibly."

"But we can. As I said, Leah could do this for her community service project."

I turned away and pulled the towel hanging off the stove.

Debbie filled the silence with talk. She wanted Cliff and me to have some time alone. She tried to convince me to let her ask the Unitarian Society if they would help us with meals. I shook my head no, with my face in the towel. Debbie said, "You must learn to take help. It's your time."

When I looked up, her eyes were wet, but smiling.

Two nights later I was scheduled to meet a friend for dinner. I hadn't been out in a long time, but Cliff came home early to watch the children. My friend, whom I'll call Lauri, and I met at Café Amanouz, a Middle Eastern restaurant. We had the Royal Feast, with hummus and falafel and tabouli and marinated eggplant, and I told her that the social worker wanted us to accept meals from the Unitarian Society. We'd been talking animatedly, face-to-face, scooping up hummus with pita bread triangles like people at a cocktail party, when her face fell, registering disgust. "I would never accept meals from other people," she said. I tried to explain why it was necessary. We weren't poor of course, but we were poor in time.

"My neighbor says she doesn't believe I should either," I said. "She insists it only takes ten minutes to broil a piece of fish, but what she doesn't see is how long it takes to bring that fish to the table—to the table with everything else." She hadn't included the vegetables and potatoes—the shopping, the planning, the boiling, the broiling, the serving, the washing. The what of the next meal. Given how often we ate and how diverse our needs were—sometimes I was preparing three separate meals—it could take an average of two hours a day to keep my family in dinners, maybe more. (Four floor times a day.) Add that to answering the phone, arranging playdates for Elizabeth, giving Elizabeth time, cleaning the rest of the house, doing research on Walker's problem, calling doctors, going to appointments, and the whole day would be gone. How to clear the way?

"What about the grandparents? Couldn't they do some of this?"

"Mine are in California. Cliff's want to help, but floor time is athletic work. I know they'll help with whatever they can—some meals. But how much can we ask?"

"Tell me, wouldn't you accept meals yourself, Lauri?" I asked. "I mean, in a crisis."

Lauri said, "No." She wouldn't.

When we were saying good-bye, she hugged me and asked what she could do. I couldn't think of anything but what the social worker told me I should do. "The only thing that comes to mind is . . ." But no, I remembered her disgust. I could see her weighing the possibility of making meals for us. Could she even manage the logistics—a busy mother with a part-time job and two demanding children, a house? . . . No, clearly she didn't think she could do it. I knew I wouldn't have been able to cook for someone else myself.

That meeting was the last time I saw Lauri for over a year.

And so, the meals began to come. Twice a week the doorbell rang. Women arrived at the door—housewives with casseroles, women in skirts and coats on their way home from work stopped by with something they'd made and frozen, standing in the entryway explaining how to heat it. There were vegetarian casseroles, quiches. There were baguettes and peasant breads, and dinner rolls, chicken breasts, and stuffed shells, tabouli salads and macaroni salads. At times we didn't have time to talk and chat (one conversation might represent half a floor time, or time away from Elizabeth, or I was on the phone with some professional). Still, the meals came. Women came in leather jackets. Women with nose rings. Women in coats who seemed to be coming by on their way to dropping the kids off at school. Women in jeans. Women with children leaning on their knees. Elizabeth and I were fascinated to see all the ways salads were presented, salads with almonds, salads with oranges, salads with tomatoes wrapped separately. Croutons wrapped separately. One package included a bottle of salad dressing.

A woman pulled up in a pickup truck. She was large, with dyed blonde spiked hair and several nose rings, and wore a motorcycle jacket. She held a large box on her hip and passed it to me casually. I could tell she didn't want me to feel embarrassed. Not a word. But when I opened the box, I found an expensive take-out meal for four, two candles, and a pack of matches inside.

The Ladder

EVERY TIME WE THOUGHT we had the hang of floor time, it changed. It had to. It was about growing, about moving up the ladder. The idea was to gain a rung at a time. Cliff and I knew next to nothing about child development. I don't know what we would have done if Dawn and Arlene had not been there to present the next level.

Arlene and Dawn both understood Greenspan's concepts far better than Cliff and I did. Arlene and Dawn continued to do research. They attended conferences and stayed on top of new developments in the field of child development, but if you took a peek into the dining room window, you would never have guessed that they were doing anything but having fun with a kid.

Still, that didn't mean it was easy.

Dawn explained that she was working from a model Greenspan had created, his map of emotional development in children called "the developmental ladder," which has discrete stepping-stones, or as he called them, "The Six Milestones."

She explained that each of these milestones builds on their fore-runners. A human will need to master each fully before being able to successfully move on to the next phase. It is the work of becoming an emotionally healthy individual. She pulled a paper out of her notebook and handed it to me. I posted it in my kitchen, where it remained for years, until I took it down to write this book. Following is my abbreviated version of Greenspan's developmental ladder:

Milestone 1: Self-Regulation and Interest in the World
Amidst the hubbub of the whirling, turning, noisy world, a child must learn to stay calm and pay attention.
Milestone 2: Intimacy
Baby is in love. Nothing in a baby's world comes to be more significant than the chosen caregivers.
Milestone 3: Two-Way Communication
Baby realizes that "what I do matters." He begins to open and close circles, and enjoys caregivers' reactions.
Milestone 4: Complex Communication
Baby learns that by using gestures he can show feelings and interact with the world to get his needs and wishes met.
Milestone 5: Emotional Ideas
The child begins to imagine worlds that do not exist. The beginning of play. He might feed a baby a bottle, or use a bit of dialogue.
Milestone 6: Emotional Thinking
A child begins to act out stories—gestures, motions, words—they grow complex, are no longer isolated, but connected into stories, scenarios, worlds. The child puts on a play for a stuffed animal. He stages a long rescue scene. This is the beginning of all higher order thinking.

Dawn said that "keeping the interaction one-on-one limited Walker's stimulation while giving him maximum awareness, maximum emotional engagement," but that first milestone—keeping calm when being stimulated, even though we had reached it—was a tenuous rung in the ladder. Still, Walker's desire would tell him and us what he was ready for and what not. It may be the fundamental truth of all human development and decisionmaking: that we know in our guts what we need.

By January, when we had been working with REACH for eight months, Amy was home in Mississippi and would only be coming once or twice a week when she returned. Walker, by that time, had

dropped his gesturing for "all done" and "more." Words were coming so fast he no longer needed them.

Still, while his peers were toddling and walking around the house,
Walker was merely crawling and just learning to pull himself up to
standing with our support. He was still disoriented by touch and by
being held, and though his appetite for it was great, his ability to be
engaged with people for extended amounts of time was shaky. He was
also loving people, but I still wondered about Arlene's early question:
"Does he notice a difference between you and other people?" Dawn
had told us that Walker would need to master each phase of the
developmental ladder. Yet if at his fundamental core, he was always
struggling with level one, to stay calm, how could differences matter?

———

REACH sent Lisa LeBeau to be Walker's ten-hour-per-week tutor.
Lisa, a warm and friendly woman with dark brown hair and piercing
eyes, held a teaching credential in special education. Since she had left
her full-time teaching job and was in the process of sending out
résumés, she agreed to come every weekday afternoon from 4 to 6 to
feed Walker and socialize with him; she would take over where Amy
left off. Dawn provided Lisa with a list of goals and teaching strategies:

GOALS FOR WALKER

1. To become more emotionally expressive (animated facial
   expressions, range of emotions)
2. To demonstrate complex non-verbal problem solving (bring a
   book to dad, place on lap, vocalize to get it read)
3. To be capable of rapid back-and-forth interactions
4. To be capable of mental representation (emotional symbols)
   pretend play or words that convey emotional intent
5. To imitate words and sounds
6. To build bridges between emotional ideas (me mad because you
   leaving now)

Lisa kept a list of teaching strategies on the back of her daily log sheets. They read:

STRATEGIES

1. Build on Walker's natural interest, draw toy into yourself so that emphasis is on relating, rather than on the toy itself
2. Use animated facial expressions, enthusiasm, and playfulness
3. Exercise Walker's initiative, try not to direct him too much
4. Try to sometimes play music in background (to teach him to interact while distractions present)
5. Keep constant flow of communication going
6. Entice Walker with opportunities to practice motor skills (such as pulling to stand)

From January into the springtime, evening after evening, five days a week, Lisa sat in the kitchen feeding Walker avocados, applesauce, chicken, hamburger. Often I was there in the room with her and Walker listening to them chat and play and eat—or try to eat—while I was frying onions, cutting vegetables, and tossing salads. We tried to keep Elizabeth and Walker separate, particularly when Walker was eating. She was perky, happy, ready for games, and excited by Walker's new ability to react to her, excited that he had something to give. He grew so excited to be with her, he couldn't keep his food down.

One of the clichés of early childhood is that kids don't eat their food so much as paint with it. They are all aspiring abstract expressionists. The way Walker ate, however, was beyond art or self-expression. If he was painting, he was more like a house painter, covering surfaces with sustained thoroughness. If he was eating avocado, for example, green slime covered his entire face and arms. Goo was smeared all across the base and frame of his broad tray, slime was dripped onto the legs of his high chair, clumps gathered in globs all over the floor. Arlene joked that we needed a dog to keep the floor clean. Lisa quickly learned to wear jeans and sweatshirts to work. Walker was messy not necessarily by choice, but because his motor skills were rudimentary. There was a sensory explanation as well. Walker was not able to feel the food on his cheeks. In this regard he was hyposensitive, undersensitive.

Yet what Walker may have been lacking in manners, he made up for in joyful interaction. It sometimes took two hours for him to eat. During her sessions, Lisa was gentle, enthusiastic, loving, affectionate—everything one could hope for in a sensibility to help dispose a baby toward loving. Walker was getting under her skin, making it into her dreams. Lisa told me she had a dream that she had her own baby son. They'd laugh together, his face trained on her eyes; he was learning to be funny, charming. He was learning to ask for what he wanted. Walker was climbing over level two. Perhaps even nearing three.

Dawn came weekly to supervise Lisa, to keep her goals growing as Walker grew. That winter, Dawn, Arlene, Lisa, Cliff, and I began to notice various emotions. One day in late January, Dawn refused to give Walker an electronic piano that was in her bag. He grew angry; we had never seen anger before. Walker was not just showing the "positive" (as Arlene had once noted). We saw more quality to Walker's emotion. Laughter continued to grow more joyful, less maniacal. Inflection grew in Walker's voice, the flat tones were growing more fluid, more expressive.

After Lisa had been working with us for a month or so, I called to ask her a question. When Walker realized who I was talking to, he grew animated, crawled into the kitchen, and cried out "Sa!" "Sa!"

"I heard that," said Lisa. "Is he saying my name?"

"I think he is! My God, Lisa," I said. "He misses you." *Had he ever missed anyone before?*

By late February, we saw other emotions: surprise, sadness, irritation.

Walker strengthened his ability to pull himself up to stand. By March, Lisa and Cliff and I walked him around the house, holding his hands for support.

We enjoyed the same vertical learning curve in Walker's progress that Amy had recorded. He seemed to have mastered level two, intimacy. Lisa's reports were glowing, filled with large words written across the page: "Doing well today!" "Very interactive." "He learns almost any word you use!" "Learning fast!"

To Paradise Pond

FOR MONTHS WE had been keeping Walker inside the house as much as we could. He came with me to bring Elizabeth home from school, occasionally visited his grandparents, went for doctors' appointments, and had taken an occasional walk around the car in the driveway, yet I hadn't liked to take him out. The winter was bracing. Who knew what effect zero-degree weather would have on an immature nervous system. It was certainly trying for mine. I didn't go out much myself in it. Anyway, taking him outside was disturbing. I could feel him disappearing. Lost moments, him slipping into shadow. In the car he looked blankly out the windows. Clearly, the movement and all the light were still too much for him.

It had been months since Arlene suggested our first walk around the car. At the end of February, Arlene said, "Why don't we take him for a walk?"

"You mean outside?" I said. "You mean, around the car?"

"Maybe further," she said. "It's almost spring. It might even be forty-five degrees outside."

"Do you mean a long walk?"

"Yes," she said. "Perhaps he can handle it."

I lumbered up the basement stairs with the stroller. It was way in the back now. I hadn't thought I would ever use it again. We walked to the nearby campus, past the college president's mansion, through the gardens, usually engulfed in white in February, which showed patches of earth among the small heaps of snow, buds of crocuses beginning to emerge. We made our way beyond the gardens to the crest of the hill overlooking Paradise Pond. The water was a light gray, still covered with a thin sheet of ice, yet from below shimmered a slight luminous rainbow. The clouds were bright white in the foreground, yet black storm clouds behind them cast a purple hue on the mountains beyond. I looked at the pond and held Walker up into the air. "Do you see the water, Walker? That's ice there. And up there, the clouds. And over there at the end—that orange line that looks like it's holding the water down. It's a Japanese bridge. There's a waterfall, but we can't see it." Walker was looking out toward the lake, smiling and moving his arms excitedly. Yet there was no knowing what he saw or thought.

When we arrived home, I asked Arlene, "What do you think he saw?"

"I assume," she said, "he saw what we saw."

The walk was a success.

From that day on, Lisa began taking Walker outside. They took the same path Arlene and I had taken, passing the president's house. They stopped and gazed at the gardens and the large pond, crossed the road to a small frog pond filled with carp, set next to the greenhouse. They began calling it "the fishy pond." Walker began calling Lisa "My Lisa."

Pretend tea parties, hiding games with blocks, looking at spring flowers together, sorting shapes, staring into our faces, showing fascination without reactions: such was the stuff of our work together— yet now it seemed more like play. I was actually beginning to enjoy floor time.

That March, we took a day off and drove Walker to a medical appointment in Vermont. The next day, Lisa came over to work with Walker. As she appeared in the doorway of the dining room that afternoon, he looked up at her and wept. "Mommy, I want Mommy."

I came around the corner and Lisa and I stared at each other; we found ourselves looking back at Walker, then back to each other. Suddenly we were both smiling and broke out laughing. Seeing us laugh made Walker cry more. But we continued to laugh.

Walker was sixteen months old, and he had never cried for me in his life.

Walker cared if I left the room.

As Walker began to be more and more connected to the events of the day, he began bumping his head inadvertently on tables. It was that way with him—heaven's feast and hell's picnic at the very same moment; we couldn't separate the sense that he was going backward and going forward at once. Was his new emotional awareness bringing a backlash—imbalance? His excitement levels rose, suddenly a once-sleepy baby now seemed impossible to settle down. He was grabbing at things and throwing them down. He was laughing sometimes and banging his head against the high chair more often so it rocked dangerously. It was hard to enter that level of excitement, hard to slow him down to make eye contact and get him to listen. He would crawl away or take a handful of plastic building blocks and arbitrarily throw them. Was he trying to shake us off? Increased intimacy seemed to me to be making him more sensitive. One day I was in the kitchen putting groceries away. I crumpled a plastic bag. He screamed out in pain yet crawled into the kitchen for me to comfort him. *What a strange instinct! To come into the room with the frightful sound. Should we be relieved he wanted to come to me? Or saddened he seemed even more sensitive to this sound than before?*

One day in March, Dawn came over with some bad news: Her superiors at REACH had decided to discontinue Lisa's services. They also planned to remove one of Dawn's days from Walker's schedule. Walker was simply doing too well.

They would be withdrawing twelve hours a week of help. I leaned against the stove. Dawn stood on the other side of the kitchen table, smiling awkwardly, sheepishly. "I didn't expect this," she admitted. Dawn was in a difficult position. To admit it was a bad plan would be to suggest that her superiors were at fault. I'm still not sure what she thought, but she didn't seem comfortable with the decision.

"Do you realize what this means? I have to keep doing it mostly by myself?" I said, turning away.

Debbie Roth-Howe, our REACH social worker, came to help me try to put in place a plan to keep Lisa on. She would call some local social service agencies, find some funding.

In the end, she was able to keep Lisa with us for a short time. REACH would phase Lisa out; she would be able to come a couple of days a week for the next two months, and then she would be gone.

"Doesn't REACH understand?" I said to Debbie. "Just because someone's doing better, you don't take away their medicine."

Her eyes were wet again.

⌒

"Remind me again," I said to Arlene one day. Walker was across the room from me, laughing and looking me straight in the eye (but maddeningly far away). "Why doesn't he like my body?" My nagging fear, in spite of everything I knew about Walker's sensory processing, was that Walker might have some innate repulsion to me, but her answer was simple. "It's no mystery. Bodies move too much. Think of it," she said. "A car is predictable, it goes forward and backward, and makes a few broad turns, but no machine, object, or toy comes anywhere close to being as unpredictable as a human being. Never mind people and the choices they make. There is nothing more erratic than the human body. Imagine you're sitting next to someone. You don't know what she'll do from one second to the next. Every movement is different— arms flying around to express a point, legs moving. In some ways that knobby toy that bounces erratically around the floor is easier for Walker to get his mind around than a human body."

She thought for a moment. "He needs to get acquainted with your body," Arlene added.

I sat very still in the middle of the rug and did as Arlene instructed me to do, not to move much. She wrapped Walker's legs around my waist. I sat breathless, hoping I would be acceptable, tolerable in that state.

Within the instant, he was arching backward as if he were profoundly uncomfortable.

"Being close to you disorganizes him," she said.

"But I'm not moving."

"You're breathing. You still have skin."

"Skin," I said, through my teeth. "The most tactilely stimulating substance known to mankind."

She laughed.

Over the next few days I held Walker, rocked him, let him lie in my arms in the crescent moon shape; he seemed to like it. Other times, he became very squirmy, muscles all seeming to want to shoot off in different directions. I invited him to come toward me, enticed him to come toward me. One day, as I was practicing, Arlene stood and put Walker's legs around her waist, positioning his hands around her neck. "This is a game I used to play with my daughter, Jenna: 'Be a baby koala!' I'd say, opening my arms, letting her hang from me like a monkey. Jenna used to hold on furiously, as if she were velcroed on." Arlene let go of Walker. He slipped immediately, couldn't or wouldn't stay velcroed. She caught him halfway to the ground. I wondered if he had lacked the strength to support his own weight (his muscles seeming to turn to soup), but I also had the profound impression that something else was at play. It seemed as if Arlene had almost pulled the plug on Walker's awareness.

I picked him up, wrapped his legs around my waist, his thin arms around my neck. The hold wasn't what I would even call weak; It wasn't a hold at all.

"He doesn't understand your body yet."

"But why doesn't he?"

"Because he doesn't understand his own."

For months after that day, I encouraged Walker to hang on me any chance he had, to wrap his hands around me, to cling to me. He worked hard, harder than I ever imagined a baby could work. He tried to hold on, and eventually his grasp tightened. Over time, he learned to hold on a bit with his arms. When we invited his legs to join in, the arms let go. But eventually they both began clinging together. Remembering Arlene's words—that it was the unpredictability that was challenging to Walker's motor system—we often threw in odd movements, feigning a fall, stumbling forward, leaning precariously backward, moving quickly and then slowly. If humans were unpredictable, Walker would need to meet that unpredictability head on, to know and relate to other people one day with agility, alacrity, insight, flexibility. Indeed, the task for most infants is learning about how to be human in all of its unpredictability, to hold on when someone moves unexpectedly, to laugh when you almost fall, to greet unpredictability with energy and joy.

Flexibility was the kind of thing you learned in your bones. Walker would not learn it from his bones—or from his muscles as they were. His sense of himself in space was weak, disorienting; adjustments would need to be made slowly. Yet we wanted him to be able to make quick adjustments and snap decision all the days of his life. He would need them the first day of kindergarten, he would need them meeting kids, he would need them when the teacher switched from art to circle time, he would need them hanging out in the school yard. He would need them if he was ever to play soccer, chase a girl, order food in a restaurant. I couldn't resist projecting further: He would need flexibility if he was ever to drive a car on a road, throw a baseball across a field. I dared to think further: He would need flexibility for job interviews (when the prospective boss would look at his every movement to gather information about him, would discern if he really was on the same wavelength). He would need it if he was ever to woo a girl, or make love. Body speaks a language as much as voice and intonation. Playing "Baby Koala," we understood we were teaching Walker a language.

Exotic Poisons,
Unusual Connections

In 1996, a child with autism and gastroenterological complaints underwent a routine exploratory GI procedure. Within days of the procedure, remarkably, the child, who had not spoken for two years, could speak. The parents discovered that their child had been given a hormone called Secretin, which was originally designed to improve absorption to catalyze the diagnostic test. The parents struggled with the medical community to receive legitimate acknowledgment that it was indeed Secretin that had helped their son. Now, a doctor was giving their son Secretin for unprecedented purposes: so that a child who had looked away might look, so that a child who had spent months in silence could talk.

We were beginning to learn that the patterns we were seeing were not particular to Walker. Some people were noticing a connection between GI problems and the autism spectrum population. At Margaret Bauman's lecture, Sidney Baker, a doctor now specializing in autism spectrum disorder, stood up at Bauman's invitation and began speaking about the connections between GI dysfunction and neurological dysfunction. He excitedly talked of the queer substances found in the urine of children with autism—one of them an exotic poison found in the Amazon taken from the unlikeliest of places, the skin of frogs, which aborigines used for poisonous darts; another, the residue found in wine barrels after fermentation. Some people theorized that the bodies of these children do not metabolize food properly, allowing chemicals to slip into the bloodstream and make their way to the brain as opiates. Yeast might be one of the culprits. "Removing wheat and dairy can be an effective treatment," said Baker.

Dawn was interested in Secretin, but cautious. She warned us against believing in miracle cures, which surfaced occasionally in the field but often proved limited. Yet what fascinated me and relieved me when I researched the theories about poor absorption was that some-one was finally asserting that there was a connection between GI distress and autism spectrum disorder.

The disorder was so multifaceted that it was difficult to find one expert who could help us with all concerns: Ground, however, was being broken on several fronts, and we along with other parents were scrambling to find answers. It seemed the answers came from disparate corners, different camps, conflicting sciences.

Shortly after Walker turned two, Cliff and I took him to see the gas-troenterologist once again. We waited interminably in the waiting room in the same unearthly silence, waited with Walker again in the examining room for another twenty minutes. When the doctor entered, I was surprised that he was fluent in English. For some rea-son, I had remembered him as having a thick accent. Yet when he began speaking, I realized why I'd made the mistake; he was hard to talk to. Our words seemed to hover just in front of him and fall away. He didn't answer a question he didn't like, or he mumbled an answer, vague and dismissive. When Cliff mentioned the idea that wheat and dairy might be detrimental to those with autism spectrum disorder, he grew visibly angry. I mentioned a book I was reading called *Biological Treatments for Autism and PDD,* which described the benefits of removing wheat and dairy for kids like Walker. He said, "There's no scientific proof to that notion at all. You give him anything you can. He's too small and frail for you to limit his diet."

"But isn't it possible that allergens are responsible for Walker's frailty, for his behavior, his poor absorption?" asked Cliff.

The doctor looked at me skeptically. "Are you telling me you want me to give him foods we know he's allergic to?" I asked.

"His reactions are minimal," he said. "Feed him whatever you like. He's got to gain weight."

Cliff and I nodded to each other and left, deciding to consult an allergist.

When we finally did find the time to go to another appointment, we found ourselves waiting in the reception room for forty-five minutes and in an examining room for another thirty. Walker sat on another high examining table fidgeting and grabbing at us, going wild with boredom, as any child would. Next door, the allergist was laughing and chatting heartily with someone. He finally came into the room, heard our story, studied Walker's records, looked at Walker, and visibly upset, began lecturing us.

"This kid is too thin. You'd better expand his diet!"

"We've been keeping him from wheat and dairy intentionally," said Cliff.

"You're endangering his life," said the allergist, his voice rising.

"Wait a minute," said Cliff, growing red. "You know next to nothing about us or our child. You know nothing about how far we've come. You stand there and tell us we're threatening his health?" I was fearful they might come to blows.

The doctor backed off, and Cliff calmed down.

On the way home, Cliff said, "That was a disaster."

"You're not kidding," I seconded.

"That's not what I mean," he said. His tone was clipped.

"What did you mean?"

"Us."

"Us?"

"The doctor may have been right. We just haven't been approaching this diet problem with a plan."

"No plan! You've got to be kidding! I've been reading, I've been researching. We're not supposed to give him wheat and dairy. Am I wrong?"

"We need to give foods a fair try."

"I have. So you do think I'm wrong!"

"We're just not approaching this scientifically."

"Fine, you try something!"

Through Another Door in the Wall

BY THE TIME WE WENT to Greenspan's office for a second visit, Walker, at twenty months old, was in many respects a different child. In the nine months since we had first seen Greenspan, Walker's face had softened to reveal dimples. He smiled and laughed often, seemed a passionate child, affectionate, cuddly. We noticed a growing quality of emotions—surprise, sadness, irritation. He used many words spontaneously, could identify verbs by observing pictures, recognized all of his friends and family in photographs. He had improved his tone, improved his speed of motor planning. He was crawling up onto furniture. He was beginning to support his weight on wobbly feet, with help. He was less sensitive on walks, and he could focus more.

Yet at a year and eight months old, a time when most kids were flying throughout the house, able to cope with whatever sensory assaults the world wanted to throw out there—the circus, parties, crowds, malls—Walker was still a very sensitive child who, though he was learning, couldn't walk. He was still weak, though no one could fully explain why. In the middle of play, he might inexplicably lie down from fatigue and suck his thumb vigorously. When he sat, his back curved and shoulders drooped, leaving him in a slouch, a sign of his low tone. We still had to work to win his attention. If we didn't work at it, he might miss us. His levels of attention were erratic, often dependent on the skill of the adult playing with him, but we were hopeful Greenspan would see the progress we'd made—hopeful that he would agree that REACH had judged correctly that Walker needed no more intensive services. Especially now that Lisa was gone, I lived for this hope.

Cliff went to the floor first in Greenspan's office. He sat in front of Walker, but he was somehow stuck, couldn't get "inside" the play. He was trying to get into the clubhouse, but Walker wouldn't let him in. Still, Cliff sat close to Walker, giving all he had, putting his voice down close near Walker as he played with plastic pots and pans, talking constantly, but the talking was only occasionally getting through. Cliff was more of a narrator, a sports commentator talking about Walker's play: "Oh, so now you're cooking. Must be hamburger," he said enthusiastically, while Walker pretended to stir something in a toy pan.

Greenspan sat behind the camera watching, quiet for several minutes.

"What you need to do here," the voice finally said from behind the camera, "is think of the challenge. You're playing to his weakest trait instead of playing to his strengths. What you need to do is challenge him to be more assertive, get him talking, looking, and doing all at once."

Greenspan put his voice into high range, raised his excitement level, and said, "Where do you want that one?"

Cliff looked pensive for a moment. "Challenge," he repeated to himself. "So I need to do things so he'll want to come and get it?"

"Keep him constantly talking, responding," added Greenspan.

Walker was holding a doll. Cliff pulled it away and said, "What's this?"

Walker looked up at Cliff and answered, "Doll."

"You want her?" He jiggled the doll up in the air, higher and higher, raising his voice into an elevated octave.

It was as if we'd been attending a solo performance and suddenly an orchestra rushed on stage to join Walker—only the players were all Walker and his abilities. With that single exchange, Walker changed his tone, his facial expressions. No longer slouching downward, he firmed up his back, lifted his hands, grabbed the doll, smiled, made eye contact with Cliff, and spoke, saying, "Yes, yes, yes," all at once.

"See, before," said Greenspan, "what you were doing was *not challenging* him. It would be like somebody asking you to xerox a hundred pieces of paper, instead of asking you to participate in a debate.

Cliff responded, "I feel like it's like asking someone with no arms to xerox papers."

"If you have that attitude, it's not going to help him."

Now it was my turn. I jumped down onto the oriental rug, no longer afraid of the string, which had so beguiled Walker nine months before. I was eager to show what I could do. I'd been doing floor time for a year now, every day for hours. I thought I knew how to keep Walker going, was eager to show what I could do. I raised my energy, my excitement, revved as high as I could, moved into the Mickey Mouse falsetto, took the truck, and gave it to Walker.

"Wait," said the voice behind the camera. "Why did you do that, Mom?" (Four seconds on the floor and I'd already fouled.) "Why did you put it so close?" Greenspan was bemused, but insistent. I smiled, casually said okay, but I was nervous. Suddenly, I couldn't bear the scrutiny.

Greenspan gently explained that Cliff and I needed to be careful of our attitudes. "You see," he said, "children with special needs are always having things done for them. You've got to watch yourself. You want *him* to do the work. You don't want to be telling me or him that you don't think he can do it. He can. Pull the car away," he directed. "The way you can help him here is with your affect." I placed the car on the oriental rug between us. "Farther!" he called out. "Challenge him. Put it in a garage!"

I quickly backed up against a pile of toys near the wall and tucked the car under a plastic bridge, leaped to my knees, and called out like a barker at a county fair, "Get the truck from my garage! Come on, get it from my garage!"

Walker raced across the room and grabbed the truck, turned and put it in front of me. I looked up at Greenspan. Walker had crawled faster, and with more agility than I had ever seen him crawl. I was stunned. I looked up at the face behind the camera, proud of Walker, yet an inexplicable exhaustion came over me. Perhaps because Greenspan had made me work so hard that moment, and there was the tension of being judged.

But the voice behind the camera came right back: "Keep going. Send it back, send it back," he directed, and then added, laughing, "This isn't a one-response class! Tell him it's coming back!" I thrust the car back to Walker. At first it landed a foot from him. Experience told me that Walker might not be inspired to play if the toy weren't direct-ly in front of him. He paused for a moment.

Greenspan raised his voice into a high playful octave and prompt-ed me: "There's the car, buddy, there's the car. Come on, send it back."

I followed suit. "Give me the truck. Give it here." I said energeti-cally, urgently, like a cartoon character in desperate need of trans-portation.

Walker raced to the car and threw it back.

I was ready to go home, but Greenspan pressed us to do more. We did. "Why don't you hide a toy and ask him to look for it?" asked Greenspan jauntily. I hid a car when Walker wasn't looking—put it into a shoe and shoved it under the rug.

"Can you find the car?" I said. "Can you find it?" Walker began looking around the room. He crawled a few steps and stopped. "Can you find it, can you?" I squeaked. But I had lost his attention. Walker was sitting very close to the bump in the rug, a huge bump. Yet he saw nothing. *Arlene said she assumed he saw what we saw, yet he clearly doesn't. Not exactly what we see,* I thought. I wasn't sure what not seeing the bump meant to Greenspan, especially since he was still suggesting we up the ante.

"Why don't you have him hide a toy on you," he suggested.

"What?"

His voice rose to the Mickey Mouse high again. "Say: Hide the car from Mommy. Hide the car from Mommy." (*How could he expect a one-and-a-half-year-old to play such a game? Why not just break out the chessboard?*) Finally, in response to my constant high-pitched pleas that Walker hide something for me to find, he began circling into a cor-ner, disoriented and dizzied.

"Actually picking up on the idea that he needed to put the car someplace where you couldn't find it would be difficult for any child Walker's age," said Greenspan.

Why did we do it then? I wanted to say! Yet as he spoke about Walker's motor system, somehow something clicked. I got it. Greenspan was forcing forward, ever forward, probing for strengths, pressing for interaction, pushing beyond a child's level of mastery, *even beyond what might be expected for any child that age.* The point was always to expand the envelope, to search for strengths and make them pull their weight and more, to set new standards on all fronts. He wasn't being a bully (wasn't bullying Walker, at least). He was more like the driven coach sitting at the front of the raft as it makes its way down thunderous rapids. Everyone was going to have to do his share. Strengths were going to have to do double duty. Weaknesses were going to have to pitch in and lean forward. It wasn't enough that Walker could do fifteen circles of communication in a row, Greenspan said he wanted Walker to be able to do thirty or forty. It wasn't enough that Walker was in some ways "bright, possibly even gifted"; Walker needed to bring other skills up to the mark, because one system would, or could, bring down all the rest.

It wasn't enough that Walker was a cognitive Titan; if we didn't improve visual spatial perceptions, his conceptual skills might easily be diminished.

Language might be good, but Walker's challenged physical abilities might weaken his spatial reasoning, could even affect language itself.

Greenspan's mandate was what Lenore and Arlene had taught us months before: The point was always to integrate every action. "If you want to improve one system, go in through another," he said. "If you want Walker to learn a word, you must use the body to teach it."

"Remember," he continued, "it's by moving that we come to understand space. You understand concepts by looking and doing at the same time, not by reading."

The message was clear, spelled out in lists of how many floor time sessions per day (eight to ten, as many as before), with added directives: peer playdates, several a week; four, to be exact. Greenspan wasn't lowering the bar. He was raising it.

For the months between June 1998 and April 1999, from the time that Walker was twenty months old to thirty months old (when we would visit Greenspan again), we saw Walker ride a roller coaster of ups and downs. He grew in his tolerance for our constant back-and-forth play, for what Dawn and Greenspan called "circles of communication," and even began to approach us himself. He had a charming little habit of saying everyone's name after he addressed them ("It's a bunny, Dawn"). Dawn explained that his initiative to come to us meant he was approaching milestone three. Still she was concerned about certain discrepancies. "Perceptual skills are zooming ahead of his motor system and visual-scanning skills."

"What?"

"I mean he can imagine doing something, but executing it with the body or literally seeing it fully through is difficult for his visual skills. He might be able to conceptualize a little figure pretending to put a fire out, but that doesn't mean he can do the steps."

Arlene worked on tuning Walker's visual system. She said that in her years as a physical therapist she had not understood—not before Greenspan—"how much vision drives the motor system." Formerly, she might have worked on a child by standing behind him and altering the position of his feet and legs; but now, using Greenspan's method, she was always in front of the child—all the children in her caseload—driving them forward, enticing the senses, inviting curiosity, challenge, and exploration.

Georgia DeGangi had done some groundbreaking work on sensory integration for infants and toddlers. Arlene admired her work and used her ideas, yet Arlene found herself inventing ideas even as she was implementing them.

If visual processing leads motor skills, she would begin with light. One day she came with a flashlight, turned the lights low again, and encouraged Walker to follow the light on the ceiling, on the floor, on the chair. To further drive action through vision, Arlene, taking her cue from Greenspan, had Walker play endless hiding games—hiding puzzle pieces all around a room, having Walker find them and bring them back to complete the puzzle. I spent hours each day playing hiding games with him, hours and hours and hours of hiding games. We began with a small five-piece wooden puzzle, hiding the pieces in relatively easy-to-find places: on a tabletop, in a corner, on a chair, all in full view. It was a format that must have been divined from floor-time heaven: looking for pieces worked on visual scanning, moving around the room worked on gross motor skills, always coming back to us engaged the emotions (we praised him and relished his success), the puzzle board itself insisted on a continuity of experience—we were playing the same game. The puzzle-based hiding games increased Walker's ability to focus and concentrate. Within a few months, we were using twenty-piece puzzles, concealing pieces in drawers, under cushions, in boxes. Arlene raised the bar every chance she had. She put a rocking board near a table; Walker had to crawl over a rocking surface to retrieve the piece. She placed ramps in his way—he needed to scale them to reach his goal. Playing hiding games, Arlene was able to work on pivoting, on "sitting to stand," (standing up from a sitting position), on balancing, on trunk control.

As Walker grew motorically, we began to see some psychological changes. He began roughhousing with us in a rather aggressive way. Where once he had been overly timid, now he was seeming bold, at times even too bold. He was grabbing at us, approaching us, laughing, clapping at our smiles, insisting we give him food, toys.

While he began relating more and more, we upped the ante on stimulation—using vibrating pens and vibrating massage toys. He climbed wedges, crawled under tables.

Yet I was still plagued by the images invoked by some of his behavior. His head seemed consistently heavy, as if it were dense with matter, seeking other solid objects. He was always banging into things, he arched occasionally, began moving his arms up and down, up and down, when he was excited.

⟿

"Sensory" described what came into the organism. "Motor" described what came out. They were the alpha and omega of the nervous system, and nearly every letter in between. Quite simply, taken together, they represented most of what the brain did.

When everything is working, sensory and motor operations are partners in a dance. Yet if one partner is weak, the dance might be awkward. How can I give out an appropriate response if I don't understand the message?

Arlene was an athlete. She chased soccer balls on weekends, coached for her son's teams. Strength and agility informed the confidence in her hands, in her dark doe eyes. One day in June she said, "We're going to play with balls today." She pulled out of her bag a peculiar baseball-size ball with plastic sherbet-colored knobs. "Look, Walker," she said. She flipped a switch and the ball began bouncing erratically around the room, ricocheting off of walls, moving off-center.

Walker moved away, spooked.

"What's wrong?" I asked.

"Moving with a still world is easier than moving with a moving world," said Arlene.

She took a rubber doll out of her bag, placed it on the carpet. She pointed to the doll. This is the easiest kind of toy to play with. It doesn't move and requires very little movement from the player. Walker swept up the doll and began chewing on it.

Now she placed the doll out of Walker's reach. "Another load." Arlene was implying by the word "load" that each element added to Walker's stress. "Another load. Walker has to move." Walker crawled to the doll.

She pulled out of her bag a small electronic merry-go-round and flicked it on. "This is another load. A moving object."

"But this. This is the greatest load of all to the nervous system."

She pulled out of her bag a small superball. She pulled her wrist back and flicked her fingers, sending the ball spinning through space. It fast-forwarded toward the wall, ricocheted to the ground, and then flew halfway across the room again.

"Go get it, Walker," she said.

Walker looked around, almost dizzied. He wasn't looking where the ball was at all. It was almost as if he'd missed the motion completely.

He picked up the doll.

That night I did something I had never done before. I put a taped football game into the VCR. I studied the players as they ran back and forth on the field. Thousands of people were cheering in the stands. Football had never interested me, yet now I watched, rapt, understanding what everyone in the stands had always understood. Back in high school, my friends and I, who tended during breaks to sit in a circle on the grass and read or talk, were not interested in athletics, the life of the body. Only one of us was an athlete, a runner, and he rarely talked about the sport, may even have been slightly apologetic about it. Yet now, suddenly what athletes did seemed important to me. Walker would need to learn this. Besides, it wasn't just about the body; athletes were doing nothing short of training their brains to quicker and quicker response times, to making faster synaptic connections, pushing the envelope of electrical virtuosity.

A player was running. He turned to look at the ball far above him in the air. It seemed to be just where his mind and imagination had calculated it would be. He ran across the field, pulling away from grasping hands, dodging moving bodies, avoiding the heads charging toward him at rocket speed. Still, all the while, he moved like an arrow in some shared imagined destination with the ball. At just the last moment, the ball dipped toward the ground, he turned, reached forward, and the ball fell into his arms like a billiard into a pocket.

The athlete had, like a computer, calculated his own movements with respect to a moving object—the ball—as well as other errant and unpredictable moving objects, his defensive opponents. Included in his calculations were not just the dimensions of space, but also those of time. The brain was required to understand or somehow calculate how much time it would take the ball to reach a certain, though not-yet-known point, all the while directing movement, trying to make adjustments in "real time" while calculating future time (where the player would be in a minute, when the ball would reach the peak of its arc). Neurological pyrotechnics.

I suddenly had some insight into how some children with sensory-motor difficulties might view a typical person. Did we seem like superhuman athletes? Able to calculate and execute maneuvers beyond what a child might imagine he could ever accomplish? Was it such neurological pyrotechnics—though not as quick and grand—that made typical people seem unreachable to some people on the autism spectrum?

The comparison works the other way around as well. Might it be the slowness of an impaired motor system that makes people on the spectrum seem at times unreachable?

Still, as we played hiding games with Walker, and he moved more and more through the dining room, looking under rugs and crawling under tables, he began to master his space. Walker grew to master his body moving though that space.

On June 18, just ten days after our second visit to Greenspan, Walker took two steps across the dining room by himself. Seven days later, he took four steps by himself. On July 1, he could stand in place on his own. Within ten days, at the age of twenty-one months, he was walking independently.

We were on a roll; we could smell the end.

It was enveloping, a high like none I'd ever experienced. Cliff and I and Dawn and Arlene reveled in Walker's progress—his abilities: to say his own name, to speak four- and five-word sentences spontaneously, to be able to search for toys from increasingly complex directions ("Walker, look in the toy car that's under the blanket"). The play had grown fun. It was obvious we weren't going backward; obvious Walker was not likely to regress. ("The car under table, Arlene"). We decided to have a party for Walker's birthday—a large party—something to make up for the last one, when we sat around watching him eat hamburger. We invited seventy-five people, REACH professionals who had worked with Walker, friends and family. We all gathered in the living room and Cliff and I thanked all who had helped. We gathered around Cliff's mother, who sang a song and read a poem she wrote, and our friend Ron played a Bach piece for solo violin. Walker sat in Cliff's arms and exuberantly moved to Ron's music. Elizabeth, Cliff, and I toasted family and friends who had been instrumental in Walker's recovery. On the invitation we said that Walker wanted no gifts. Instead, we asked for donations to REACH. We were skimming the top of the world on Walker's birthday, buoyant. It almost didn't matter that toward the end of the party, Walker grew weary of our guests and began to look away.

PART 5

Imagining the World

CLIFF WAS SPENDING more and more time at work, rushing out before eight, sometimes not home until seven. There was a crackle in the air between us. His body, when I passed it in the hall, seemed almost hot from anger (or was it mine I was feeling?). "Why aren't you doing all the floor time sessions you're supposed to?" I wanted to say. I said it once. It didn't help. "Why don't you even look at me once in a while?" he probably wanted to ask. We didn't talk much. Sometimes we could span the gulf—other times . . .

Debbie Roth-Howe suggested we go out together. I called Donna, our day-care provider. She agreed to watch the kids at her house from 6:00 to 10:00. Exactly what I was hoping for from this "date" is difficult to define. We'd have the whole evening to ourselves. Anger was melting away to excitement. We would be together, the way we had once been together. I washed my hair when Arlene came over (even though technically she was supposed to be training me). I found myself looking in the mirror for the first time in months. I didn't like what I saw. My eyes looked popped out, almost scared, encircled in a gray shadow. I took a few minutes to blot the shadows with cover stick, put on mascara, a dress, nice shoes. At 6:00, the time we were supposed to be arriving with the kids together at Donna's, I sat in the kitchen with Walker and Elizabeth, waiting for Cliff to come home. Elizabeth began making jokes, poking at Walker, putting her face up to him and making faces. He began laughing hysterically. I couldn't calm him down. I kept looking out the window, staring at the driveway as if looking could make Cliff come home. He was twenty-five minutes late when he finally rolled in. My excitement dissolved into rage. *He really didn't care about us, did he? Or care about me? He was just hanging out at work, playing that game that working people play—as if the world began and ended with the writing of a report, the success of a meeting.*

He came in the door. "I'm sorry. I know I'm late. Something came up just as I was about to leave." He put his arms around me, buried his head in my neck. I barely responded, didn't put my arms back around him.

I didn't speak much at first during the dinner. Cliff told some stories from work. When I finally softened, I brought up a problem about Walker. An uneasy silence grew. After dinner we wandered through town. We used to love a stroll, a discussion, a dessert. Now we seemed aimless.

"Why didn't we plan to do something?" said Cliff.

"We're doing something," I said.

It was 10:30 by the time we arrived home, and I carried a sleeping Walker up the stairs and placed him on his changing table. Though he was nearly three, he still wore pull-ups, disposable, absorbent underwear. Arlene had encouraged me to let Walker climb with supervision, and I had taught him to climb down from the changing table. When I realized that no pull-ups were on the shelf, I left Walker up on the table and stepped away to retrieve one. While rifling through the backpack, I heard a crash.

Walker lay on the floor, panting. He lay frozen, and then he began screaming. I brought him to my bedroom next door. He was shaking, crying in broken syllables, "Wa' off, wash . . . it . . . off."

"Wash what?" I asked, searching for blood.

"Can you move?"

He didn't answer. *Had he broken his neck?*

The doctor told me to call 911. I did immediately. Within minutes, two huge men in uniforms were standing in my bedroom. "Go away, go away." Walker began screaming.

They opened a large bag and produced a stuffed bear which they gave to Walker. He didn't smile, but gripped the bear tightly with his fingers.

Within minutes, they were wrapping Walker around a board with white tape, and he was taken by ambulance to the hospital.

He proved to have broken his collarbone. The doctor explained that it would heal easily. "Often the collarbone is removed and used to replace other bones; the collarbone will completely grow back inside the membrane." Yet Walker hobbled around the house for the next few weeks in a brace. Elizabeth laughed at him, said he looked like "a little old man."

By the time Walker was two and a half, he had mastered Greenspan's first four milestones. He could stay calm enough to engage for increasing blocks of time (milestone one); he was attached to Lisa, Dawn, and Arlene and to Cliff, Elizabeth, and me (milestone two); he was interacting with his world, seeing his effect on it (level three); and he was using gestures and words (level four). And he was growing more used to balls that jumped and whirled in frantic imitation of all things human and unpredictable. Yet his play was still very much stuck in isolated moments.

Arlene was eager to bring on more pretend play.

By then, so was I. I knew that to teach Walker to use his imagination was not only to teach him to understand himself, but equally, to build the foundation for higher reasoning. If Walker could master pretend play, he would not only be more emotionally aware, he would be cognitively more sophisticated as well. Imagination, Greenspan's theory asserts, is the screen on which the mind begins to project possibilities beyond what is.

Still, looking at my developmental milestone chart was a dry exercise. Looking at a chart couldn't possibly prepare me for what I was about to learn.

When I thought about the fundamentals of early childhood education, of course, the first activity that sprang to mind for most of my life had always been the great cliché of childhood education: the alphabet. I had naively believed that besides perhaps learning about seasons and colors, a child doesn't begin his education until he firmly masters the great symbols of spoken sound. But now Dawn told me that learning the alphabet was nothing more than a "splinter skill," worthless compared to a child's ability to master other symbols—worthless compared to his ability to master the world of the imagination. Walker's education would be well underway by the time he entered kindergarten; there was indeed a network of complex operations he would need to scale before he even walked through the kindergarten door.

Imaginative play was the first and real schoolhouse, the stage on which all abstract thinking plays itself out.

With Walker we were now working in a brightened room.

Walker was acting out gestures of pretend play. He might feed a baby a bottle or run a train on the track, play at cutting a wooden vegetable designed to break in half, then switch track himself. He loved to run to the door and pretend he was going out. Dawn worked at expanding such play. "Where are you going?" she asked. He stopped and considered.

"Shopping," he said. She added more questions, more steps. Soon it became a custom for Dawn to give Walker her keys. He took them and ran to the door, pushed a key into the old skeleton keyhole and turned it. The lock didn't work, but that was the point—pretend was pretend. In Walker's mind it worked. He opened the door, already ajar, and pretended to go outside. Soon Dawn added props: a shopping bag, plastic fruit and vegetables, cereal boxes. Eventually we made it outside to Elizabeth's plastic minivan, and Walker, propelling the weight of the van with his feet, shuffled away to the store. Imagining worlds that didn't exist, Walker was taking the first step toward learning Euclidean geometry.

I attended a conference by one of Greenspan's associates, Serena Wieder, coauthor of *The Child with Special Needs.*

"But he wants to be a policeman. That's all he talks about," said someone about her child at the conference. Obsession, getting stuck in feedback loops, was a hazard of the disorder—keeping together the complex machinery of feelings and ideas and planning. Wieder said, "For some children, obsessions are a solution. A child might move in circles if he's anxious about change. You need to find a way out of that solution. Deepen the plot, create new opportunities." The way out of obsession was to keep going. "Let him play policeman. Instead of trying to escape from it, go into it. Use the passion. He likes policemen. Buy him ten uniforms, all different styles. Help him ascribe to each one a different rule, a different reason. Play policeman until he's 'blue' and had enough, but remember always to use the play as an opportunity to introduce variation, new themes, new reasoning. Don't get stuck in the same old scenarios."

If kids get stuck in the same stories, their minds, too, their psyches could get stuck. At home and at school, they might be less flexible.

There were levels of development in imaginative play. Or rather, as I understood it, the growth of a kid's imagination is like a tree, growing up and out and branching, leafing, flowering. The first level was easy enough. A child uses a toy as a prop. He picks up a bottle and feeds the doll. It's not just a small pretend gesture, but one imbued with deep significance for a child: He's exploring his first emotional theme—dependence and nurturing. The imagination, of course, does not stop there. A child learns to use nothing as a prop. The ability to use no prop is higher because it means you've moved into abstraction: Marcel Marceau clutches at a cylinder of air and drinks it; the child projects what might be onto what is not, using his body to show what the mind alone has created. "When a child can use an invisible hose to put out an invisible fire in role-play, his imagination is cooking," said Wieder.

At some point a child will begin to "elaborate" on these skills and other skills, using variety and spontaneity. As he does, the play turns from small phrases to longer episodes. One branch of growth involves using an object and pretending it's something else. Wieder encouraged parents and therapists at the conference to use objects as unlike the imagined object as possible to help the imagination stretch. A doll is a telephone; a pencil is the ocean.

One of the most important aspects of the imagination as it branches into being happens when a child begins to pretend he is someone else. He puts himself in another person's shoes and begins to explore through his own inner space the workings of one of the most important aspects of the outside world: another person's mind.

Imagination grows and expands exponentially; feelings and ideas come into play.

Another significant branch of development occurs when a child begins to project his identity into action figures. Sometimes with action figures a child can manipulate his reality more easily. He can be Batman one minute and Joker the next. He can be a little god, creating his universe anew, manipulating concepts, experimenting, evaluating, thinking, feeling.

At first, like all children, Walker had been only able to hold a bottle to a baby and pretend she drank. Shortly before he broke his collarbone, Walker had reached a state where he was donning firemen's hats, running through the house in a pretend fire truck, driving Elizabeth's van. Still, the play could be short lived, and not particularly varied. Dawn wanted to work on more complexity. She also hoped Walker would learn to use action figures to represent himself. Serena Wieder had said that children at first were reluctant to project their own selves into action figures because they didn't want to give up that desired object. *Did that mean that the child was too literal in that phase?* I wondered. But Walker may have had a different reason for avoiding action figures—if they were difficult to manipulate conceptually, they were even more difficult to manipulate physically.

Damage to bone had a dramatic effect on Walker's imaginative play. It grew quickly in richness, complexity, passion. For a full year we played out many imaginary scenarios. We were doctors together and patients together. The couch was an ambulance. I often sat in the middle and drove it. Or Cliff pulled Walker in the laundry basket through the dining room to the living room. First one of us had a broken collarbone, and eventually other bodily traumas—broken legs, head injuries, broken hearts.

One day, Walker pulled an action figure out of the toy basket and said, "This is me." He threw the little man on the ground and said, "He broke his collarbone." Walker was branching out in his imaginative play. He could move from being a character, to projecting himself into a toy character, and back again. After that day we played all kinds of ways. We pretended to be people, or we played with symbols of people—real people were patients; action figures might be doctors. They climbed into boxes that were ambulances and drove away to the hospital beside the couch.

A Close Call

By December 1998 when Walker was a few months past two, he was often affectionate, talkative, and interactive, grabbing and drinking everything that is life, full of excitement, happiness, and desire to learn. "Your son's a flirt," said several women during various trips to the market. Dawn and Arlene were deeply bonded to him, and he to them. "How's my favorite client?" said Dawn when she came one day. He was growing stronger and stronger.

Cliff and I joked that we felt like the picture of Dorian Gray. We were the aging portrait; Walker was Gray, getting brighter and brighter every day.

But the joke got old, sour. Or I was souring with it like the portrait. Though I could feel gratitude, the sense of great luck we had, I could often fall into a black space, perhaps because of the winter, perhaps because I was working too hard. We had very little help during that time—Amy was gone, Lisa was gone, and there was still so much work that Greenspan insisted must be done ("You don't stop the job in the middle!").

Still convinced that Walker's race was a race against time, I raced; we raced. I told myself that the race would be short-lived, a sprint. *Just a few more weeks. Just a few. And then we'll all make up for lost time.*

We were like great landmasses, Cliff and I, moving in different directions. After dinner, he disappeared into Walker's room, I into Elizabeth's. Sometimes those landmasses moved together into closely fitting formations that made for continuity and stability—no earthquakes. Other times the masses drifted apart, glacial.

Cliff helped in all the ways he could. He still did much of the shop-ping, brought take-out home some nights, and he always took Walker to appointments where blood would be drawn; I couldn't manage it. At night, Cliff read to Walker or they talked quietly at bedtime. On the weekends, they were beginning to roughhouse together, though play-ing rough could be so exciting that Walker couldn't settle to sleep those nights. When we went to visit his parents, Cliff took over and fed Walker. I stared straight ahead or talked with Cliff's mother and father, tried to rest.

Most of the time, Cliff and I continued to pass each other in the hall looking down at the ground—too shy or angry or too busy to look. Sometimes Cliff and I tried to go out on a Saturday night, but as often as not we argued.

I still hungered for time with Elizabeth. I spent an hour or so with her in the evenings, but it wasn't enough. I even cleared away some special time for her, but it was sometimes interrupted.

I am gone much of the time from Elizabeth. We both know it. Those hours, per-haps she thinks me as gone as any mother is gone who boards a train with a suitcase, even though I am in the next room, singing the bottle song. Gone because I am on the phone so much to doctors.

Elizabeth invited friends over after school or on weekends. When I had a moment, a break, I watched them play, though I wasn't always welcome. She and her best friend, Emmi, had a secret game they played. They insisted I not watch. Elizabeth seemed ashamed by the thought I might look. I peeked through the window, couldn't help but watch.

The first time I looked, I saw that she and Emmi were collecting large fallen branches from our maple tree, branches the size of walk-ing sticks. A half an hour later I peeked out the window again and saw Emmi limping across the backyard, with the stick under her arm as a crutch. Emmi hobbled toward the tree. Elizabeth came rushing toward her, walking efficiently, and helped her walk to the tree. Again and again, I saw them out there (I still see them), leaning on walking sticks, hobbling across the backyard. Elizabeth sometimes traded roles with Emmi; she was the patient on crutches, making her way across the yard, trying on the suit of being ill, broken.

My mother came to spend Christmas with us. We had breakfast in front of the fire in the dining room, the kids camped out on blankets near the hearth, yet I was somehow out of control—rushing, cooking, wrapping, lost in recipes, driven toward trying to make dreams come true.

By New Year's Day, Walker was in the hospital, ill with the stomach flu, dehydrated. No one knew why Walker had gotten so ill. The doctor said it was simply a flu that had dehydrated him, but it was scary to see an already frail child shrinking, sinking into illness, refusing drink. We had brought him to the doctor, who arranged for someone in his office to give Walker fluids via an IV, but no one could get the IV into Walker; his veins were too small. They sent us to the hospital.

I sat with him in a waiting room for an hour and a half, and then we were ushered into a large room with a large metal crib that looked almost like an animal cage. I found myself talking in broken sentences to the doctor who came in to interview me about the problem. What should I tell her. Autism? Was the appellation even relevant any more? Sensitive? She scribbled the words onto her chart.

I laid down on the squishy cushion of a foldout chair. It sagged nearly to the ground.

I remember my own childhood, how I used to fall into these worlds of illness, especially around Christmas. Christmas—all the colors spinning and the phone ringing and all of those loved ones wanting something, or me wanting and hoping. Excitement and feeling always did me in. Often I was very sick; once I landed in the hospital, with, strangely, the same symptoms that Walker had that day—stomach illness, followed by dehydration. Illness could make the world go away, everything seeming to change shape and form, smells growing, time shrinking so that hours alone seemed like seconds and dreams seemed like other planets, other worlds. The self would leave the body and roam elsewhere.

I watched Walker while he slept, the IV taped to his small arm, which occasionally flopped out through the bars of the crib. From time to time, through the night, I pushed it back onto the mattress. All the while they were pumping fluids into his veins. By morning he was alert and seemed well. They sent us away by 7:00. *Was he weakened by the stress of too much happening? Is this why Walker was sick? I wondered. Because sickness itself was a way out? Or does too much stimulation simply challenge the immune system in ways we haven't even begun to understand?*

Darkness of the winter grew with stress and solitude. I was fraying, though I'm not sure I realized it.

One evening—the night before Cliff and I were to meet with REACH about Walker's individual service plan, I went to a parent meeting where I saw a husband and wife I knew from REACH.

"You look tired," said the wife.

"I am."

"Why?"

"I have tons of floor time sessions to do every day," I said.

"Our son's getting a tutor to do floor time," said the mother.

"We used to get that kind of help," I said, looking around the room. My eyes stung by the fluorescent lights. I could barely think straight.

"Used to?"

"I guess they don't think he needs it any more."

Her face turned red, her nostrils flared with outrage. "Do you mean to tell me you're getting no help at all?"

"Well, Dawn and Arlene."

"Dawn and Arlene? We're getting twenty hours of floor time for our son."

"Twenty hours a week?"

"Four hours a day," said the mother. "Yes," she added, "While I work around the house."

I couldn't stop thinking of the number—*twenty*? I knew that Walker was the first child to receive funds for a tutor to do floor time. He was doing so well they were trying the program on several other clients. But twenty? We had never gotten twenty hours. Even when Walker was at his worst. Here was this mother with twenty hours of help per week and I with nothing. I feared I might be getting sick. Why?

I stayed up until 4 A.M. making a list of all my concerns about Walker. I made a chart. All the while, the snow silently fell, enveloping the porches and driveway, stacking up over a foot high in the yard. I was going to make a case for why Walker needed a tutor.

Early the next morning, REACH's director, Darleen Corbett, called me to say that Arlene, who lived in the country, was snowed in. Would we be able to make the meeting?

"Yes," I said. "We'll be there."

Dawn, the director Darleen, Claire (REACH's clinical supervisor), Cliff, and I sat on couches in a small room. The director took my chart and begin addressing my concerns. Walker needs more oral motor stimulation. Walker needs practice climbing stairs. "Pat, you can do those, can't you?" All down the list it went like that until I was weeping uncontrollably. "No," I finally said, sobbing, barely able to talk, "I can't. I have nothing left to give."

"Now wait a minute, Pat," said Cliff. "We can do some of these things on the list."

"Who can?" I said, turning on him. "Will you?"

"Yes," said Cliff.

Darleen looked at the list of things that Greenspan had insisted Walker needed. "Some of these you can address later," she said.

"We're not going to wait," I said.

The argument went on like that for a long time—me weeping and Darleen trying to figure out which of the things that Walker needed could be put on hold.

"Do you need to stop?" said Darleen.

I shook my head. I didn't want to stop. We needed help. I couldn't delay.

"Pat, I think maybe we'd better go." Cliff seemed embarrassed by me, but when I refused to leave, he began reading from his copy of the chart. "Four playdates a week. How can we start to do those, Pat?"

"Don't you understand? I can't do any more. Even the effort of calling . . ."

"I'll call Therese," said Cliff. "I'll arrange a playdate."

I couldn't master the words that would have been filled with bile. *You'll arrange the playdate, but who will host it?*

The rest of the meeting went on in a similar vein, the group figuring out ways that we could fulfill all of Walker's needs without additional help. The strategy was to decide that Cliff could do some, some could wait, and Pat could take on a few more responsibilities.

Through tears, again I tried to insist we were in need.

We knew what the problem was. REACH didn't see any signs of autism in Walker. He was making strides, dramatic ones. And as long as we worked to keep him moving forward, he would continue to improve.

When I wouldn't accept their refusal, Darleen came on her knees, held my hand, telling me, "We are not going to give you intensive services. We do not believe your son has autism. Greenspan felt he was pre-autistic at one point, but he's doing well now. Perhaps he never had autism." She grew emotional herself and said, "I know how you feel . . . I know what it's like to have doctors telling you all you need to do for your child, but we can't do it."

I wouldn't look at her. What crushed me was that she was unwilling to embrace the paradox of diagnosis in this field. If you had a diagnosis, you got help. If you didn't, you got nothing. There was no middle ground, no gray area for accepting that autism was preventable, but only with backbreaking work by a family. How could I convince them Walker needed all of the things that Dr. Greenspan prescribed and that I couldn't do it alone?

The meeting adjourned. As we left, Cliff put his hand on my shoulder and said, "Maybe it's Pat who needs some help now." I realize now that he was feeling sympathy for me, yet in that moment it felt like betrayal. It was the final betrayal, as if he were implying that they were right.

Within days, Debbie Roth-Howe was back in my kitchen, sitting at the table, trying to convince me that it might make sense for me to enter the psychiatric unit of a hospital.

"So they've decided I'm crazy?" I said.

"Well, I guess what happened was worrisome. But let's talk about you."

Debbie had not been working on our case for a while. Near the time that Lisa left, Walker was doing so well that it didn't seem necessary. She shook her head and said, "I should have seen this coming."

"How could anyone have seen it coming? Walker looked good."

I made the Dorian Gray joke. It was always good for a laugh.

"Seriously, Pat. *Have* you considered the hospital? People go there to rest, to rejuvenate when life is too hard."

"What, McLean? The psychiatric hospital?"

"No," said Debbie. "There are psychiatric units in local hospitals. You go there, spend a few days resting. It could help."

"So they think this is all my problem, don't they?"

"Let's just focus on what you need right now." Debbie went on to describe what could happen in a psych unit. I imagined *a soft bed, me floating in and out of sleep.* The thought of going sounded illicit . . . *but sleep? And someone else's cooking?* . . . I found myself fantasizing that they might even drug me—give me some lovely intoxicant to send awareness sinking in heavy water, consciousness burying itself in sand. But it suddenly occurred to me that if I checked into the hospital, I wouldn't be with Cliff.

Suddenly, I wanted nothing more than to be with him. That could be the only real solace I could have—to spend time with my husband, my closest friend. Being in the hospital would mean nothing compared with being alone with him.

I was surprised to hear my thoughts running in such a direction. I thought I had been angry at Cliff. In fact, I had sometimes imagined us divorcing, things had been so cool between us. I had almost forgotten who he was. Who I was. Yet now, my mind ran back to the days when we sat and talked for hours in restaurants and cafés, parks and museums in Cambridge and Boston. Huge, almond-shaped inquisitive brown eyes meeting me across the table, we talked about religion, about books, about philosophy. We talked about death. We talked about meaning, and we talked about the meaning of meaning. Bending down one day, watching some kids play with sticks by the water's edge in the Boston Public Garden, I said I wanted children some day. He kissed the top of my head. I thought back to Cliff and in the early days of Walker's . . . what could I call it? . . . illness?— remembered Cliff doing all the things Lenore had taught us. He still did them. He had spent hours listening to me drone on and on about sensory processing, about autism, about synapse overproduction. Cliff had not embraced the obsession of mine that had been floor time, yet now I saw that he couldn't have. He was protecting us, balancing us. He was like the guy in a football game who keeps running in front of the one with a ball to keep him from being tackled. I still didn't completely understand why he had become so engrossed in the idea of selling our house. But I suddenly felt a great compassion for Cliff. He hadn't been playing golf or watching TV. We'd both been working as hard as we could. Worrying about money was important to us. Someone had to do it. I know he longed for peace, for a moment to breathe. I wanted to do it with him.

So often when Debbie and Leah had come to give us time alone on Sundays in the past, Cliff and I had tried to connect, but it was like the vacation we had taken once at Avila Beach. We wanted to make a fire, but we had only a log, and no kindling. We couldn't get it started.

I was glad to hear myself thinking that I wanted to try again, to rekindle.

I called Cliff. For me, it was a seminal moment. The moment of truth. Cliff could either take me seriously, could either meet me where I was, or he could leave me to go to the hospital.

After we talked, Cliff hung up and to my surprise, made arrangements for the children to stay with our day-care provider, Donna. We drove out of town, up toward the Berkshire Mountains, climbing over snow-blanketed hills for miles. We passed rock formations covered with ice that rose thirty feet above the ground. On the craggy mountain faces, monstrous icicles, glass blown into the shape of pipes, sweated in the sunlight. We stayed at an inn in Lee, not far from Edith Wharton's Lenox house. Cliff booked the best room they had, with its high-bolstered queen-size bed in front of a fireplace and a large sliding glass window letting out onto the shore beside the frozen lake. I brought my *New Yorker* and the *Atlantic Monthly*—I hadn't read either in . . . how long had it been? We jumped into bed and read side by side for two hours in front of a fire, occasionally watching men ice fish on the lake. For dinner, we walked down the hall to a restaurant also overlooking the lake, ate curried soup, fresh bread, nut-encrusted salmon, drank wine. Cliff ordered champagne and said, "To us. It's good being with you." I was shocked.

Within twenty-four hours, we were picking up the kids at Donna's. I had never imagined that so little time could change two people so profoundly. When I think of that trip, I realize that it was indeed a crossroads. Either Cliff and I would live in separate worlds for good, and divorce, or we would be with each other, on the same track. I had felt that he wasn't supporting my efforts at times. Perhaps it was a test. In that one decision to make those reservations, Cliff saved our marriage. When we returned, he called REACH's director and clarified his point. He hadn't meant to imply that Walker's needs weren't important, hadn't meant to concede to the assumption that my stress was the only issue. It was a turning point for us. From that weekend on, we stayed close.

A few days later, Darleen Corbett approached me at REACH. Kneeling down beside me and Walker, who was playing on the floor, she explained that she would send our request for a tutor to her superiors at the Department of Mental Health. I knew the gesture was pro forma. Walker was simply doing too well to warrant our receiving help. Never mind that we were still supposed to give him eight to ten floor times a day. Never mind that he was supposed to be playing with four kids a week. Never mind that even Greenspan probably didn't understand how difficult such a schedule would be. Never mind that making a connection with another mother would take hours. I knew what was required: a diagnosis.

I called Greenspan's office, and we arranged for an official diagnosis, in spite of the fact that Greenspan didn't like to give them. He would review Walker's chart, and I would call back with a fax number he could send it to.

One call and we could become eligible for hours of tutor time. Yet even as I was talking to the office, a strange dizzying feeling came over me, as if I were making a mistake.

Cliff, home ill one afternoon, was standing behind me after I hung up.

"Who were you talking to? What do you mean *diagnosis*?"

"We need one for Walker in order to receive services."

"Pat, don't you think that would be unethical? Do you want to do this to Walker? Label him?"

"Cliff, I don't, but . . . do you realize what this diagnosis would mean? What kind of help we would receive?"

"Do you realize what that label means—what it would mean for Walker's records?"

I knew what Cliff meant. He meant that words shape thoughts and thoughts shape deeds, and all that goes into these shape a child. I didn't want to label Walker—not when I knew we had a chance of escaping a label. Cliff became very ill that week, and it was easy to be absorbed in making soup and tea and doing the shopping. I never made the call.

⌒

One summer morning when Walker was two years and nine months old, a photographer came to photograph him for a brochure for REACH's parent organization. A writer had come a few days earlier to hear and chronicle our story. They planned to feature Walker on the brochure, along with three other families that the company was working with. I hadn't had much time to think about the photo shoot. The night before, I ironed one of Walker's navy blue T-shirts and some shorts to match, and cleared away some toys in the living room. In the morning, the doorbell rang earlier than I expected. A businesswoman in a skirt stood in the frame; she had come to supervise the photo shoot. The executive sat in a chair while I seated myself cross-legged on the floor with Walker. I felt out of place. She wasn't at all pleased with Walker's T-shirt, nor the matching shorts, no matter how smoothly ironed.

Why would Walker ever need a suit? When would I have time to buy something like that? The photographer came, a gentle, sensitive man who also worked for *National Geographic.* He began to set up. There was such irony in the bright photographer's light, the executive in her finery watching him set up. We were going to advertise the heights the organization brings to mankind. I was happy to do it. Where would we have been without REACH? They were heroes. Their parent company was a great institution. But right here and now, this businesswoman seemed to know so little about our lives. She didn't understand that we were still struggling every day, that every second was precious to us, that we had come far with Walker but we had not completely won the battle, not yet. When Walker was in groups, he became disorganized. Sometimes, he even threw up in groups. *What kind of a student would he become if he got so excited he couldn't concentrate?*

I went upstairs and fished around for another outfit, something the executive might consider more appropriate. I quickly put Walker in a one-piece suit someone had given us, with colorful pictures of tools sewn on in primary colors. It was still far too big for his frame, but it was really the nicest baby outfit I had. (*What was I going to be dressing him for? Where were we going to go? Disneyland? To fairs? To restaurants?*) As for me, if she didn't like the dress I was wearing, I would go upstairs and change.

REACH found a volunteer named Catherine to help me. She came for about two to four hours per week. She wore a nose ring and black skirts and shirts and loved to talk. We sat in the dining room and chatted. She brought Walker gifts occasionally—books or toys. I looked forward to her visits and loved to listen to her stories. One day Catherine and I were standing over Walker's crib watching him sleep, and she confided that she had a neurological condition.

"All of sudden things will come racing toward my eyes, as if everything is sped up and it's moving toward me at light speed." I wondered if Walker had such perceptions. Was it possible to experience speed differently? Time differently?

We had other college students who helped, volunteers or workers, housecleaners—from Bulgaria, from Romania, from Pakistan. Several Americans. Somehow each drifted off as students will do at finals time, or they felt the pull of home or the draw of politics.

Companions

WE FINALLY DID IT. *Made it up the "food chain." We belong. We can make it in groups.*

Walker was growing more tolerant. We were beginning to take him to REACH for successful playgroups. The kids played in a large room full of sand tables and puzzles and toy car garages while their parents sat on the floor, joining in. But here was the delicious, the most lovely moment of my week. The first day, the educator running the group explained that after the first hour, the kids would convene at a table and eat snacks and the adults would leave to convene with the social worker.

I recognized the name of the social worker I'd dismissed from our case. I grew nervous. *She probably hated me.* As the playgroup progressed, I became increasingly agitated and self-conscious. The children gathered for snacks, and the social worker came to the doorway and stood there. Was she going to snub me? Should I apologize? I thought about avoiding her gaze, but thought I'd better look. And she did something surprising. She looked me in the eyes warmly. I saw in that moment that she had always meant to help me. That her mission was for me to take care of myself. It was a message I was ready for.

She ushered the parents into a small, cozy room with white couches. She turned the fluorescent lights off and lit the table lamps and began gently to invite us to talk about ourselves.

We might all have been at REACH so our children would gain socialization skills in the adjoining room, but the truth is that the socialization I was receiving in the room next door to Walker was more important to me. Together we five or six women were meeting now every week. We were together when one woman confided that her husband didn't take her child's disability seriously. We were together the day that a new family came in with a child who had suffered amputations. We were there together the day that one mother revealed to us that she had just received a heartless, clinical letter from a neurologist predicting that her child would not live to the age of three.

Ever sympathetic to the question of how to create playdates and opportunities for socialization, Arlene combined her appointments so she could work with three children at once. She created a session for Walker and two other boys whom I'll call Allen and Steven. She set up ball baths (a kid's pool filled with plastic balls), and tunnels, ramps, and ladders. Walker and his companions ran around following each other, sliding down slides, tossing their bodies in the balls, laughing, throwing the balls in the air, playing treasure hunt, sitting on balls in a circle, trying to balance and sing at once. She turned off the lights, gave each one a flashlight and had them touch each other's spots of light on the ceiling. Such a game would teach visual tracking and would combine verbal with physical activities. Keeping track of the adults in the room would be an added challenge for the kids. She had them listen to music together, climb stairs after one another, tricycle together, pull each other in a wagon.

Walker was often exhausted by such a level of stimulation. In the middle of the session, he would lie down and suck his thumb and not get up. Steven's mother asked, "Does he have heart trouble?"

"No," I said. "At least I don't think so."

"Why is he so tired?"

I looked at Arlene. She shook her head.

Two years later, I called Arlene one day because I was looking for information for an article that I was writing about Walker. Arlene was home from work. She said she needed to take a bath; she was having a hard day. Steven had died. His troubled heart had given out.

A Searchlight

THE IDEA, AS I UNDERSTOOD IT, was to teach Walker to be as familiar with the world as he was with the inside of his own head, and vice versa. Knowing your desires is to truly know your world; and to know your world is to know what you desire from it.

Dawn, Arlene, and Greenspan insisted we ask questions.

Questions continually sent Walker's awareness ever outward into that vast world, so intricately linked to who Walker was becoming. Questions also drove him time and again to examine, to question, to review and understand his own logic. Yet whether he was moving his awareness outward or inward, the point was always the "connection"— to connect his consciousness to the process of interacting intellectually with the world. Reflection, analysis, decisionmaking, communication. I never realized how powerful a simple question could be.

Greenspan's purpose was, as usual, twofold, threefold, fourfold. Walker needed not just a way for knowing the world and himself in relation to it, not just a language for speaking that knowledge, not just an awareness of time, and space (When do you want it? Where do you want it?). He also needed to learn the rhythm of communication. He needed to be able to answer quickly, to shoot back the ball as quickly as it shot to him. If he couldn't do this, he couldn't play the game that was social interaction. Greenspan didn't want him to be left on the bleachers.

Questions would help Walker know his desire, and know his place in this earthly maze.

And so we asked questions. We asked them in the car, we asked them at the dinner table. We asked them during play. We asked them during bath. We asked them at bedtime.

When I asked him questions, I often think I was giving a ticket to Walker, a problem that could only be answered by imaginary travel. I envisioned a searchlight, going where it needed to go on the imaginary trip of coming to a conclusion. If I asked Walker, "What do you want to eat?" I watched him, watched him think intently. This is what I imagine took place.

The searchlight first leaves Walker's body, spins its way upward and outward into the world, going to wherever it needs to go to answer the question. It may race through the house or out to the market or to any place that may have clues for what Walker might want from the world. At the same time, the light also searches his body. It moves quickly through his organs, through his heart, his legs, his gut, searching to find the right answer. What *do* I want to eat?

As Walker learns to ask questions, I begin to wonder if it might be possible that the nervous system actually holds sensory information in the place that experiences it. *What does Walker's chest tell him about how it feels to be hungry? What does his gut and his throat know about his love of sorbet or hamburger or rice noodles?* Eventually, the searchlight has collected all the raw material needed to make an answer. It returns to Walker's brain with an answer.

At first, with Walker, the process of answering a question such as "What do you want to eat?" is slow. I imagine the searchlight combing the kitchen, the supermarket, the stands at the farmers' market. Usually, after a while, he replies, "I want a banana."

Then I am supposed to up the ante: "Why?" I ask.

At first, he might not answer. Is the searchlight stuck somewhere? Is it seeing too much?

I wait for a response. "Because . . .," I finally prompt.

"Because." He pauses.

But his eventual answer has nothing to do with food.

"I want to go outside." (Perhaps the vast amounts of information he ponders and searches derail him, remind him too much of other things in the world?)

"Why?"

Silence.

Is he thinking about the first question or the second? I'm not even sure he is still thinking about either one. Yet he's intent. The search-light seems to be going back inside, collecting words this time.

"It's cold."

"You mean you want to go outside?"

"Yes."

Up the ante again. "Why? Why do you want to be in the cold?"

Pause.

". . . Because? . . ."

"Because . . ." A pause. "I like cold."

Now we're getting somewhere, but it is still not enough for Dawn, Arlene, or Greenspan, I know.

"Why do you like cold?"

"Because I do."

I cheat, I can't stand it. I want to give him some ideas. "Does it feel good on the skin?" "Do you like the wind?" The searchlight moves out into the world again, perhaps into the breeze.

"Good on my face," he says.

There were times when asking so many questions, when forcing the searchlight to stay on the move, I felt I was asking too much from Walker—from anyone his age, asking him to account for every whim.

I have noticed that most kids don't seem to naturally like "Why?" questions. They seem to live somewhere outside of why. Perhaps they want to be like parents and say: "Because I said so." Perhaps it is because rather than having to analyze, kids prefer the ever-present moment of feeling and desiring. Kid spontaneity might just want to grab up pieces of life and devour them whole cloth. Did it matter to Walker what explanations were—why, for instance, he felt love for me and Cliff and Elizabeth, why he wanted to look into our eyes and laugh seemingly at the whole farce of life and love?

No, it didn't.

Where is Daddy? When do you want me to give it to you? Which is your favorite? What's so good about that? How soon should we go?

What's bad about it? Why did you say that? Why did you choose that one? Which one is prettier? Why do you think? Why do you feel? What do you want? When do you want it? How come you're . . .?

After a year of constant questions, Walker could have held his own on any talk show.

The Senses Revisited

EARLY IN HIS TRAINING, neurologist Antonio Damasio encountered a patient who was suffering from a severe case of "refractory trigeminal neuralgia," a condition in which the nerves of the face are so sensitive that even a slight gust of wind can create excruciating pain. Since there was no help in sight and no medication to relieve the patient's suffering, as a last resort Damasio's mentor, neurosurgeon Almeida Lima, performed an operation to produce small cuts in a part of the frontal lobe (such lesions had been shown to relieve pain). According to Damasio's account, the day before the operation, the patient was nearly frozen in fear of making the slightest move, yet after the operation Damasio witnessed a man seemingly in a state of miraculous recovery, happily playing cards with another patient.

The patient was asked if the pain was gone.

Remarkably, the patient said, "No." He still felt the pain, yet somehow what he didn't feel was any emotion about that pain. There was no suffering because there was no emotion in response to the pain, even though the sensation of pain was present. Damasio calls this a "dissociation between 'pain sensation' and 'pain affect.'"

This story fascinated me when I read it because it underscores the mysterious and powerful connection between sensation and emotion. Damasio himself uses the example to explain the separation of emotion and feeling. They are not one, he insists; but I argue, how separate can emotion and sensation be if it takes an operation to separate them? What we feel in our bodies is deeply bound to what we feel in our emotions. In fact, Walker has taught me that emotions may be more bound to sensations—more bound to the way the nervous system processes information—than we ever realized.

The summer of 1999 (Walker was two and a half), we visited my mother and father in Los Angeles. One morning I wandered into my mother's bedroom and found her applying makeup. Leaning against her doorjamb to chat for a few minutes, I found myself browsing her bookshelf across the room. There, among her books from the 1960s, *The Second Sex, The Feminine Mystique, Human Sexuality*, I saw Bruno Bettelheim's *The Empty Fortress*. It had been two years since I had first found a few insulting phrases in the book and then felt compelled to close it and read no further, and almost as long since I learned Bettelheim had been exposed as a fraud. Even though he'd been dismissed by many in his field, it occurred to me that since he had studied autism, perhaps he might have observed something about the children in his caseload to suggest that they were hypersensitive. Now I pulled the book off the shelf, this time with the idea of skimming it for information about the sensory system. I knew that *The Empty Fortress* had been written almost a decade before Jean Ayres had coined the term "sensory integration," yet Ayres, it seemed to me, was merely putting to words what other professionals must have been observing. I read through the convoluted snare of words describing the deeply felt, singular moment when a child takes a breast into his mouth. I flipped through and found little on sensitivity. Briefly, Bettelheim noted the peculiar, almost mystical, capacity of patients with autism to detect the presence of a cavity before it appeared to the clinic dentist, yet he made little connection between physical sensitivity and the difficulties the children were facing. Bettelheim, as all the critics had already said, had indeed missed the boat on the subject of sensory defensiveness and the emotional withdrawal of his patients. Yet despite this, I was interested in him now because he had been an icon of his age. What was it about Bettelheim's age that made him so popular, and why had he, as had so many in his camp, missed noticing the sensitivities of his patients?

When we came home, whenever I found time, I researched the subject of sensitivity, which by then had me in its two-fisted though fascinating clutches. Dawn gave me tapes of lectures—one by G. Gordon Williamson, associate clinical professor at Columbia University in occupational therapy, and two others of individuals with autism explaining their personal experience. I cornered whomever I could and read whatever I could, including rereading Temple Grandin's *Thinking in Pictures*. I didn't have to scratch the surface looking for sensory information in Grandin's work; it is bristling with sensory impressions and thoughts about why the senses were ignored for so long. Grandin notes that even as late as the mid-1980s, many major figures in the autism community denied the importance that sensitivity plays on the behavior of individuals with autism. Ivar Lovaas himself, slow to admit that sensory processing problems play a significant role in autism spectrum disorder, was, according to one witness at a conference where he spoke, denying their importance up to the late 1990s.

Why was it so difficult to accept these simple observations and integrate them into an understanding of the behavior of people with autism? Temple Grandin asserts that looking at sensory processing problems was not compatible with the behavioral approach, which chooses to change behavior without particularly analyzing its causes, an approach that began with the work of B. F. Skinner and his followers, and in the 1980s and 1990s was increasing in popularity.

I began to suspect that the problem of not accepting sensory integration and sensory processing explanations for autistic behavior might indeed reach back much further—to the roots of our culture with its emphasis on the intellect.

Greenspan's philosophy, of course, is based on the notion that the body and nervous system play a major role in what we would usually think of as psychological urges. He is adamant that muscle tone, and the use or lack of use of certain muscles, deeply influences social assertiveness, for example. I accepted these truths reluctantly. I guess I was wired to be a Platonist.

Thinking and reading on the subject every day—between sessions when I picked up Elizabeth from dance or going to the "Y" or whatever I was doing, I drew a clearer picture for myself of how our culture has long neglected the development of highly individualized nervous systems (which we all must have).

Freud's therapeutic model and the models for understanding human behavior we've all come to embrace are largely based on the idea that the self and personal identity are forged from the dynamics between an individual and his parents during formative years. This notion—that experience forms us and defines us as individuals—is so ingrained in our philosophy that we take many of its assumptions for granted. We often explain our personalities as if they were the sum total of historical events. For Bettelheim, a Freudian, when he saw children literally hitting themselves, the answer had to be "mother."

Sensory integration theory, as well as the many discoveries being made about the various processing functions, suggests that the abilities we are born with—sensory processing capacity, ability to process language, motor-planning ability—are significant factors in the fates of children, and even in their lives as they grow to be adults.

It's clear that differences in sensory processing ability, especially if not well understood or treated, follow us into adulthood. For this reason, each of us—neurologically hardwired differently—ironically "determines," or plays a large part in determining, our own environment. As Greenspan explains, if as a baby, I frown at Mom because I'm overwhelmed, she will frown back—the cycle of me "creating" my world, and it creating me, goes on and on.

As I began attending lectures on sensory processing, I became familiar with an idea that has become widely accepted among occupational therapists—the notion that most of us don't necessarily need to rely on outside sources to understand what sensory integration, or sensory processing disorders, feels like. When the average person is ill, the brain and sensory system, absorbed with healing itself and managing pain, has difficulty tolerating "normal" amounts of stimulation. The body and neurological system are already overloaded by the illness and, like a computer given too much information to process too quickly, need to shut down some systems. This is why people who are extremely nauseated, for instance, can't stand to be touched. When we're sick, we often experience bright lights as painful. (Have you ever been so ill that you didn't realize that time had passed, even though you were actually awake?) Sensory integration and sensory processing problems distort perceptions.

Sensory integration theory teaches that the amount of sensation we are processing often determines how we feel in our bodies; the senses can determine levels of comfort, anxiety, fear, even aggression. For this reason what is happening sensorially might just translate into how we feel about ourselves, how we feel about other people; sensory processing may even inform how we learn, and even how we focus, whether we're fearful or calm, how we move.

How many of us suffer from sensory problems?

I found my answer when Walker was three. I watched a videotape of Patricia Wilbarger helping a boy diagnosed with attention deficit disorder and sensory integration disorder dramatically change his behavior and functioning levels merely by having his mother brush him firmly with a surgical brush once every two hours and apply pressure to his joints.

Wilbarger estimates that 15 percent of the general population suffers from tactile defensiveness, a catchall phrase describing sensory problems of all kinds. "That means that 15 percent of people will walk the streets in 'alarm pain.' They don't know how to keep themselves calm." They dwell in a persistent state of overstimulation. As the camera focuses in, Wilbarger makes an urgent call for health-care professionals to rule out S.I. disorder before they make diagnoses that may, in fact, be incorrect. Of such misdiagnosed or ignored individuals, she says, "They will suffer their whole lives, walking the streets, not knowing what they have. To cope with tactile defensiveness some will take drugs, alcohol, will need to jog, or will only feel better after a fight. And they will never know why."

Other estimates regarding how many people in the general population suffer sensory integration problems run as high as 30 percent.

New discoveries about sensory processing suggest that each of us—not just those with the disorder—experiences our senses differently, depending of course on how sensitive or insensitive we are in various areas. Combinations of sensitivity and insensitivity are as varied in the human population as are shape and color in nature. Some people, for instance, can't stand loud music; others crave it. Some don't want to be touched. Others need to be touched. If someone—anyone—wants to be touched or doesn't, it's not necessarily a sign that he or she was physically neglected or abused as a child, or is emotionally cold—it can be a condition of the nervous system. Each nervous system is unique.

As Walker emerged from his separate, internal landscape and began to share every waking moment, I began to wonder what exactly we were sharing. I began, too, to wonder what experience I was really sharing with Cliff and Elizabeth. If we are all experiencing the world of sensory stimulation and overstimulation at different rates at different times in vastly different patterns, this information suggests that it is not just those with hypersensitivity or hyposensitivity who are living "in other worlds." We must all, whether in subtle or dramatic ways, be experiencing very different lives even while sharing them.

One of the hallmarks of severe sensory integration disorder, for instance, is "stimming"—an individual's need for repetitive behavior to soothe himself. People with autism, for instance, spin in circles or flap their arms up and down to stimulate the vestibular sense. They spin plates or move their hands in front of their eyes, as a form of visual stimulation. They bang their heads to receive input to the proprioceptive sense, perhaps to provide deep pressure. Any such form of stimulation is an attempt to calm a stressed nervous system or to stimulate one that craves input. Yet I learned that we all "stim." We all engage in repetitive activities to soothe our nervous systems. Nail biting is stimming. So is chewing on the ends of pens, chewing gum, and manipulating small objects repetitively in the hands (such as bending a paper clip or fiddling unnecessarily with a pen). The difference between people with profound S.I. problems and the rest of us may just be the level to which we need to participate in self-stimming activities, and the social acceptability of the activities we choose. Many of the actions that typical individuals take to calm their nervous systems, may be, in fact, more destructive than hand flapping, though of course not as self-destructive as head banging, or smoking cigarettes, drinking alcohol, drinking too much coffee, and obsessively eating. Chewing is a form of proprioceptive input to the jaw (at mid-line). The mouth is the portal through which we first experience the world—a powerful focal point for the nervous system, and as such furnishes a profound source of calm to it. Safety may not be a priority for people with severe S.I., but can we say that the rest of us take our health into consideration when we engage in rituals to calm an overstressed nervous system?

———

Those who study sensory integration posit that all sensory input is "information." Light is information. Color is information. Voices are information. Moving pictures are information. Information is information. The more detail, the more information.

———

Consider this experience: You are standing in the vegetable section of the supermarket trying to figure out how many mushrooms you will need for a quiche. Standing next to you is a man on a cell phone talking to someone. "I'll be home, but I have to go out again," he says. There is a momentary pause during which you locate some on-sale mushrooms, when he begins to yell, "What do you mean?" You are trying to listen now, intent on understanding why he is so upset, but then suddenly on the loudspeaker an announcer begins to speak, "Shoppers, it is our sincerest goal here at Shopper's Square for you to know that we value your patronage above anything else. We hope to make your shopping experience as pleasant as possible. If there's anything . . ." The announcement is cut off by a loud female voice that says: "A two-year-old child named Nathan has been lost. Anyone who finds him, bring him to the service desk please." When she cuts off the loudspeaker, the recording is advertising the two-for-one sale on fall floral arrangements at the florist's shop. A woman passes by, offering you a flyer on a car wash fund-raiser. The man on the phone says, "I'll do it this time, but stop pushing me."

Humans, as the study of autism and sensory dysfunction has taught us, have a logical response to being overwhelmed: we retreat into more internal worlds. The Information Age may be presenting to us, as a culture, this unique problem of the person with autism: we are at once isolated and overwhelmed. Like autistic individuals, we are often inundated with information that our nervous systems may not be well adapted to handle, particularly since massive amounts of information not well integrated with healthy emotional interaction can be corrosive to a healthy nervous system. Furthermore, the "older," more atavistic parts of our brains may simply not be prepared for massive amounts of stimulation. If this is true, then S.I. theory, and other theories penetrating the mysteries of the sensory system, will offer important information about how we carry tension, who is most susceptible to anxiety in an overstimulating environment, how we can relieve stress and lead calmer, more fulfilling lives in an age when autism may be becoming a metaphor for how we all live.

Right now, I sit in the basement of a coffeehouse. It has overstuffed couches, dim lighting, as if it were meant to be a saloon—instead, it's designed so that patrons can come, sit at small tables by themselves, access the Internet, or plug in their own laptops. Across the way sits a man working on his laptop. I don't say anything to him and I probably won't. He is biting the sides of his finger. Next to me is another man. He plays with his beard and stares at a screen I can't see. I play with my lips a bit, look at these words. We all manipulate our information, doing our best at parallel play. This could be the autism ward of a special school.

Just as extremely overstimulating situations help us understand autism, understanding autism helps us see the ways that overemphasizing "information" and the manipulation of information in our culture may be unhealthy for us, might be leading us down a path away from healthy social interactivity.

Arlene was on the floor with Walker. I was on the couch dreaming, pondering something that had happened the night before.

Not being able to sleep, I had gone to the bookcase where I keep my favorite books. There, on the middle shelf, were two by Walker Percy. I stared at them for a long time before I picked them up, an old dog-eared paperback of *The Moviegoer*, his first novel, and a book of essays, *Lost in the Cosmos*, one of the few hardbacks I had splurged on when I was in college. I felt an old thrill looking at the title on the spine: *The Moviegoer*. I hadn't had the time to read a book in months. Years. Almost three years since I'd read a book that didn't have to do with medical issues or sensitivity. I pulled them off the shelf. A publicity picture of Percy fell out. There he stood—the guy we'd named our son after—smiling before the camera in a herringbone sports jacket, a tie, a black knit vest, smirking as if to say, *Does any of it really matter?* Why had this man been Walker's namesake? What kind of a son had we been hoping for? I asked myself. I remembered, of course, vividly the sorts of images that came to mind when I thought of Walker Percy. A medical man. A writer. A thinker. I imagined a man in his twenties walking through the park, wearing a sleeveless knit vest, casually toying with the keys in his pocket, talking intently with his girlfriend or his best pal, dishing jokes with a straight face, a wry wit.

Now I looked at the picture of Percy again. Is that really who Percy was? *"So you named your son after me?"* he seemed to be saying. *"Do you really know who I am anyway? For starters I'm dead. You named your son after a dead man. A very traditional thing to do at least in some faiths, your husband's faith. I like that. I think of myself as an honorary Jewish man—a spiritual wanderer. But the difference is that in your husband's tradition they name after relatives. But I think I know why: I'm onto you. You were looking for certification in far-flung places. Trying to fend off the everydayness, the stench of so many Sunday dinners. Or are you like me and just have a repulsion to anything associated with yourself? So you fought your malaise, tried to stake a claim, bucked the old boys."*

I guessed he was right. What did Walker have to do with Walker Percy, a man who was just an author I liked? Yet hadn't there been a scene from *The Moviegoer*? A scene when this character Binx (a thinly veiled version of himself, I suspect) was staring at light, or looking out the window.

I flipped through and found this:

I became bewitched by the presence of the building; for minutes at a stretch I sat on the floor and watched the motes rise and fall in the sunlight.

. . . and this . . .

Not in a thousand years could I explain it to Uncle Jules, but it is no small thing for me to make a trip, travel hundreds of miles across the country by night to a strange place and come out where there is a different smell in the air and people have a different way of sticking themselves into the world. It is a small thing to him but not to me. . . . What will it mean to go moseying down Michigan Avenue in the neighborhood of five million strangers, each shooting out his own personal ray? How can I deal with five million personal rays?

I began thinking about the connection between sensitivity and the artist. It seemed to me that so many artists and writers I had read about were highly aware of light and smells and textures, sometimes too sensitive to exist comfortably. W. H. Auden apparently needed a high degree of deep pressure to calm himself; I had once read that he pulled rugs off the floor on top of his body in order to sleep (like kids with autism who squeeze between mattresses at night). Didn't Thomas Merton also have some visual sensitivities? Hadn't I once read that when quite young he had a "deep and serious urge to adore the gas-light in the kitchen with," as he said, "no little ritualistic veneration"?

But he was a mystic. Was there a connection between not just the artistic life and sensitivity, but between spirituality and sensitivity? Did mystics choose a reclusive life for biological, not just spiritual, reasons?

Now, sitting with Arlene, I began to wonder how much of religious experience was sensory experience. What is the meaning of a symbol if it isn't in part known by the body? *Frankincense, a smell of the divine. Music, the sound of God, human feeling translated into the auditory. Prayers, hands moving to the mid-line, to the most centering part of the body, the mouth; fingers touching lips, touching sense, touching sound, whisper of wishes.*

"You know, you might want to think about yourself."

"What?" I said. I had suddenly awakened from my reverie to realize that Arlene, who was on the floor gently spinning Walker in the saucer-shaped disk, was speaking to me. It was the summer of 1999, not far from Walker's third birthday and his final REACH evaluation. Arlene's hands were on Walker, but her head was now turned 180 degrees away from Walker, toward me.

"You might want to consider your own sensitivities."

"My own?"

"Yes," she said. "You seem distracted."

Of course she was right. I hadn't been watching her work with Walker. *But didn't Arlene understand that I had worked with Walker all morning? A person needed some refuge.*

"I think," said Arlene, "that toward the end of the session, it's sometimes difficult for you to notice Walker's needs."

"Walker's needs?" *Wasn't I always thinking of Walker's needs?*

"What kind?"

"He needs some direction now. We need to find out if he's hungry or tired."

"So you think I space out too much?"

"You do retreat at times. I've noticed it, noticed it more and more."

Sensitivities . . . you mean I might have sensitivities, too?

"Often we tell parents that they might want to look at themselves," explained Arlene. "Sometimes the children we are working with are just exaggerated versions of their parents."

Dam burst. Banks flooding. I was halfway down the river—Walker's river, Walker's experience—but I must have known, must always have known it was my river, too. . . .

In the beginning, it hadn't mattered, finally, where Walker's problems came from. If there was a way to reverse them, reversing was where our energies must go. Yet now, occasionally, there was time, time to delve deeper, to go backward into the past, to ask questions about etiology. New discoveries about autism were burgeoning, appearing every day, and still are, many of them in the area of genetics.

Twenty years earlier, in the late 1970s and early 1980s, Dawn and her colleagues tried to discuss the issue of genetics and autism spectrum disorder with neurologists and other researchers, yet neurologists insisted there was no connection. Dawn herself was perplexed by such an assertion because she often found strains of her clients' traits in their families. One father whom she visited years ago was so rigid and obsessive that one afternoon when she was late, he wouldn't stop talking about her lateness. "He would barely let me alone to work with his son." She couldn't shake the certainty that such rigidity was in fact the same phenomenon as the son's "perseverative" tendencies. Because of his disorder the child would obsess, get stuck, loop back into an experience or mood and stay there. Yet the father of Dawn's client, peculiarly, was exhibiting a similar tendency toward obsession, though perhaps he was more able to function in the world.

Later, of course, Dawn's suspicions proved true; genetics were indeed a deciding factor in the disorder. (If parents have one child with autism, their chances of a second child having the disorder rise from 1 in 500 to 1 in 20.)

The line between pathology and normalcy is a fuzzy one at best in the world of "the spectrum." Where does it end? Begin?

As geneticists study autism, they are discovering that autism isn't merely passed down by people with a diagnosis, but it is also passed down by parents with a few autistic characteristics. Geneticists call people who do not fit into all the diagnostic criteria "broad autistic phenotypes."

Time and again when I have been talking to women with children with autism, I hear a resonant story. I heard nearly the same story twice from two different mothers who had never met. The couple goes to a lecture on autism or visits a therapist shortly after their child receives a diagnosis. The couple learns that people with autism have systematic minds, like things in certain orders, have trouble with transitions—that people with autism are not social—that they may be good with math and music, or they are highly visual. The husband walks out of the classroom, or office, and says, "My God, they've just been describing me."

Parents may share strengths associated with the disorder. The popular press occasionally theorizes that certain individuals celebrated for their technical genius, but lacking normative social skills, may be on the spectrum: Bill Gates, Albert Einstein, and even Thomas Jefferson are among them.

Recent studies reveal that people on the autism spectrum have superior minds for understanding systems. For this reason an inordinate number of children with Asperger's syndrome (high-functioning autism) as well as other kinds of autism are appearing in California's Silicon Valley, where many parents are programmers. Simon Baron-Cohen, a clinical psychologist at Cambridge University who studies individuals with autism and their families, discovered that the parents of children with autism often share some of their talents, talents that are often cornerstone gifts associated with the disorder, particularly their visual strengths. Baron-Cohen says that parents and children with high-functioning autism are often so good at embedded figure tests (tests for picking out specific geometrical shapes within a complex picture) that "you hardly have time to get the experimental materials out on the table before they've spotted the target." Baron-Cohen has found a "significant overrepresentation of engineering among the fathers and grandfathers of children with autism (12 percent, as compared to the 5 percent of engineers in the rest of the population)."

Cliff in some ways fits the broad autistic phenotype. He has significant talent in certain areas. He is an architect, has an extremely high aptitude for math and acute visual awareness. He, like Walker, solves puzzles easily and has a gift for pattern recognition, and in temperament he is an introvert. (Is it a coincidence that the last two books I read on autism were written by mothers of children with autism whose husbands were architects?)

Maybe such distinctions don't matter. Still, Walker seemed to share some exaggerated gifts and foibles that Cliff and I both possessed.

Arlene's words were a revelation—they sent me into my own past, where I started researching and reviewing my own issues with sensory processing. I was revising, revisiting the question of who I was, remembering, searching, researching—but remembering now, suddenly now, with my body.

Memories of my childhood is Southern California are defused with a flooding, headachy light. In my memory, light mixes with sadness, with a feeling of powerlessness. Light was everywhere: dodging off of cars on the road, radiating in the rearview mirror, sunset like the orange of the orangest of migraines blasting into my forehead as we drove home evenings on the Hollywood Freeway. Sunlight came into the bathroom in the afternoon and made taking a bath at that time almost nauseating—too much sensation, too much warmth.

I began remembering sensations I craved when I was little. One odd night I lay in bed and longed to find a scab to scratch off. I loved the feeling of resistance that pulling off scabs gave my skin, loved the tearing feeling around my skin—the sensation of unusual resistance somehow made me feel more alive. I also used to bite my arms. When we sat in the back of the station wagon on long trips, I bit my arm hard, studied the teeth marks. Afterward, I sucked on my skin and let the fine hairs tickle my lips. Dad used to say, "You weren't meant for this world, Patsy. Neither was I." It suddenly occurred to me that he too might have a sensitive nervous system. Perhaps the whole family did.

One day, during this time, Cliff and I attended a choral concert. On the way home I was tense, distracted. Cliff wanted to know if anything was wrong. For the first time in my life, I looked first to my "sensory system" to see if anything was amiss. I felt a subtle, uncomfortable energy in my body, a slight headache, a barely perceptible metallic humming sensation in my ears. I looked back over the experience listening to the concert and realized that about halfway through the second half, I had actually turned inward. I had no memory of the second set of pieces, either visual or aural, though I could recall many details from the first half of the concert. Something about the pitch of the high voices, or perhaps the sheer quantity of music I had been exposed to, or maybe the acoustics—the reverberations of the voices resounding off the walls of the high cathedral where we sat on hard pews—something had sent me into an internal world, a dreamy state.

At the end of the concert, I left to find the ladies room, having told Cliff I'd meet him at the front of the cathedral. I wandered downstairs through an Escheresque labyrinth of halls looking for the bathroom. On the way, details emerged from the Gothic wood-paneled walls—

an incongruous sign reading "Pool and Gym," the odor and rough look of the dank boiler room. In the bathroom I stood reading a sign near the sink, explaining in explicit detail the protocol for removing "soiled clothes from preschoolers." Somehow the sign took on as much importance as the concert, as my waiting husband: It was all of my universe. In a dreamy state I stared at the sign, considered the lettering, wondered how the children were treated as they were changed. Eventually I broke my concentration. Upstairs, I stood in the foyer with three or four geriatric couples waiting for Cliff while a frigid wind whipped in through the open door. As I left the church with the couples (thinking Cliff might have moved outside), I found myself awash in sensation again. A hard wind—well below zero with the chill factor—seemed to take arms, pounding the top of my head. The large wooden doors were locked from the outside, and feeling pursued (I have always been sensitive to cold), I rushed through the wind to the back of the cathedral, nearly running into Cliff as I opened the back door. He began a story, but I couldn't listen; I turned and began running toward our car.

On the way home I could barely talk. Eventually Cliff asked if I were all right. Was it him? "Well, yes," I challenged. "Where were you?"

Cliff was silent.

I tried my best to apologize. Yet I couldn't sustain an interest in conversation for the rest of the evening. I was irritable and couldn't concentrate well until after a full night's sleep.

I began to consider how simple exchanges that happen every day between people who are close—or trying to be—can be difficult between people who are sensitive in different ways. So often, people and children with sensitivities are challenged to be present when "the show"—their show—may really be happening internally.

The first few years of his life, I was perplexed by the paradox that is Walker. How, for instance, could a child who can barely stand to be touched not be bothered by a vaccination shot? How could a child who bumped up hard against us at bedtime also cry and ask to go inside when the wind came up? The answer to these questions came slowly. They came as I begin to unravel the complex tapestry of sensory integration.

The answer is that people can be hyposensitive and hypersensitive at the same time. Going backward into my life, I began to understand that I have indeed been both hypersensitive and hyposensitive. As an adult with children, I could barely stand attending a concert, could not function well in the grocery store. Yet when I was in high school, I surrounded myself with people. I went to movies, watched television, could barely stand the silence that sometimes used to creep in from my own internal wanderings, often could not tolerate the quiet of reading.

It had been dim in the living room with Walker when he was an eight-month-old baby and I was learning floor time. I feared tedium. I was afraid it would be boring at first in the way that boredom can seem almost frightening. I knew my encounters with Walker would have to "be me"—if not about me, at least from me—our connection would have to be inspired from some inside energy that I might possess. I was scared I didn't have it.

My friends tell me now that I had receded, that I had been hard to reach. I was thinking all the time. I had unzipped a door and entered an airless chamber that included only Walker and me and his illness. I went into the dark room and seemed to somehow enter Walker. Was I joining his world? Was it the only way to bring him out, I wondered now, like Orpheus going to the underworld to retrieve Euridice?

The phone was off the hook. There would be no retreating to thought, to music or books. My husband was at his office, Elizabeth was miles away with friends. Yet with Walker in those dark rooms on the hottest of summer days, I realize, I had found a stillness, a calmness to my nervous system I might never have come to know as an adult. What entered, at least during certain moments, was a quiet I can't remember having experienced before—something that I may have been longing for and working to cover over, a stillness gone unheard.

Walker's plight began to teach our family that the Golden Rule can be meretricious, a deception. We didn't need to do for each other as we would have done for ourselves—that wreaks havoc and misunderstanding. Instead, we started seeing that each individual likes to be "done to" individually. We are becoming a closer family for relating to each other through the senses, so to speak, knowing each other first as sensory beings.

On an escalator in a department store, I put my arm around Elizabeth. "Mom, would you not do that?" she complained.

"What?" I said.

She flung my arm off. "Don't touch me."

"Really, you don't want me to touch you?" I said.

"I do. I do. It's just, you put too much weight on me. Try it lighter." I put my hand on her.

"No. No. No. That's too light, it tickles." I relaxed, leaned my head in toward her.

"Perfect," she said.

We all began to grow more gentle, tentative, and watchful with each other. We learned to recognize contrasts and similarities in the yearnings of our separate nervous systems. Cliff likes jazz. I find it too stimulating. There are times when I feel like "mixing it up" (Greenspan's term) and Cliff feels like being calm. Greenspan taught us to read the signs, to be as sensitive with each other as we might be with Walker, to play to one another's moods. Greenspan taught us that playing to the nervous system of a loved one is a matter of being mindful and watchful. Perhaps it is like courting the trust of a deer or a bird. We peek first from behind the tree.

PART 6

I Have a Prob'em

BY THE THIRD VISIT to Greenspan in April 1999 (Walker was two and a half), Walker's green eyes had deepened to a dark hazel brown. His skin was clear, his forehead broad, and his gaze intelligent. His shapely mouth puckered as he talked. There was a childhood charm and softness about him as if he were being filmed through a filter. He was approaching us, taking social initiative, and was beginning to play with Elizabeth, to be able to bear the intensity of her effervescent giggles, her precipitous, animated gyrations, though occasionally they proved too much for him.

Still, we were concerned about Walker's ability to tolerate groups. Though Walker had graduated to attending REACH's playgroups, he tended to regress in crowds. In a group, he seemed at a peak of excitement, overly happy somehow, giddy. A box filled with small toys (such as a Lego set) could be too exciting. After playing for thirty seconds, in a passion of impulse, he might throw them off a table. We worried about how he would fare in preschool and kindergarten. Arlene felt Walker was at risk for ADHD (attention deficit hyperactivity disorder), that he was still overwhelmed and might have trouble sitting still in school. He was also still significantly behind in his motor skills—sometimes had trouble handling small objects, picking them up and setting them right when he was tired. We wondered if he would be able to learn to write or use scissors.

In spite of our worries, there could be little doubt that Walker was gifted socially and intellectually. He was becoming something of a master of verbal repartee—fascinated by strangers, and drawn particularly to adults in his world. He was so much more engaged that we had even flown with eight-year-old Elizabeth to Maryland so she would learn floor time, too. At his third visit with Greenspan, Walker was more interested in playing with the man behind the camera than with us.

Walker ambled over to Greenspan's packed toy box and unearthed a broken school bus. The chassis was missing, making the toy somewhat useless. It was a shell of a yellow bus—doors, windows, windshield, but no wheels. What was it about the toys in Greenspan's toy box that so many of the toys in there were broken? The bus was not the only casualty in there: We saw horses with missing legs, dolls with no heads, tubes jammed with toy balls. Surely there was a reason to plant such toys. We were soon to find out.

Walker moved directly to Greenspan:

WALKER: My school bus has a prob'em.
GREENSPAN: Who should help you?
WALKER: (Turning and pointing to me.) Mommy.

I jumped to the floor and tried to fit the shelled-out school bus over a smaller truck, which was intact, but the bus kept falling off the truck. I laughed and shrugged. Walker took the truck out from under the bus and began tugging at the wheels so he could put them on the school bus. But the wheels wouldn't budge.

He went back to Greenspan, who was still holding the video camera.

WALKER: I have a prob'em with . . . (Pause.)
GREENSPAN: What's that? What's your problem, sweetheart?
WALKER: I have a prob'em with the wheels.
GREENSPAN: (In a gentle voice.) Why? What's your problem? Why do you have a problem with the wheels?
WALKER: Because I ha' to take 'em off.
GREENSPAN: (Innocent, inquisitive.) Because you want to take them off?
WALKER: Um hm.
GREENSPAN: Why do you want to take them off?
WALKER: Because. (Pause. Thinking hard.) I want. . . . (And he stops.)

GREENSPAN: Because you *what?*

WALKER: Because I wanna. . . .

GREENSPAN: Because you want to? (Pause. Walker looked at Greenspan, then the truck.) Well, are they better on or better off? (He prompts.)

WALKER: Off. . . .

GREENSPAN: What makes it better to have them off?

WALKER: I don't know.

GREENSPAN: Huh?

WALKER: I don't know.

GREENSPAN: Well, once you get them off, what are you going to do with the wheels?

WALKER: Take them off. . . .

GREENSPAN: *After* you take them off, what are you going to do with them?

WALKER: I don't know.

GREENSPAN: Oh. (Pause.) So, er . . . what should we do? So it's hard to take them off?

WALKER: Um hm.

GREENSPAN: Well, what should we do?

Walker paused for a long while. Finally Greenspan prompted:

GREENSPAN: Who's going to help?

WALKER: I want *you* to help. . . .

GREENSPAN: *Me?* (Playfully surprised.)

WALKER: (Looking into the camera.) Um hum.

GREENSPAN: Well, I can't do it. I'm not too good. I've got to hold my camera. You know who could help you? I think your . . . sister might be able to help you. What do you think?

Walker ran to Elizabeth, who was coloring, sitting on Cliff's lap on the couch. She had dressed for the occasion—a blue, flocked dress, a sweater with fashionably too-long sleeves, and gold pumps.

"Can you help me Elizabeth?" he called out with emotion, and threw himself affectionately into her lap.

ELIZABETH: (Now picking up on Greenspan's method.) Sure,
what do you want help with?
WALKER: A truck.
ELIZABETH: What do you want me to do with the truck?
WALKER: Take the wheels off.
ELIZABETH: Why do you want me to take the wheels off?
WALKER: Because I want . . . because I was going to put them on
the school bus.
GREENSPAN: (Surprised.) What did he say?
CLIFF: He's going to put them on the school bus.
GREENSPAN: That's pretty sophisticated.
CLIFF: I guess he remembered all this time. I didn't think he had.
ELIZABETH: How do you want me to do it?
WALKER: Like this.
ELIZABETH: I'll try.

She pulled and pulled but couldn't pull the wheels off, and
laughed. Walker ran back to Greenspan.

WALKER: (Looking into the camera.) Elizabeth can't do it.
Elizabeth can't do it.
GREENSPAN: Maybe Mommy or Daddy can do it.

Walker ran to me, and I was the one who finally broke the circle
of circles.

ME: Let's get a new toy and just not worry about it.

I knew I had made a mistake. The word on floor time was that you
were supposed to avoid ever cutting off an exchange with a child,
since the idea was to keep the circles winding and winding around
one logical event as long as you could; expanding interaction expands
the mind, increases attention span, reinforces logical connections. I
couldn't bear the going-nowhereness of it. Still, this was unquestion-
ably my favorite visit to Greenspan thus far; we had a chance to see
the man himself engaged in floor time. I often wondered what he
would be like if he ever came out from behind the camera to play
with a child. Had he been hiding back there? Now I had my answer.

I was fascinated to see Greenspan working the conversation. He kept Walker present to his one goal, present to one question or problem, yet all the while moving outward—going to his sister, going to me, asking for help, opening circles, and keeping them going. The circles were spinning and spinning back. I didn't know Walker was capable of so many—fifty in that one exchange.

Walker had passed milestone five—he could imagine a world that does not exist—and he was beginning to make the logical connections associated with milestone six.

We worked hard at floor time for the following six months, focusing on visual scanning skills—more hiding games—and fine and gross motor activities. The results were staggering.

On the day Walker was scheduled to receive his three-year-old assessment at REACH, six adults—Dawn, Arlene, Jean (a speech therapist), Walker's prospective preschool teacher, Cliff, and I—congregated around him in a small clinical testing room. Cliff held the video camera. At different times during the assessment, each of the therapists put herself in front of Walker to test him in her area of expertise. Dawn and Arlene would be using the Michigan Early Intervention Developmental Profile. Dawn presented puzzles and diagrams and toys to test cognitive ability. Arlene asked Walker to jump, to draw, to stack blocks. Jean used the Preschool Language Scale to test both receptive and expressive language. She put a large book on the table in front of Walker and showed him pictures. Each page of the book contained exercises for increasing levels of skill. She asked Walker to repeat a string of words. He did so, beaming proudly. She pointed to a picture of a bicycle, a broom, scissors. "Which do you ride? Which do you cut with?" He passed the three-year-old mark. She turned a few pages. He passed the three-and-a-half-year-old mark while flirting with his examiner. She turned some more. A three-year-old who might never have spoken had acquired the language proficiency of a near-four-year-old. But when Arlene had asked him to jump, he couldn't.

Nine months later, after receiving regular physical therapy in pre-school, Walker could jump and run, though perhaps not as vigorous-ly as most. He could cut paper with scissors and do particularly well-aimed and sneaky things with a squirt gun.

He still suffered from food intolerances and occasional gastroin-testinal difficulties. At times he was a sensitive child. He didn't want to swim in a cold pool, and he was occasionally annoyed by loud nois-es, yet I would argue that his experience and education, or perhaps some inherent gift related to his sensitivity, afforded him a high degree of emotional intelligence—ironic, given his early patterns. He under-stood a lot about this life.

When Walker was three and a half years old, he once came into the kitchen holding the beige plastic body of Mr. Potato Head puppet-style.

"Hi!" he said in a high, squeaky voice. "I'm Mr. Potato Head. Actually, no," he corrected himself, still in the potato voice. "I'm not Mr. Potato Head . . . I'm Mr. Nobody."

"Why Mr. Nobody?" I asked.

He showed me the body. It was blank. "Because I have no eyes, no nose or mouth. I'm sad and lonely."

"Why are you sad?" I said.

"I want my whole self."

"Then you'll be happy?"

"Yes," he said.

Imagination, sensitivity, inquisitiveness, ease around other people's bodies—these gifts made closeness possible. Yet Walker and I grew close in ways I could never have anticipated or indeed have imagined. We shared the "juicy" intimacy that Greenspan had entreated us to seek on that first day we'd met him in 1997.

We had a repertoire of things we did together. One of them was to take bike rides to Smith College. One day, on the way down the steep hill that leads to his favorite location, the "fishy pond," he was laughing and raising his face to feel the wind. He called out, "Oh it feels so good, Mama." I warned him that he would have to use his brakes because gravity would be pulling him. He rode down the hill without falling. He took me by the hand to his favorite refuge. "My house," he called it, a tree with leaves that bowed to the ground, form-

ing a secret tent underneath. We played house, walked in the herb garden. Two hours later, he lay on the grass, head in hands, looking out
over Paradise Pond.

"What's gravity, Mama?" he asked.

"It's the force that keeps you down," I told him. "You're not floating away right now because of gravity. Gravity keeps you on the
ground, bound to this earth."

He jumped onto his tiptoes, extended his arms, and said, "Mama,
pick me up, please."

"I can't think of anything I'd like better," I said.

Epiphany

I WAS STANDING AT the slightly cracked-open door of the office of Timothy Buie, M.D., a gastroenterologist who specializes in children with autism spectrum disorder at Massachusetts General Hospital in Boston. Elizabeth and Walker were in front of me, Cliff by my side. Cliff and I had heard that Buie had attended Yale Medical School and was now leaving his private practice to work with Margaret Bauman's L.A.D.D.E.R.S. program. We hoped that he would have more insight into Walker's problems with absorption and with potential food intolerance than the professionals we had been seeing.

Now, as I stood in his doorway, eyeing the room, I saw a navy backpack lying in the middle of his desk. Oddly, I felt relieved; I had the sense we must be in good hands. Everyone had backpacks at college—was I just responding to an icon of my generation? Yet a backpack often suggests that books are inside. A backpack also means "movement." Perhaps I was thinking that there were no trap doors out of this pediatric GI's office the way I had imagined there were in our other GI's office. Or perhaps I was thinking that here was a man who was on the move, who might be part of the zeitgeist, perhaps even at the forefront of autism spectrum research. I just had a feeling this doctor would know his stuff.

Buie proved to be everything his backpack promised. He spent an hour with us, explaining in detail the scientific theory supporting his position that we must, given Walker's history, continue to keep him, at least for the time, away from wheat and dairy. "There's not a lot of hard, scientific proof, but that must not be mistaken for lack of truth or justification to our theory—it just means that the jury's still out.

And there's plenty of anecdotal evidence that removing the major allergens from a child's diet can help health and behavior. One of my little guys came in here and could not sit still long enough to talk to us; when the parents removed wheat and dairy, he calmed down and gave us his attention."

Walker was sitting on Cliff's lap, eyeing a red model Volkswagen.

"Look, Elizabeth, a punch buggy," said Walker

"What?" said Buie.

"A punch buggy! You pass one and you punch," said Walker, who turned to hit Cliff in the arm and laughed heartily.

"It's a game Elizabeth and her friends play," explained Cliff. "They call Volkswagens punch buggies. When you pass a Volkswagen you punch your friends."

Walker was still laughing, looking around the room at other toys and models and chatting with Buie. He punched Cliff again.

"Do you have a bathroom?" asked Walker, smiling at Buie. He and Elizabeth left the room together.

"We're eager to know about Secretin," said Cliff. The autism community was still abuzz about the child who had suddenly talked after taking the drug. "Of course, Walker doesn't have a problem talking, but we heard that the drug helped with absorption difficulties."

"Well," continued Buie, "I think I've probably done about as much testing with secretin as anyone and what I've learned is that the more you go looking into the gut of children like these, the more you find."

"Can you test Walker with Secretin?" said Cliff.

"You can't get it," said Buie. "Several people have bought it up believing in its value."

"You mean they're hoarding it?"

Buie nodded, put his hands in the air. "In any case, it's not a problem. There are other drugs we can test with."

Cliff and I were eager to understand the connection between brain functioning and the GI tract. Buie began talking. He talked so fast we could barely keep up. Following is what I remember from his discussion:

"We believe that what we may be dealing with here is an allergic-type response, or an intolerance. One theory is that the gut of these kids doesn't properly digest certain allergens—specifically their proteins—wheat and dairy being the big guns. Some people theorize that opiates or other harmful substances may be released in the bloodstream of children in this population. Andrew Wakefield, the English researcher, posits that measles immunizations are responsible for causing damage to the gut lining, leaving it permeable. As you probably know, they've found evidence of measles in the ileum of the small intestines of patients with autism spectrum disorder. They posit that the virus is inflaming the colon or intestines, letting opioids pass through to the bloodstream, making their way to the brain. Other researchers are shooting Wakefield down, trying to prove that immunizations have nothing to do with autism, but I'm not sure that's the point."

It was Buie's contention that we may discover that immunizations may well be hurting some kids on the spectrum. "We don't know yet. My general feeling is that immunization on a vulnerable child may set off an immune or inflammatory response." But Buie felt that the etiology of the problem may be something other than vaccines. When he presented his theory to Wakefield at a conference, Wakefield wasn't interested.

"We still don't know if the problem originates in the brain or in the GI tract. But I was taught in graduate school that one should always try to see a cluster of several symptoms as being related, as being part of a whole system."

We could hear the sink turn on in the bathroom next door.

Buie leaned in on his desk, moved toward us, pointed in the direction of the bathroom where Elizabeth and Walker were and said, "This guy is great. What a personality! I love this guy."

Walker and Elizabeth entered, and Buie straightened.

"What I propose we do," said Buie, "is to test this little guy." He smiled at Walker. "Let's see what's really going on in the GI tract. I'd like to schedule an endoscopy."

Cliff and I were concerned about giving Walker anesthesia. How would a kid who still threw up occasionally for mysterious reasons react to a drug that was potentially lethal to some? Was he too sensitive to go under? When we were allowed in to see him after the procedure, he was still unconscious, thirstily breathing the mist of oxygen that sprayed in his face. After forty-five minutes, he still wouldn't come to. The nurses were worried, but he finally did. He began to stir, and at last, he spoke—complaining.

Buie's endoscopy showed that Walker was suffering cell damage due to allergic irritation, cell damage to both his stomach and esophagus. He prescribed an antihistamine called Cyproheptadine.

Within an hour of taking the antihistamine, Walker's life changed. My records record that Walker ate the following:

7:20 P.M. A banana
7:35 P.M. Five rice-cracker sandwiches with soy cream cheese and jelly
8:05 P.M. Applesauce
8:20 P.M. Seconds on applesauce
8:40 P.M. Three hot dogs (no buns)

The kid who never wanted food was now finally eating like a kid, and with the antihistamine, continues to do so.

In May 2000, Walker and Cliff and I visited Greenspan's office once again. By that time, Walker was three years and seven months, a preschooler no longer under the auspices of REACH. Greenspan did as he always did; he filmed us playing and working with Walker. In the past he had usually filmed us twice, correcting our floor-time method during the second round. This time he filmed us once, turned off his video camera, and sent Walker out of the room.

He told us that Walker was doing wonderfully by any standards. "He's intelligent, a great problem solver, creative thinker, has a can-do attitude. More important, he's got that spark in his eye. You don't see the average kid looking this wonderful."

The feeling in the room was electric. We all began to talk excitedly about child rearing in general.

"It's great when parents spend a lot of time with their kids." He was looking at us intently.

When parents *spend time* with their kids? I would have slugged the man if I hadn't been so grateful.

Out of the woods. Buoyant. Cocky.

If there is an epiphany to this story, this one day was the epiphany. What Greenspan said, "wonderfully by any standards," told us we had succeeded, we'd won the race against time. Elated, a bit overconfident, we left the appointment. Well, of course there was a bit of floor time to do, and those maddening playdates—but I think we both secretly decided we were done with floor time. We were done. We could relax, be a family.

We would never worry again that our son might someday have autism. He was social, more than social—he was alive with a glint in his eye. He was a rich and complex little boy. And he was mentally healthy. We rolled the windows down and the southern May breeze blew against our faces. We hadn't rented a convertible, yet in my memory we had as much fun in the car as if we had. We stopped at McDonald's and bought Walker the biggest bunch of greasy French fries we could find.

What we didn't know, couldn't have known, was that our story wasn't over.

What Wrecks This World

OF COURSE, GREENSPAN KNEW that our story wasn't over. Though he was thrilled with Walker's progress, he still had presented us with the usual endless and impossible laundry list of activities. He knew that Walker still needed to work on his sensory-motor skills, because sensory-motor skills could dog a kid like Walker long after he became emotionally and developmentally healthy. Ever the taskmaster, he insisted that we not slow down. Walker needed to be involved in: four playdates a week, running, jumping, kicking, and throwing, as well as speech therapy (since he was such an advanced speaker, he needed help keeping his tongue up to his thoughts), occupational therapy, and physical therapy. Cliff and I could limit our floor-time sessions to about two or three a day, however.

On the way home from our Greenspan visit, Cliff, Elizabeth, Walker, and I were driving up the coast of New Jersey and had stopped to sleep in a seaside town called Spring Lake. Thinking we'd treat ourselves to a celebration, we found a large room in a cozy inn near the ocean. Elizabeth, in third grade, sat outside on the porch and wrote a letter to a friend. Walker fell asleep between Cliff and me while we drank wine in bed watching TV. The next morning we drove toward the shore, against the wind barreling down the coast— and parked at what we thought was a deserted beach. The wind was so forceful we could barely get the doors open. As we walked onto the sand, Cliff held Walker in his arms, and Elizabeth and I ran together. We turned the corner around a stucco pavilion, and saw a bulldozer pushing sand. Elizabeth and I ran toward the water to the roaring waves while wind thrummed against our ears. We couldn't hear each other speak, but we assumed Cliff and Walker were behind us. When we reached the water we began picking up shells, admiring them, throwing rocks into the water, but soon we realized that Cliff and Walker hadn't followed. We turned back to investigate and found Cliff running toward the car. Walker was in his arms kicking and evidently crying. It took a while to discern what Walker was saying through his tears, but we finally made out his words: "It's going to wreck the world. It's going to wreck the world!" He was shaking and flailing, and we finally had no choice but to drive away from whatever it was that was wrecking the world.

All that summer, Walker was nervous about going outside, fearful now of noisy outdoor machinery—lawnmowers, construction equipment, leaf blowers. He wouldn't go to assemblies at school, avoided music presentations. It took us a while to piece together what had happened that day on the beach. Apparently, Walker put all the sensory events together—the crashing waves, the roaring wind that was thrumming his eardrums, and that noisy bulldozing—and believed that they were one terrifying and overwhelming event. He must have decided that the machine alone was responsible for a sensory experience so intense that it was nearly traumatic.

The public school in Northampton agreed to send Walker to an occupational therapist at nearby Cooley-Dickinson Hospital to work on "auditory sensitivity." There we met an occupational therapist named Elizabeth who suggested we try a desensitization technique that she explained was developed by Patricia Wilbarger.

The protocol seemed too simple to be effective, but after all we'd been through, why not believe it might help? Elizabeth taught us to rub the gumline just behind the top front teeth of Walker's upper palate, and then press quickly and firmly on his lower teeth. The process, to be repeated twice, five to six times a day, took seconds. "You might see some changes within a few days," said Elizabeth.

"Like what?"

"It differs," she said cryptically. We decided to make a list of Walker's quirks. We sat on the floor and discussed what separated this four-year-old from the average child his age. I listed some traits I thought were still troublesome: (1) excessive sensitivity to loud noises; (2) afraid to go outside, fearful of construction equipment; (3) excitability, especially at night (Walker sometimes didn't fall asleep until 10 or 11); (4) hard to get going in the morning, a bit disorganized (Walker wouldn't put his coat or boots on when I asked him to—he might lie down on the floor or throw his boots belligerently); (5) poor appetite in the morning; (6) excited in proximity of other kids, pokes and pushes.

Elizabeth explained that we would need to do the protocol before meals, snacks, and brushing for a week (six times a day), after which we would taper down to fewer times a day, diminishing to using it before stressful events.

Cliff and I were willing but, frankly, skeptical. The protocol seemed counterintuitive. We knew that spinning kids could help desensitize them, but spinning was directly related to the sense of movement it was treating. *What did the upper palate have to do with irritation from noisy lawnmowers?* Still, we were willing to try.

On Friday, October 24, we began the protocol. Six times that day, we rubbed Walker's upper palate (one, two), pressed on his teeth (one, two), and repeated the process.

The next day, Saturday morning, Cliff and I were sleeping in bed. Walker silently entered, stood beside us, and began speaking: "Time to get up. Time to get up!" He called like an eager boy scout. "Look, I dressed myself," he added. I sat up in bed to see the small figure on the other side of Cliff wearing pants, a well-matched shirt, and socks. Walker had never dressed himself without one of us standing over him, encouraging, daring, enticing him to put each piece on; yet on this morning, he had not only fully dressed himself but had performed the unprecedented act of choosing his own outfit (a high degree of organization for any preschooler).

In the following days and weeks, Cliff and I saw changes that we couldn't imagine to be related to the protocol, yet they were so dramatic, we were convinced they must indeed be. Toilet training had dragged on for months, yet this first morning Walker's pull-up was dry. He volunteered to be toilet trained (*and was* within days).

"Can I have breakfast?" he asked after he woke us up that first Saturday on the protocol.

Cliff and I looked at each other as if to say, "Who is this kid?" In spite of Walker's increased appetite with the antihistamine, he still hadn't been able to bring himself to eat breakfast in months, perhaps longer.

Within days, we noticed Walker could suddenly tolerate sitting next to other kids on the couch without acting restless or poking. While riding in the car, he usually refused to listen to anything beyond conversation or children's tapes. Now he would listen to any radio station I wanted, even news radio. Usually he was so excited around guests that he wanted to be the only person engaging with our visitor—he talked excitedly, making his interactions, charming though they were, dominate the evening. Yet that first Saturday night, he sat quietly during dinner with our guest injecting intelligent questions, as if he'd grown by years. Walker no longer stalled to leave the house. He pulled his boots and coat on faster than I could. To our utter surprise, one of the most profound changes did indeed happen to Walker's sense of hearing. Within the first day of the protocol, he became inured to noisy lawnmowers. A friend blew a horn in his ear; he didn't mind. He could (and remains able to) spend hours in a noisy arcade without complaint.

When I saw Elizabeth the O.T. the week after we finished the protocol, I asked what the gums could possibly have to do with noise tolerance, with organization.

"A major nerve runs directly to the brain from that place in the mouth," said Elizabeth. "The trigeminal nerve."

"Wow." I said, remembering that Arlene had taught me that the mouth is the most organizing part of the body.

"Do you think that's why it helps when kids suck their thumbs?"

"Yes," she said.

Walker's progress with desensitization therapy was so transforming that it made me wonder whether sensory problems might be responsible for a host of behaviors we attribute to immaturity and "naughtiness" in all healthy children. The nervous system may play a more vital role in our children's focus, temperament, and learning than we ever imagined.

Cliff and I sensed that our years working with Walker had, in large part, served as a paring away at sensitivity. It came away in pieces or layers over time. Life was still not easy, however, because what remained was Walker's agitation in the evenings and at bedtime. Cliff no longer held Walker in a ball to help him relax at bedtime. Instead, one of us lay beside him until he fell asleep. On the worst nights, he was a caricature of restlessness. He could spend one to three hours struggling toward sleep. He stood and flopped down hard on the bed, bottom first. He got on all fours, raised his body for leverage, and pushed his head into our stomachs, banged his head into the pillow— was this an adaptive form of head banging? Or he would knock his hip against any hard surface he could find—our bones, our hips, the pillow, the mattress, the wall even.

Tonight—July 3 (Walker four and three-quarters years old). 98 degrees today. 85 at sundown. Air so humid it seems it could grab hold of your lungs, wrap itself around your organs and drag you down. Walker feels it, it makes him unbearably restless. It is as if there is a worm in him that he wants to knock out.

9:00 we go downstairs for a snack. I think, if he eats, he'll sleep. At least I think so.

9:30 down for canned pears.

10:30 down for toast.

Around 11 he is still tossing and turning, trying to get some kind of resistance out of the bed, bang! Hitting his hips hard as he turns. The bed is a trampoline. He's trying to wrest a massage out of it. (He is so uncomfortable in his skin. Yet how much more comfortable am I or Cliff? I guess this is what it all boils down to for all of us: how comfortable we are in our skin. How easy it is for us to reconcile the fact that we long to be still in a world that insists on turning dizzily about.)

"Mom," he says, "When's morning?"

"It doesn't come until after you sleep."

Silence.

He sucks frantically at his thumb. The worm still eats at him.

"Mom, please, tell me how to sleep." More bumping up against me.

"You need to go inside, into where your head is and think about your day. Then your thoughts will turn to dreams and your dreams will be sleep."

"Okay," he says.

He lies awake for twenty minutes. I begin to sleep myself when out of nowhere he jumps up.

"I did it!" He says, jumping still. "I did it!"

"No, no," I say, pulling his body down from the back of his pajamas, fighting this being that struggles fiercely to move through space. "You only had thoughts, not dreams, not sleep."

"But I can see the light coming!" he insists.

"It's almost midnight, Walker."

He stands up, "The sun's rising, Mom."

"The sun will rise only after you sleep, Walker."

I pull him down again.

Silence. Sucking. Frantic sucking.

"Mom, can you sleep instead of me?"

"No, Walker, you need to sleep for yourself."

"I'm trying Mom, I'm trying."

When he says this my heart folds over, watching this little four-year-old trying to master himself, and I know that it's true what the philosophers say: that mastering ourselves is the hardest task of all tasks. I'm beginning to wonder how it's done. How it's ever done? How is it that the mind, the brain, can learn to change itself? I still can't get my mind around the idea that the brain stands over itself and sees beyond itself. What part of the brain sees all that it is and what it can be and decides to change? Where is it in the brain that it can transcend itself?

The next day, Elizabeth (eight and a half) was dressing for a basketball game, feeling sad because she'd have to play the team she used to belong to last year. Uncannily, she said, "I guess that's what we always do in life. Play against ourselves. We're always remembering what we were and seeing what we are."

A Car Turning Off the Road

WE TOOK A RISK and brought the children to Northern California to visit my sister and friends who live there. Walker was four years and nine months old. He proved a good traveler—flexible and enthusiastic, yet what thrilled Cliff and me was the quality of his engagement even as he was experiencing new environments. Walker sat in the back seat of our rental car and talked to us. He made up stories about dinosaurs, laughed at jokes, thrilled as our car spun across the Golden Gate Bridge, loved the man at the toll booth who joked with us about the Red Sox. When we stopped to stay with friends near Sacramento, Walker fell in love with their same-age daughter, Melissa. Walker and Melissa disappeared upstairs into the playroom, sat on the couch shoulder to shoulder watching TV. Yet he was overenergetic at times. And when the family served broiled salmon at a formal dinner, Walker, sensitive to the smell, vomited on their white rug.

Still, Walker was maturing, growing in depth. Complexity. Developing layers through time. We continued to observe a deep quality in his emotional expression, even an intensity. We were having a lot of fun, telling stories and goofing around. One night at a restaurant, I was sitting next to Walker and he jumped up and said to me, "Mom, my heart is just bursting with love for you and for Daddy. Now that my heart has burst, the love is moving all through my body."

Later I held him in my arms and told him he was my sweetheart.

"I don't have a heart," he said.

"You don't? What happened to it?"

"It broke," he said.

"Why?" I queried.

"Because we had to leave Grammacita" (his pet name for his grand-mother).

That night, we lay in bed playing a game called Brain Quest, a series of brain teasers for kids, graded by age-appropriateness. One of the cards showed a picture of a chair with only three legs; it looked like it was a form of high design, as if it belonged in the Museum of Modern Art. "What is missing from this picture?" I asked, reading the prompt.

"A person," said Walker.

It was around this time—the year 2001, the summer before Walker turned five—when we began to notice that Walker had some uncannily strong cognitive skills. One was a prodigious interest in time. One morning at breakfast, he began singing a made-up song about the subject. He was learning to tell time (and later at five and a half would read an analog clock).

"Tomorrow is the day that never comes, because when tomorrow comes it's today," he sang.

⸺

By that summer, Cliff and I had grown lazy about floor time. In fact, we hadn't done it formally in some time. We played together, but not as therapy; we played for fun. The truth is, I sometimes found myself avoiding play. As joyful as it could be, I'd had a surfeit of it. The very thought of it could nauseate me. I so longed to be just a mother, or a friend to someone else. I hung on the moments I could sit with friends at the park or in the living room and chat while our children played.

I had the luxury of indulging a passion for spending time with Elizabeth. Because I only did floor time once a day, at bath time—and because Cliff and Walker spent enormous amounts of time together, building elaborate train scenes, making fantasy scapes out of Legos and blocks—I finally found the time I had always wanted to be with Elizabeth. We went to craft stores, looking for little scarves or trinkets, or to movies, or took walks. We fell in love with East Heaven, a hot-tub salon in town. In our hot-tub room, we listened to Enya and Sade and blues. Listening to that slow, sultry music we lay on our backs, letting our feet dangle in the water. One afternoon in the winter when we were lying on the cedar deck with our heads together gazing up at the snow-filled skylight, I realized that away from home it's possible to talk about absolutely nothing. *I'm doing it, I'm actually talking about nothing!*

"Mom," said Elizabeth, "Did you ever notice that when The Backstreet Boys sing slowly they're always apologizing about something they did to their girlfriends, like why they didn't show up?" We laughed for a long time.

One day, we shopped (for nothing, too, nothing in particular), went to a movie, and on the way home talked about philosophy, about politics, about black holes and the life of stars.

The next day, Walker and Elizabeth and I were driving through Hadley, a nearby rural town, past the farm stands and the fields, when I noticed in the car in front of me a pair of arms on the passenger side flapping up and down repetitively. The car bobbed along, straight and quiet, the arms continued to flap. Whoever belonged to those arms must have been a large teenager, or an adult. The arms continued to flap as we stopped at a light, flapped when it turned green. *This passenger must be very ill with autism.* The head of the driver—I could tell it was a woman from the hair—seemed calm, still, even resigned. All the while, the arms bobbed up and down, up and down. The car was an old fifties car, the head of the mother behind the wheel so upright, the way women were supposed to be in the fifties. Her hair was well groomed. The car pulled into a turning lane. *How in the world can a car just go on like that?* All of the implied feeling in that still, motionless, matronly head, driving straight on, keeping the car on the road—all the while, chaos, or controlled chaos, the hands moving up and down, up and down. That car bouncing so subtly, like a plane over pockets of air. There wasn't a note of judgment or anger or exasperation in the mother's head. Just acceptance. She had accepted the flapping hands. The car turned into a nearby parking lot and disappeared, floated away, out of sight. I thought for a minute of turning around, of following it, of chasing it down. The arms of that passenger seemed grown, well worn, and used to motion. *"Stop and chase them,"* a voice insisted, but I didn't. I didn't pull into the Hadley

Garden Center parking lot, I didn't flag the car down and motion for the mother to roll down her window, as I did in my imagination. I didn't talk to her about vitamins, about occupational therapy and sensory integration therapy (though she probably knew about those). I didn't talk about essential fatty acids, about some of the more cutting-edge therapies I was learning about. I didn't tell her about all the healing hands we'd met. I didn't tell her about movement therapy—that we had learned that it's possible to reach the mind through the body, and the body through the mind. I didn't tell her that Dr. Buie insisted that this disorder requires "a multi-tiered-sandwich approach. One does everything one can." Perhaps most important, I didn't tell her about Greenspan's interactive therapy. Instead, I let the car disappear. It was the kind of thing some highway drivers do in the middle of the night in a snowstorm, watching a car slide off the road, pretending it didn't happen, just driving on.

Eyes of a Stranger

IN JANUARY 2002, the winter that Walker was five years old, a mutual friend introduced Walker and me to Drew, a child diagnosed with Asperger's syndrome (a high-functioning form of autism) and his mother, Linda. Drew was a tall, handsome boy with large eyes, who moved like a sprite. Linda was tall, athletic—the kind of corn-fed beauty you see on the track or in health-food stores. She had thick hair and large eyes like her son. Drew was hiding a bit when we first entered, but then he came out and said, "Hi," without quite looking right at us. There was an intensity about Drew that I was immediately attracted to. His speech was slow, and though he wasn't engaged in circles of communication with us, he seemed passionately attached to Linda, if not quite verbally, then with his body, which followed her and joined her consistently. It was as if they were dancing together, though Drew needed to withdraw occasionally when things got intense. Emotionally, there was a feeling that he still stayed on the periphery, at least when we were there. Linda showed us the sensory integration gymnasium she had made in the basement. We watched Drew tumble and jump and kick, a five-year-old as spry a gymnast as a boy of seven, or older. Linda had gone after Drew's sensory problems with ferocity; this child who supposedly had at some point had a physical deficit was now a master of balance, poise, and skill. At just about 5:00 P.M., she suggested Drew help chop onions. He jumped up onto the kitchen island and sat perched on the side of the counter, chopping onions with a large cleaver I wouldn't let an eleven-year-old wield. It was obvious that she had a genius for the body, for developing it. I could see that instantly. (It was only later that I learned that

Linda was in fact a bodyworker, a teacher of yoga and a Shiatsu practitioner.) It seemed instantly clear to me that the approaches she and I had taken were opposite to each other—or, rather, complements to each other. She had focused on the motor system and intensive sensory diet; I had focused on the emotions. I could see that Linda had a lot to teach me, and I wanted to learn it. I wanted to give Drew's command of his body to Walker—something that I, a skinny kid, had lacked my whole life. I wanted to give Linda what Greenspan taught me. There was something about Drew that made me think he intended to be social, longed to be connected, but just didn't fully have the tools to manage it. Linda gave Drew a lot of direction. It seemed she was more in the mode of managing, though expertly so, a child who could be explosively frustrated. She was uncomfortable when he got angry and hit the pillows of the couch. Drew needed a lot of time going inward, playing with an electronic toy, or leaving to go to his room. She told me, "Walker is imaginative, but Drew isn't; he's literal. I have to instruct him what other kids know instinctively." I didn't believe it. It seemed to me that he just needed practice. I had an urge to try floor time soon.

A few weeks later, on February 14, Valentine's Day, Walker and I went to visit Linda and Drew again. Drew said, "Hi," and was friendly, but distant, needing to play solitary games. He was lying on the floor playing with a toy car wash. Walker was playing with the one next to him. Linda and I agreed that I would try floor time. I took a deep breath and went down to the floor, pulled a blue matchbox car from a pile, prepared to raise my voice to a higher register, revved up my engine. I asked Drew in a squeaky voice if he would give "me" (the car) a wash. Drew ignored the car. But as Greenspan had taught me, I was insistent. I kept asking him to wash me.

"Please wash me, please," I squeaked. "I'm an absolute mess." My voice rose higher and higher. "You must wash me! I'll get in trouble if you don't wash me."

No response.

"Please, please, will you?"

Drew didn't look at me, but he took the car and started washing.

"How much do you charge?" I asked.

"A hundred dollars," said Drew. I pretended to give him the money. He took it. He took the pretend money. And so it went like that for several minutes, until once, after my asking how much he charged, he said, "It's free. Costs nothing."

"No money!" I exclaimed, laughing. "Man, oh man, I'm comin' back here!" Drew looked up at me; his eyes met mine for a long draught. I thought of a term Darleen Corbett has used, "drinking in my depths." Not only was this the first time Drew had ever given me any eye contact, it was the first smile I had ever seen from him. What was the synapse that fired that moment? A chill ran over my arms. It was eerie, exquisite.

Drew and I played hard for an hour. Still, when I left the house, Linda seemed cold somehow, distant. *Had I shocked her? Did she think I was crazy playing with her son so intently?*

For the next two weeks, I wasn't able to stop thinking about Drew—while I was giving Walker a bath, or while writing this book, or making dinner. Why was I so intently focused on a child I hardly knew? And anyway, wasn't I ready to be through with floor time? There was a time when I would have begged never to do it again in my life—never to have to do that floor-dusting voice-grating work of it again. And yet something came back to me with Drew that I'd forgotten—the old feeling: excitement, maybe even elation, the endorphins spinning out of control, seeing, feeling the effects of millions of synapses firing. That day I had the sense that myelin was being laid a thousand miles an hour in Drew's brain. Walker may have been nearly through with floor time. But I wasn't.

Drew was quite a remarkable child, very bright. He connected faster than I ever imagined a child could. I was convinced he was capable of a lot—maybe even more than the typical child. Driving home on Valentine's Day, I wanted to turn around and drive back and do floor time with him again. *What was wrong with me? What was I looking for? The gift of shaping or changing a child's life?* I was hooked into something so human, so elemental. Doing floor time with Drew, a rushing had come over the tops of my fingers and hands and sank into my throat. The feeling was electric.

Eventually I made up some pretext and called Linda. On the phone, she said she was grateful. Tears welled in my eyes when I learned that she had been doing floor time every day, that she was seeing a different child. She saw humor, tenderness, things in him she "had never seen before, and didn't miss because I didn't know they were missing." And then she told me a remarkable story.

"On that day when you came over and did floor time with Drew, when you left," Linda said, "I was drained, devastated. I saw how much work floor time was, how much energy it took. I just didn't think I had it in me to do it. I actually called my partner and cried. I know I was acting strangely. I would rather have run ten marathons than do that kind of work. But after school, Drew came to me and gave me a valentine. After school he made me another one. He hugged me and then he did something he had never done before. He pulled away to look at me. He held my face in his hands, looked me long and straight in the eye, and said, 'I love you Mama.' I wept from happiness, and I was determined to do floor time. I'm very grateful."

She'd said she was grateful, but I said, "It's I who owe you gratitude." I didn't know what to say. How to take all the history—everything that was me in that moment, everything my son had become (Linda had called him perfect)—and roll it up and somehow push it into that small phone and offer it to her. "I felt joyful when Drew looked at me that first time and smiled. Emotion bloomed on his face." It was like breaking the wall in Berlin. Watching someone come alive. And all the time I was talking to Linda, my mind was rushing to Walker's babyhood, those dark eyes finally turning toward my own.

The Fate of Babies and Pirates

WHEN WALKER WAS FIVE, we visited Dr. Greenspan again. Cliff and I were expecting a full bill of health, to be discharged. Instead, Greenspan spent forty-five minutes alone with Walker and then called us in to play with him. He was, of course, thrilled with Walker's progress, praised his emotional and cognitive development, adored his sense of humor, marveled at his verbal accomplishments, but something concerned him. He worried that Walker was, in a sense, too nice.

"Your son has no abstract representation for aggression," he said.

"No *what*?"

"Walker can talk six ways to Sunday about love, but he can't talk about aggression. You need to help challenge him in the pretend play. Help him deal with themes of aggression. Mobilize his gumption."

Cliff and I looked at each other, a long look across the room, raised our eyebrows simultaneously.

"He needs more time with you," he said, turning to Cliff, speaking emphatically. "You need to be closer. He's too identified with his mother." He turned to me. "Be supportive as you can be, but don't be overprotective. Let him be the assertive one. If he's upset, be available, but let him come to you. Argue with him sometimes. Don't always give in." Greenspan recommended Cliff spend several hours on the weekend and at least one each weeknight with Walker—possibly even change his work schedule.

"He needs to be aggressive?" I said.

"No. I didn't say that. We're looking for a balance in his play. He needs to play out loving themes as well as more assertive ones. We are looking for kids to play out tea parties and dolls and getting along, as well as scenes of conflict, arguments—even wars need to be played out in pretend play.

We both realized it was time for Walker to move beyond wherever we were. It was time for him to leave the apron strings, to be closer to Cliff.

"I work hard," Cliff said to Greenspan in his office. "I do as much time as anyone I know with my kids, but I'm not sure how much more I can do. I come from a family of strong women who have always taken the lead taking care. . . . "

"The dynamics you're fighting have been played out for generations in our culture. But you can reverse them," insisted Greenspan, looking at both of us. "You can do it for your son and you can do it for yourselves."

As for me, Greenspan seemed to be implying that I had been babying Walker—that all that great juiciness between us was no longer appropriate. *So you're not so great at letting go*, I told myself. *You're going to have to.*

That night, as Cliff and I lay in bed together, I didn't say anything for a long time, but I was thinking, I was thinking about the drama that we'd been living. In some ways, we had a larger-than-life son, a larger-than-life psychiatrist following his progress, a man who saw us too clearly, far too clearly. Daunting. He saw our faults.

I finally spoke. "This is about us, do you realize that, Cliff? It's no longer about Walker. "He's telling us we need to change. Did you notice?"

Cliff was silent for a long time. He turned to me, put his arm around my waist. I was nearly in tears, and I suspect Cliff wasn't too far behind. His silence said, *After all we'd done, it still wasn't enough?*

The next day at the pool, I tried to introduce an aggressive game to Walker, as Greenspan suggested I should. I proposed I become a "slimy boat monster" who was going to try to attack him. I bared my teeth playfully. He cried.

I held him.

What am I doing, I thought? All these years since even the early months, when Walker began to learn to look at me, to look at us, he's grown to be a spark, a star, a meteorite of energy and interaction. Greenspan said he wanted Walker to be closer to Cliff, maybe even to like him better than me, or at least to favor us equally. We had a private world. Now I'm supposed to give some of that up?

A woman swimming nearby stroked over and said, "God, your son's cute. I want to steal him and take him home with me." Walker gave her a sweet look; it could have made the sun tremble. They smiled at each other for a long time.

I heard this everywhere, at the market, at school. Walker beamed up at strangers, asked questions: "Hello, what street do you live on?" or "Do you want to play with us?" At restaurants, Walker often jumped up onto his knees and had conversations with people at the next booth. At my mother's hotel on her last day after visiting for two weeks, three waitresses and the restaurant hostess stood around him, giving him their fond good-byes. "Remember me?" asked one of the waitresses. Of course he did. He knew her name—knew all their names.

Why is it that Walker doesn't want to play "slimy boat monster"?

I worried that his aversion was my fault. I was never very good at aggression myself. Perhaps I had avoided it in our play.

Greenspan seemed to be implying that Walker and I were too close, mother and son were too close. Could I deliver, let go? Let my son go places where a mother may never follow? All this time I'd been fighting to bring him into my world, to keep him with me, to keep him close. Now the directive was to switch gears. To let go and turn away. I knew what Greenspan meant. He made it clear I needed to stay there, be supportive, to be there, but as for myself? There's a lot I had to let go of. It was almost as if I needed to let go of some deep part of my very self. I needed, at least in part, to dust my hands of the job I'd been doing these past years, and, in doing so, to say good-bye to this intense dyad I was in with Walker. It was time for him to grow up—this lively sprite who darted love with a palpable, beaming force from his sweet, large eyes. Over the following weeks, I struggled to pull away more often to give Cliff lots of room. Cliff spent hours and hours with Walker—most of the weekends, and a solid hour or two every night after dinner, their "special time." Walker came to expect and ask for it. Cliff was devoted to Walker.

For all of August I worked hard with Walker, making animals do aggressive acts. His answer was to look at me pleadingly, as if I were forcing something unwanted on him.

I fought against my desire not to play such games, talked to other mothers about it. None of us liked our kids to play rough. In fact, during playdates, several mothers rushed in and tried to stop any imaginative play that involved aggression. "Don't cut the pirate with the knife. Let's get along!"

Yet after several calls to Greenspan's assistant, I began to understand that Walker needed to play out aggression, ironically, to free himself from the bonds of aggression. A child needed to explore all aspects of the emotional self in order to separate himself from the tyranny that repressed feelings could be. Or was it to find a voice for feelings that may be too frightening even for the imagination?

So I was no longer in the world of disability—this was the world of child development, of normal child development. Some of it had to do with helping my son learn to separate himself from his anger enough to give it a name, I told myself, grappling with understanding why Greenspan was taking us down this path. Aggression, I knew, could go deep down under the rug and seethe there in passive frustration. *But why play out aggression?* Somehow, Greenspan seemed to be suggesting that if Walker could play out aggression, he could feel it, and recognize and accept it in himself. Only when a child can play out emotional themes could he really be free of the yoke of that emotion. Play could somehow teach a child that feelings neither own us, nor are us. Aggression was Walker's bête noir, but perhaps some other kids needed to play out the feelings that Walker was most comfortable with, feelings of tenderness, or whatever they might be denying. The goal was to move toward a full range, a broad and vivid palate in the imaginative world. The point was to move toward wholeness.

I am beginning to wonder about myself. Is Walker not able to abstract about aggression, in part, because of some lack of my own? Has my own lack of ability to come to terms with anger kept my son from learning to show it, feel it, imagine it, and talk about it?

I began working with Walker every night for half an hour while he was in the bathtub, my dinosaur attacking his.

But now that every day I had begun playing games about aggression, odd changes began happening in my own life. Suddenly, figures from my past began flooding into my dreams. Those who had hurt me (or whom I thought had hurt me) peopled my dreams in new configurations. For years, perhaps even for most of my life, I had grown familiar with standard nightmare scenarios. In nightmares I was always the passive character—the person trying to run with frozen legs, the person aching to scream and finding no voice. Let's face it, in dreams I was a wimpy protagonist. Scary scenes and scary people made me shrink. In dreams I sometimes lost my body. Nightmares from the worst periods of my life showed me hovering over this planet like a disembodied soul.

Weirdly, now that every day Walker and I were doing dinosaur play, I discovered a change. I began fighting back in my dreams. No longer a hovering soul, I became a body incarnate. Actually, I was more like the terminator. In one dream, I broke into an enemy-harboring cabin perched peacefully in a meadow and began hacking at the people with an ax, their blood pouring like something out of a Monty Python movie.

I began waking up early, feeling unusually refreshed, ready for a day of dinosaur war.

One evening Walker was in his bath as usual, and he picked up from his basket of bath toys a rubber baby doll and began pushing her under the water. He held her there with a strange smirk on his face, as if to say, *I'm killing her, Mom. What do you intend to do about it?*

I was alarmed by the obvious evil in his intent. "Let's call the rescue squad," I called out quickly, and a rescue helicopter hovered over the water, dropping a line to the drowning infant.

The next night, Walker drowned the baby again. I tried to pretend I was her and cried out, "No, no," in a high squeaky voice. Finally I suggested we rescue her again.

Walker was now drowning babies every night, and I was suggesting we rescue them. After a week he began rescuing them on his own. I called Greenspan's office to find out if I was doing the right thing. The next day, Greenspan's assistant, Sarah, called me back to say that she was eagerly awaiting Greenspan's reply herself. She had several parents calling her with kids doing things like hanging up dummies by the neck and choking them, and she was wondering about her own son's vivid imagination. She called me a few days later, saying, "I can't wait to talk to you about what I learned."

I returned the call to discover that, according to Greenspan, I had done the wrong thing by saving the drowning babies.

"Pretend play is not about moral teaching," she told me, repeating Greenspan's words. "It's about living out unconscious feelings." So I had interfered with the unconscious process—hijacked it for my own purposes.

"The goal of this kind of play is to encourage the child to feel the feelings, but the ultimate goal is to bring the child to a place where he can talk about those feelings," said Sarah.

"I'm not sure these are feelings I want to talk about," I said. "Walker always seems to have a smug smile on his face while he's drowning babies, as if he's just stuck his hand in the pie. Are you sure he won't become a serial killer?"

She laughed and said, "No. Quite the contrary."

I thought hard about Greenspan's original words: "Your son has no abstract representation for aggression." Now, with this new information that talking was the ultimate goal, I suddenly understood that the framing of words made it possible to separate ourselves from a feeling, or rather, that separating ourselves from feelings made it possible for us to put feelings in words. A person who can abstract from his feelings can make imaginative representations of such feelings, can use play as a way to express feelings. The ultimate form of abstraction for Greenspan, thus, was language itself, which is a developmentally high form of representation. Feelings grow into symbols, and symbols form into words. The feeling is expressed through conversation, not through fighting or acting out, not through burning down buildings or attacking. If Walker could talk about his feelings, it would mean he had reached the highest level of emotional maturity for his age. I began to see, as well, that talking about his feelings at five might help lay a future for Walker as a healthy man. He might learn not to act out aggression: He wouldn't punch kids in high school, wouldn't walk away from friendships, or when he was older, he might not lash out unreasonably at his children or cheat people. It was a tall order, this "abstract representation of aggression." So much was hanging on the drowning of a baby.

I started stacking the deck, slipping baby dolls into the deep of Walker's bubbles. In early spring he insisted on rescuing the dolls, the way I had unfortunately taught him to.

One day in mid-April, however—Walker was five and a half— about a month after I spoke to Sarah, Walker began holding a baby doll under water, purposefully drowning her with that smug, defiant look on his face all over again.

I stepped away, turned my back, and let him do it.

He drowned her for several nights in a row, each night, me turn- ing not to watch, though eventually I did learn how to stomach it. During the day at play with friends, he started playing pirate, suggest- ing that they drown the pirates in a moat around the castle. Later, in the evening, after Walker had been drowning babies, I did as Sarah suggested and asked a question: "How does it feel when you drown the baby?"

Walker's face grew serious; he leaned back in the tub, pensive, soft- ened. He took on a depth of expression that unnerved me. He said sadly, "We don't know when we're going to die, do we, Mom?"

"No, we don't."

Neither one of us spoke. I could see he was thinking. He might be thinking about his own death or the death of his great aunt Debbie, which had disturbed him.

"I'll always remember you, Mom," he said, looking up at me, "Even after I die."

"You will?" I said. "What will you remember?"

He looked at me, speaking with his eyes, too, and he said, "I'll always remember the way you played with me."

Epilogue

IN THE SPRING OF 2002, I called Darleen Corbett, REACH's director, to ask her something about Walker's history, information I could use for this book.

I couldn't resist thanking her for the insightful "diagnosis" she had given five years before, when she gleaned that Walker was suffering from sensory integration disorder. I knew from my research that even children receiving early intervention are sometimes misunderstood or wrongly diagnosed, or are merely treated for physical delays by well-meaning professionals who may know little about sensory processing. Darleen did Walker a great service by assigning Arlene to his care, and her level of professionalism was not lost on Cliff and me.

"Tell me something," I said to Darleen. "What do you think would have happened to Walker if he hadn't received intervention?"

Silence, for a long while, from Darleen, and then she spoke. "Well . . . I suspect he would have been left behind."

I knew what she meant by the laconic answer. He might not have grown, might not have learned, might not have interacted with us much; he might have been painfully shy or so introverted as to have a serious learning disability. He might not have scaled any, or many, milestones. Yet as things stood, he had reached them all. He was a "juicy" kid who could play imaginative scenarios with us and his friends for hours. That was the intention of milestone six, as I understood it. The foundations for higher reasoning had been laid firm. Cliff and I knew that there was no way anyone would ever mistake our child for someone on the autism spectrum, and we were convinced that it was indeed possible to work one's way off the spectrum, toward health.

In his great tome, *Phenomenology of Mind*, Hegel, the grandfather of the social sciences, writing nearly 200 years ago, asserted something fundamental about self-awareness: "Self-consciousness exists . . . in that, and by the fact that it exists for another self-consciousness." We can be complete, conscious beings only when we have known ourselves through the eyes of another. To call this process the healing power of love would be sentimental—especially since, in Walker's case, so much energy and work was involved in forming a relationship, in spite of his biological obstacles. Still, early human interaction is the starting point of all knowledge. How important it is, we understood, to teach a sensitive child to bear the often unbearable light of another person's gaze.

We also knew something else, or suspected it: that as long as we visited him, Greenspan wouldn't leave us alone—he would always be challenging us to be better parents. "The gaze" is never over, for any parent.

In 2000, Dawn and REACH were awarded a contract from the state of Massachusetts as an "approved speciality service provider" to specifically treat infants and young children for autism. They earned the contract on the basis of Dawn's work with Walker and other children who began improving from a floor-time approach; the new program would be designed around Greenspan's method. Dawn would be head of the program.

The last time that Walker visited Greenspan, he was five and a half and was developing his amazing capacity to understand time. He was more reliable than I was for remembering what day of the week it was. He could calculate how long he would have to wait until his favorite show would air; he had exhausted his passion for *The Wizard of Oz* books, moving on to other "chapter books"; he possessed a huge vocabulary and spent hours and hours each week with Cliff creating, building, and having fun. They went to the hardware store together, to the market; they went miniature golfing, bicycle riding, to the movies, to T-ball practice, to soccer.

Perhaps most important of all, Walker had by that time a highly developed sense of moral thinking and empathy. He worried that his great aunt Paula might be lonely now that great aunt Debbie had died. At the dinner table, he turned to me and said, "But you haven't had a chance to talk about your day yet, Mom."

One day he asked, "Do bad people know they're bad?"

"What do you think, Walker?" I asked.

He shook his head. "No. I don't think they do."

<hr />

While we spoke at our last meeting, Greenspan ate stir-fried vegetables and rice out of a large bowl. (The prior patient had kept him overtime.) When he finished the bowl, he loaded a tape into his video camera and asked Cliff and Walker to go to the floor.

Walker was a pilot; Cliff was copilot. As Walker and Cliff entered a pretend world of radio telecommunications and missions to Atlanta, Los Angeles, Mars, and beyond, Walker began jumping up onto the couch so his airplane would fly higher. Greenspan seemed almost enchanted watching them play. As they filled up the room with laughter and broad assertive movement, a generous, almost childlike smile spread across Greenspan's face. I watched him watch Walker and Cliff for several minutes, the smile never leaving his face.

When Walker jumped down from the couch and made his airplane fly over me toward Cliff's, Greenspan turned his head slightly toward me. He was still smiling the biggest smile I had ever seen on him. Now the smile was a gift to me, to us. He was acknowledging our work. He looked into my eyes smiling softly, joyfully. There was something satisfying about that smile, as if he were registering incredulity.

After the game was over, he turned to Cliff and said, "You and Walker are very close; I could feel it. And now he's flying."

We began to leave the office, and as we turned to look back at him, he gave us two thumbs up.

If I didn't know better, I might have thought he was telling us we were done.

About the Author

Patricia Stacey, a writer, college teacher, and former editorial staff member of *The Atlantic Monthly*, lives with her husband Cliff and her children, Elizabeth and Walker, in western Massachusetts.